DATE DUE

AUG 11 1968			

THE WEALTH OF
THE GENTRY
1540-1660

ALAN SIMPSON

THE WEALTH OF THE GENTRY

1540–1660

EAST ANGLIAN
STUDIES

THE UNIVERSITY OF CHICAGO PRESS

CAMBRIDGE · AT THE UNIVERSITY PRESS

1963

PUBLISHED BY
THE SYNDICS OF THE CAMBRIDGE UNIVERSITY PRESS
Bentley House, 200 Euston Road, London, N.W. 1
AND
THE UNIVERSITY OF CHICAGO PRESS
Chicago 37

AGENTS
For Canada: The University of Toronto Press
For Australia: Georgian House Pty Ltd

Printed in Great Britain at the University Press, Cambridge
(Brooke Crutchley, University Printer)

PREFACE

IT is a pleasure to acknowledge the stimulation and help I have received in my excursions into the economics of family history. My debt to the historians of the gentry—rising or otherwise—is sufficiently obvious and my dissent from some of their views argues no lack of admiration. I owe my introduction to estate documents to my friend and colleague R. C. Bald, who drew my attention to the Bacon manuscripts which the University of Chicago acquired from Redgrave Hall a generation ago and in which Professor Bald discovered the materials for his study of *Donne and the Drurys* (Cambridge University Press, 1959). My efforts to familiarise myself with the East Anglian scene and its archives were greatly helped by the courtesy of Mrs Alan Rowe, The Elms, Ixworth, Suffolk; Mr Martin Statham, of the Bury St Edmund's and West Suffolk Record Office; Mr Dereck Charman, of the Ipswich and East Suffolk Record Office, Mr Hepworth of the Norwich City Library, Captain Anthony Hammond, of Mousehold House, Norwich; Sir Edmond Bacon, of Raveningham Hall, Norfolk; Mr R. W. Ketton-Cremer, of Felbrigge Hall, Norfolk; Mr John Holt Wilson, of Snape Hill, Rickinghall, Suffolk; Mrs John Holt Wilson, of Broomhills, Rickinghall, Suffolk; the Earl of Iveagh, of Elveden Hall, Suffolk; Mr Basil Cozens-Hardy, of Letheringsett, Norfolk; Mr T. F. Barton, of 16 Albemarle Road, Norwich; Professor Bruce Dickins, of Corpus Christi College, Cambridge; and others whom I have tried to thank in the text. I trust that the occasional solecisms in local allusions will be forgiven to a stranger.

I also trust that the charity which the ablest blunderer in estate documents must ask for himself will be extended to other perplexed pilgrims. The possibilities of error in the attempt to reconstruct the finances of the gentry are large and forbidding. For the delays in the publication of this study, and for any unfamiliarity with very recent work, I have only myself to blame; a change in duties obliged me to set it aside.

Preface

My particular thanks are due to one or two others: to Professor Michael Postan who taught me how to read a medieval roll; to Professors H. J. Habakkuk and Herbert Heaton who read this manuscript; to a succession of students who shared in my encounters with accounts—Kenneth Dodd, Ronald Matthias, Ernest Sandeen, James Farnell; to the Social Science Research Committee of the University of Chicago, which made my visits to England possible; and to my wife, whose indulgence for these researches was only equalled by her incredulity that anyone should undertake them.

ALAN SIMPSON

UNIVERSITY OF CHICAGO
14 September 1960

CONTENTS

ABBREVIATIONS

The following abbreviations have been adopted in the footnotes:

E.S.R.O.	East Suffolk Record Office
W.S.R.O.	West Suffolk Record Office
H.R.O.	Hertford Record Office
N.C.L.	Norwich City Library

CHAPTER I

ENCOUNTERS WITH ACCOUNTS

O NE of the liveliest controversies in recent academic history has been the argument over the fortunes of the gentry in the century between the dissolution of the monasteries and the civil wars. Though deprived of some of the conditions which would make it an epic battle, such as an equal zest for warfare among the combatants, or issues with a simple human appeal, it has compelled every serious student of the period to re-examine a century which he thought he understood. It is unnecessary here to retrace the history of the argument, but a mere statement of its leading questions will furnish some idea of a debate which has ranged from highly technical issues of estate management to sweeping generalisations about the dependence of political and religious upheavals on the economic experience of social classes. Did the gentry rise at the expense of the peerage by enlarging their share of lands? Did the medium-sized estate develop at the expense of the very large estate? Was there something about the peer's position that handicapped him in the struggle for solvency during a period of inflation? Did the gentry owe their success to more 'bourgeois' methods of land management? Was access to office, rather than the management of land, the real key to enrichment? Was there a declining gentry of 'mere' landlords? How far is the English Revolution—the whole of it, or any part of it—to be explained in terms of alterations in the balance of social power?[1]

This is an argument in which anyone with a good general knowledge

[1] Writings directly involved in the controversy are as follows: R. H. Tawney, 'Harrington's Interpretation of His Age', *Proc. British Academy* (1941); 'Rise of the Gentry, 1558–1640', *Econ. Hist. Rev.* XI (1941); L. Stone, 'The Anatomy of the Elizabethan Aristocracy', *ibid.* XVIII (1948); H. R. Trevor-Roper, 'The Elizabethan Aristocracy: An Anatomy Anatomised', *ibid.* 2nd series, III (1951); L. Stone, 'The Elizabethan Aristocracy—A Restatement', *ibid.* IV (1952); H. R. Trevor-Roper, 'The Gentry, 1540–1640', *ibid.* supplement no. 1 (1953); R. H. Tawney, 'Rise of the Gentry: A Postscript', *ibid.* VII (1954); J. P. Cooper, 'The Counting of Manors', *ibid.* VIII (1956).

of the century, and a clear head, can have his say. Some of the evidence proves nothing. Some of the assertions are wildly improbable. Some of the theories identify their authors as economic determinists of one persuasion or another. But when this cleansing operation has been performed, as it now has,[1] the simple fact remains that the economic history which the whole controversy presupposes has still to be determined. It is an argument about incomes and expenditures, and the number of economic biographies which exist can be counted on two hands, with a few fingers to spare.[2] It is an argument about land management, and there are even fewer studies of that, which clearly demonstrate its methods and its profits.[3] It is an argument about movements upwards and downwards among the ruling classes, and there is not a county in England for which the attempt has been made to compare the leading families of 1640 with those of 1540 and to explain the differences. This is not to say that the authors are not to be congratulated for their bold flights of conjecture. They have defined problems whose existence was barely recognised before they began their brilliant skirmishings. They have flung a mass of information as well as misinformation into the common treasury. And they have stimulated a patient attack on ignorance by people with less imagination than themselves.

How does one find out what a man was worth in the sixteenth century, and how he fared over the years? There is naturally a good deal of contemporary testimony of one kind or another. Perhaps we can roughly distinguish between four sorts. There is the observer who is trying to classify his impressions of the wealth of Englishmen in a general way. Of these the classic example is Sir Thomas Wilson, the civil servant, whose 'State of England' contains estimates of the income

---

[1] One of the ablest general reviews is the article by J. H. Hexter, 'Storm over the Gentry', *Encounter* (May 1958).

[2] The best recent example is M. E. Finch, *The Wealth of Five Northamptonshire Families 1540–1640* (Northamptonshire Record Society, 1956). See also: J. M.W. Bean, *The Estates of the Percy Family* (Oxford, 1958); G. R. Batho, 'The Finances of an Elizabethan Nobleman: Henry Percy, Ninth Earl of Northumberland', *Econ. Hist. Rev.* 2nd series, IX, no. 3 (1957); J. P. Cooper, 'The Fortune of Thomas Wentworth, Earl of Strafford', *ibid.* XI, no. 2 (1958).

[3] Besides the work of Finch, Bean and Batho, already cited, see also E. Kerridge, 'The Movement of Rent, 1540–1660', *Econ. Hist. Rev.* 2nd series, VI (1953), and K. J. Allison, 'Flock Management in the Sixteenth and Seventeenth Centuries', *ibid.* XI, no. 1 (1958).

of various classes in 1600. Next there is the individual who writes of his own affairs, or of those of people close to him, with no special motive for misrepresenting them, though some of the frailties of memory, vanity, or family pride may have affected his work. The well-known examples in this class are the memoir writers: the earl of Northumberland's *Advice to his Son*, John Smyth's *Lives of the Berkeleys*, Gervase Holles's *Memorials of the Holles Family*, or the *Life of the Duke of Newcastle*, by Margaret, his wife. Then comes the individual who may be reporting his circumstances in some detail, but under obvious pressures to distort them. A royalist in the civil war would try to understate his income if it were a question of paying a fine to a Parliamentary committee, and then perhaps to exaggerate it, if it were a question of impressing his sovereign with his losses. Finally, there is all the gossip; the vague allusions to 'great', 'fair', or 'mean' estates; the tittle-tattle about wealth, extravagance, and debts.

In the aggregate, these sources yield a mass of information. Some impression of its variety and piquancy was conveyed by Mr Stone's article on *The Anatomy of the Elizabethan Aristocracy* and its sequels in the recent controversy. It is a body of material which helps to determine the limits of various income brackets[1] and to highlight problems; but it is very uneven, both in range and quality. There is far more for the end of our period than for the beginning. Regional differences are no more than suggested. And the treachery of table talk or tax returns needs no emphasis. Valuable as some of this comment is, there is no one who would not prefer a look at the books to the most reliable 'say-so'. It is, however, when we look at the books of this age that our problems begin.

When we examine the records of income, we find ourselves confronted with two kinds of accounts which have survived in quantity. The first are those of manorial bailiffs, which in any large household were engrossed on parchment. These officials were responsible for various items of income associated with the manor. If we ignore

---

[1] The estimate of the wealth of the English peerage under Charles I, compiled by Mr J. P. Cooper, was partly based on this material (H. R. Trevor-Roper, 'The Gentry', *op. cit.*, Appendix, pp. 54–5). See also Miss M. F. Keeler's analysis of the wealth of members of the House of Commons in *The Long Parliament 1640–1641* (Philadelphia, 1954).

industrial properties, which were not found in East Anglia, and some commercial properties, which do not appear in our accounts, a comprehensive list would include the following sources: (1) rents of assise—that is, the fixed quit-rents paid to the lord by copyholders or freeholders; (2) leasehold rents—paid by one or more tenants who were farming the demesne lands or the mill; (3) profits of court—including both the fines imposed on copyholders when holdings were transferred in the lord's court and a number of small dues or mulcts; (4) the profits of woods, warrens, quarries, tithes, and so forth, where they existed. To this we might add franchises like hundreds, which were not manors, but were often included in manorial accounts.

The second class of records consists of receivers' accounts. Small and medium-sized estates could dispense with the services of receivers. Thomas Buttes, of Riborough, Norfolk, who had a part interest in a group of small manors on the borders of Essex and Suffolk, simply called the bailiffs to his own, or his brother's house, took their deliveries of cash himself and kept the records in his own notebook. On a large estate, like Sir Nicholas Bacon's, there were usually two receivers, and there might be more. It was their business to collect revenue from several sources. First would come the deliveries of cash from the manorial bailiffs on their charge. These would be entered on their accounts as gross sums, with no more detail than the name of the bailiff and his manor. These sums were known as 'livery money'. A distinguished historian who came across this term in the household accounts of Sir William Cecil, assumed that it referred to income from the Court of Wards and Liveries, of which Cecil held the position of Master.[1] But 'livery' was simply the English for 'liberatio' and the reference was merely to the deliveries of cash from Cecil's manorial bailiffs. Among the other revenues found on receivers' accounts are (1) the income from lands held by the lord for a term of years—an important source frequently omitted from bailiffs' accounts, where they deal only with lands of inheritance, or lands held for life; (2) the income from offices, stewardships, pensions, and wardships; (3) the income from the

---

[1] Conyers Read, 'Lord Burghley's Household Accounts', *Econ. Hist. Rev.* 2nd series, IX, no. 2 (1956), p. 346, n. 1.

'foreign' account—an ancient category in medieval records, which tends in our period to become a catch-all; it may include anything from the profits of the home farms or the receipts from the sale of lands to occasional wood sales or windfalls like dowries.

Examples of these two types of accounts can be found in almost any large collection of estate documents, and we are sometimes lucky enough to find them in a continuous series. The Bacon manuscripts at the University of Chicago, which were purchased from the sale of the muniments at Redgrave Hall, contain sixteen receivers' accounts for the period when Sir Nicholas was at the height of his prosperity as Lord Keeper (1559–75), and a series of bailiffs' accounts which run consecutively for almost a century (1556–1648). There are, however, two questions which have to be faced by anyone who wants to use these records as a guide to income.

First, how does one derive a statement of income from accounts whose form is determined by the medieval preoccupation with the liability of the collectors of revenue? These accounts, like those of all the preceding centuries, are organised on the principles of 'charge and discharge'. A rough analogy may be found in the accounts of a modern store-keeper, such as a quartermaster in the army, who takes various stores on his charge, and then accounts for them by showing the deliveries he has made under duly authorised warrants, the deductions he is allowed for depreciation, and the inventories of the balance that remains. However, bailiffs and receivers were charged with revenues, not stores, and there are various complications which prevent the analogy from being more than rough.

An example will help to explain the problems. Assuming that the collector starts a new account, uncomplicated by any responsibility for arrears, he begins by listing the properties on his charge. If it is a manor, the rents of assise are worth so much, the leases so much more, and the sum of the charge made up from these values represents his formal liability. But this is only a theoretical income. If some items, like the proceeds from a wood sale in the current year, are real enough, the money may still have to be collected from the man who arranged the sale; and other items may not be real at all. Some rents of assise may not have been collected for years; some fines imposed in the lord's court may not be leviable; some year-to-year leases may not be yielding anything this year because the land is in the hands of the lord; and some income may still be on the bailiff's charge after an order has diverted it to somebody else. Periodically, there will be efforts to tidy up the charge, but it soon becomes untidy again. And there are always expenses such as repairs and stewards' fees which reduce the gross receipts. So the sum of the charge almost invariably exceeds the real income.

If we proceed through the 'discharge' sections, we find a record of the 'liveries' which the collector has made to the lord or his steward. These figures are real enough, but for our purposes they are a statement of minimum income. How much more must be added? To find out, we pursue the collector through his allowances—which may be quite a labyrinth in a complicated account—and examine them. Some turn out to be acknowledgements of the fact that the theoretical income cannot be collected; some are necessary expenses. But there is always a chance that others are a diversion of real income. A sum which a bailiff has been ordered to give to the supervisor of works on a nearby manor, where a house is being built, will not appear among his 'liveries' to the lord, and consequently will not appear in the receivers' accounts, where all the liveries are consolidated; but it is obviously part of the income. Finally, we end our journey among the collector's debts. After reducing the gap between the sum of the charge and the deliveries of cash as far as he can, he is left with unpaid sums which have still to be collected from various individuals, and with the cash on his hands which he has not yet surrendered. Together, these debts (which are duly itemised) constitute the arrearages with which the 'charge' begins in the next account, and they quite often amount to considerable sums.

The real income is therefore distributed among the 'liveries', the allowances, and the debts. Where we have nothing but accounts for scattered years, it is impossible to tell the margin by which the real income exceeds the 'liveries' to the lord, or whether the 'liveries' themselves have been inflated by irregular windfalls. Given a continuous series, these difficulties tend to disappear. Arrearages will be paid up in the form of 'liveries' to the lord, or eliminated if they are bad debts; and the 'livery' figure, adjusted by the addition of any income which may be concealed among the allowances, becomes a reasonable approximation. The incidence of windfalls like fines, or of heavy expenses on repairs, also becomes apparent.

There are of course other kinds of evidence with which the testimony of bailiffs' accounts can be compared. The concept of 'clear annual value' was the basis of all purchases of manors, and documents known as 'particulars' survive in which the net income is estimated by deducting necessary expenses such as out-rents and administrative fees from gross receipts. The 'particulars' prepared by the Court of Augmentations for the sale of monastic lands are well-known examples. The same principles were incorporated in the *Valors* which were prepared from time to time for the manors of large estates; and estimates of the income which would be produced by a manor over an indefinite period were regularly made in marriage settlements, mortgages, and other transactions. However, though always an interesting commentary, these records are obviously inferior to the actual accounts. The irregularity of some sources of income, like fines, created one kind of difficulty for the predictors, the inflation another, and, when we have a chance to compare a lawyer's estimate of the value of a property with the real figures, we are often struck by the gap between them.

So far our examples have been drawn from bailiffs' accounts, but the same principles also apply to receivers' accounts. The 'sum of the charge' may be freer from unrealistic elements, as the manorial income consists of the actual sums handed over by the bailiffs, but it does not follow that all the items are real; we may find that a rent, or a pension from the crown, or a fee from a bishopric, which appears there, is always in arrears. Necessary costs have also to be deducted. Here, again, the 'livery' figure is the best guide to the net income, but it usually needs a bigger correction from the allowance section, because a receiver's allowances are more apt to conceal income than a bailiff's. He is a spender as well as a collector, and when he claims an allowance for the annuities which he has paid to various dependents of the lord, or for any other purpose which cannot be regarded as a necessary cost, this amount has to be added to the 'livery' figure. It will also be clear, from what has already been said, that where income has been diverted at the bailiff's level, before it ever reached the receiver, any estimate which is based on the latter's account, alone, will fall short of the actual total.

So much for our first problem. On the whole, and always assuming that we are content with reasonable approximations, it may be regarded as a soluble one, provided that we understand the system and have enough of the accounts in series. But after we have extracted the income from these records, how close have we got to discovering the *whole* income?

The bailiff's accounts which we have been considering are invaluable as far as they go; but they deal only with landed income (if we except a few franchises), and they do not exhaust that. Besides the omission of leases (that is, rents from lands held by the lord for a term of years), they may also say little or nothing of two profitable activities which are someone else's responsibility—the management of the home farm and the management of sheep farms. In those accounts we have seen, the home farm is never mentioned; there are indications elsewhere that this was the business of a bailiff of husbandry who accounted separately, and we have not been so fortunate as to come across a useful series of his accounts in this region. In the same way, sheep accounts were the responsibility of a sheep-reeve. There are a few references to his activities in the immense series of bailiffs' accounts for the Bacon family, but only in one instance do they incorporate the records of a sheep-manor. These farms abounded in the foldcourse region of Norfolk and western Suffolk, and we have attempted in chapter v to form some estimate of their profits from a few records compiled by sheep-reeves. But with the solitary exception in the Bacon manuscripts, bailiffs' accounts have been of no assistance.

These deficiencies in the bailiffs' accounts are only partially repaired, if at all, in the accounts of receivers. Bailiffs of husbandry, and sheep-reeves, may stand outside their system. If their profits do fall within it, they appear in the folds of the 'foreign' account; but there are 'foreign' accounts among the records of receivers which say nothing about farming, and there are receivers' accounts which contain no 'foreign' receipts, because the lady of the household, or perhaps the steward, is responsible for them. The possibility that some officer is accounting separately is one which dogs our whole study of income and expenditure.

But there is another omission from the receivers' accounts which may be of vastly more importance than any so far mentioned. This is the heavy silence about the gratuities given to office-holders. The role of the gratuity in a society where public servants were not maintained at the public expense, and where high and low expected to be tipped, has been brilliantly demonstrated by Professor Neale.[1] Receivers' accounts have nothing to say about this; they simply record the formal fees, and no historian has so far been able to show an account of the informal ones. This is a little surprising. If our first impulse is to suppose that politicians would be as careful then to conceal their irregular rewards as they are now, we quickly discover that many of these gifts were not considered irregular at all. The distinction between gifts and bribes was drawn with a large latitude for the interested giver. Everyone expected to pay for the benefits of influence. The records of a Dean and Chapter will show that a 48-ounce cup of silver gilt had been given to the Earl of Leicester for a word in season.[2] The duchess of Suffolk had a suit in the London courts—she ordered three cups at ten or twelve pounds a piece, one for Sir Robert Catlin, the chief justice, one for Valentine Browne, another judge, and one for the Queen's attorney.[3] There are letters between courtiers explaining that £500 has been offered for a service and suggesting a three-way split among highly respectable people. There are contracts in which a well-connected squire accepts £50 from a neighbour in the country to prefer a suit, on the under-standing that the money will be returned if nothing happens. Finally, in every expense account of a large household there is a section for Gifts and Rewards in which a political gratuity may be recorded as inno-cently as a tip for a gift of strawberries or a hand-out to the poor. However, there was no comparable section in the records of income, so

---

[1] Sir John Neale, 'The Elizabethan Political Scene', Raleigh Lecture, British Academy, 1948.
[2] Blomefield, *History of Norfolk*, IV, 569.
[3] Lady Goff, *A Woman of the Tudor Age* (London, 1930), p. 279.

we are very much in the dark about the actual earnings of an office-holder.

It may be assumed that informal records will turn up some day. The particulars which could be collected for the impeachment of Sir Francis Bacon show that such records were kept, and it is unreasonable to suppose that they have all disappeared. But until they do appear, we have only two alternatives. We can note the real values which contemporaries assigned to various offices; or we can try to make some guess for a particular individual by comparing his recorded income with the scale of his expenditure. We have attempted the last in the study of Sir Nicholas Bacon, but all that is being said here about the limitations of the evidence is a sobering reminder of the hazards of guess-work.

When we turn from the records of income to those of expenditure, we are struck by the curious chance that has given us more of the former than of the latter. On the face of it, the accounts look equally likely to survive. At least they are often equally big. The huge pages of the weekly stock account which produce, when bound, a magnificent volume like *The Brome Household Accounts, 1594–1604*[1] are as impressive in their way as the membranes which the clerks stitched together to make up the bailiffs' or receivers' accounts. Yet somehow the whole class of household accounts, from the journal books of day-by-day expenses to the annual summaries of 'all my lord's charges and expenses' have been much more ephemeral than the estate records. Perhaps it is just another commentary on the inferiority of vernacular records compared with those in Latin, or on the prestige and durability of parchment. So far as our experience goes, the most formal household accounts have been kept in English and on paper. But whatever the reason, our knowledge of income, limited as it is, is less inadequate than our knowledge of expenditure.

This is not to say that we do not have a great deal of scattered information about different items in the budget. We have seen that the receivers' accounts tell us something about the cost of supporting dependents. We can use a variety of documents to find out what some of the lands cost. Important incidents in the life of the family, such as a

---

[1] Iveagh, MSS., Elveden, Suffolk.

marriage, or a funeral, or the building of a house may be quite precisely recorded in terms of pounds, shillings, and pence. And there is certainly no lack of isolated bills or fragments from kitchen accounts. What is missing is the top-level account which allows us to form some impression of the whole expenditure.

On all estates, big and small, it was presumably someone's business to record disbursements as they were made day by day, and then to consolidate them periodically. On a small estate this might be done by the squire or his lady, but we have not been able to find any such record among the papers of Thomas Buttes, of Riborough, Norfolk, the only owner of a small estate to be considered in this study. On a large estate, the superintendence of spending was usually the business of a 'steward of household'.[1] This official—the highest in the hierarchy—would be charged with some spending himself, and with disbursements to several other spending officials—the lady, the clerk of the kitchen, the yeoman of the stable, the bailiff of husbandry, the surveyor of works, and so on. Where the nature of the estate, and its traditions, made for centralised control, he would be expected to 'cause them all to bring their several defrayments and reckoninges to his examination and insert them emonge his accomptes at the time of my audite, therebye to avoyde confusion of accomptantes'[2]—as we read in one set of household ordinances. Then, from this amalgamation of accounts (each organised on the principles of charge and discharge), it was common to abstract a summary of the year's expenses.

A series of these summaries, covering the forty years from 1557 to 1597, each bearing some such title as 'A Briefe Collection of all the Accompts for the Charges and Expenses of Sir Thomas Cornwaleys, knight, for one whole year', is analysed in chapter iv. They show the division of duty among the officers of a large household, the standard items in the budget, and the changing patterns of expenditure as family circumstances altered. Similar accounts seem to have formed the basis for a recent study of the estates of the earl of Northumberland.[3] They

---

[1] 'A Booke of Orders and Rules of Anthony, Viscount Montague in 1595', *Sussex Archaeology*, vII (1854), 185–9.   [2] *Ibid.* p. 185.

[3] G. R. Batho, 'The Finances of an Elizabethan Nobleman: Henry Percy, Ninth Earl of Northumberland', *Econ. Hist. Rev.* 2nd series, ix, no. 3 (April 1957).

were as much a matter of routine as the receivers' records, and more of them may be expected to appear, whatever the ravages of time. When they do, we shall have clearer ideas about a whole range of questions which are now enveloped in fog—the proportions of the typical budget, the impact of inflation on the different items, the expenses of office-holders, the alleged hardships of mere landlords, the scale of aristocratic extravagance, and perhaps even the scope of gratuities.

However, these master accounts of expenditure are no more immune from problems than those of income. Without the quarterly 'books of titles' from which the gross totals were drawn, the precise scope of a particular category is often obscure. There is also the same possibility, here, of separate accounts which have been lost. A journey of any duration was usually accounted for separately by an officer who accompanied the lord, and we shall see how impossible it is to be sure that all of these have been incorporated in the Cornwallis summaries. An estate with more than one centre, or with divided control at the summit, introduces more complications. Finally, just as gratuities could be put into the money bags without any official recording them, so presumably money could be taken out. Did every lord feel obliged to acquaint his servants with his withdrawals? Did every servant record all his own withdrawals? There is an anecdote about Sir Francis Bacon's servants which illustrates the extreme possibilities of confusion—a visitor was startled to see one after another come into the room and stuff his pockets with cash.[1] Without postulating these conditions, we would doubtless be wise to rise from the best accounts of expenditure with a few reservations.

So much for the difficulty of determining income and expenditure from the different kinds of record. But were there no records which compared the two sides of the account in such a way as to enable us to see at a glance the condition of the estate? Were no balances ever struck? Presumably on a small estate the simple record of receipts and disbursements might have ended with a balance at the year's end, or at some other seasons. But we have seen none. On a large estate, a 'book

---

[1] James Spedding, *The Letters and the Life of Francis Bacon* (London, 1872), VII, 563-4.

of livery money' seems to have been kept, in which all withdrawals were acknowledged by the spending officers, and all receipts from receivers and others were probably entered.[1] But again we have to admit that no such record has come our way, so it is not clear what balances, if any, were struck there. The large estate seems to have relied for routine guidance on a monthly record of receipts and disbursements which was kept by the steward. The household ordinances already quoted contain the directive, 'I will...that he exhibite unto me att every moneths ende his own booke of particuler receiptes and disburse-ments, to the ende that I may better understand my domesticall affayres and householde charges'.[2] A fragment of this type, dealing with the three months between 24 June and 29 September 1618, was exhibited during the impeachment of Sir Francis Bacon. As printed by his bio-grapher,[3] it consists of a brief record of gross receipts, amounting to over £4000, followed by a detailed record of disbursements. Of the latter, those consisting of 'Gifts and rewards' were grouped under one title (about £300 in small tips) while the rest—payments to tradesmen, money-lenders, household officials, and so on—were simply left as an undigested chronicle, with the observation at the end that the sums paid amounted to £3711. 4s. 2d. A record in this condition could be inter-preted, no doubt, but it was far from being an intelligible balance. Nor does the annual audit seem to have yielded a balanced statement as a matter of routine. None, at least, has been found.

It is clear that balances of some sort or another must have been struck in the course of meeting commitments. A simple lesson in book-keeping was once given by Sir Nicholas Bacon, the subject of chapter II, to a son-in-law, Sir Henry Woodhouse, who was obviously having great difficulty in meeting his. As an unpublished letter by a man who

---

[1] *Sussex Archaeology*, VII, 185. On the estates of the earls of Northumberland it was the duty of the Cofferer (who elsewhere might be called Treasurer or Steward) to record receipts and deliveries and to report a cash balance weekly (*Northumberland Household Book* (London, 1905), p. 383). But on the same estates revenues from receivers amounting to about £1000 p.a. were assigned directly to certain household officials, so the Cofferer may have been by-passed in this way. Whatever their limitations, a good series of Cofferer's Accounts would be highly instruc-tive; but those available to Mr J. M. W. Bean, for 1514–26, were very hard to interpret (*The Estates of the Percy Family 1416–1537* (Oxford, 1958), pp. 137–8).
[2] *Ibid.* p. 187.
[3] Spedding, *op. cit.* VI, 327–36.

was a model of method in his own affairs, it is worth reproducing in full.[1]

Sonne,

Dowbting lest you showld not be carefull enowghe to kepe appoyntment with me at Candlemes according to the bond made unto me by you and Mr Townsend, I have thowght good by this my letter to put you in mynd of it because thinges stond so with me, as I must of necessitie occupie that money at that tyme for otherwyse I shalbe dryven to as great an extremytie as you were when you borrowed it of me.

And besides yf my counsell may do anything with you, you shall call to remembraunce and put in wrighting all manner of somes of money that you owe to any person, and therin to note also, every severall some by itselfe, and the day when it shall be due and the forfeiture that will growe for none payment and the interest that you be chardged with all, untill suche tyme as you have payd it.

This beyng done, you are also to cause to be set downe in wrighting in another note, all the debts that be owyng unto you, and the tyme of these payments, and all the goods which you have that you may convenyently make money of, and then you are to consider howe much the debts dewe by you do exceede the debts and goods due unto you, And so knowyng howe fare you are runne behind you are then to examyne what land you may best spare to make mony of to paye that surplusage of debt owyng by you exceding that owyng to you, And then to establishe and proporcon your contynewall chardg equall to your revennewe, And except you do this suerly that will followe that will bring great disquyetnes and greife to yourselfe and to your frends, which were great pitie.

The like counsell to this, and somewhat more at lardg, I gave unto you a fower or fyve yeres since, but fynding by the declaracon of your state at your last beyng with me that such regard and care was not had of the advise as I wish there had bene. I have thowght good once agayne considering how near you be to me, and those that shall come of you, to counsell you that you would by the advise of your frends take some such course to preserve your calling and your credite and estymacon in the world as may sownd bothe to your commendacon, and to the establishment of your howse, which suerly must nedes fall and decaye without some good foresight in this matter.

And for the better doyng of this, yf you and Mr. Townshend and some such other of your frends as yourselfe shall make choyse of will repayer

---

[1] I owe this letter to the courtesy of Basil Cozens-Hardy, Esq., of Letheringsett, Norfolk, who owns it. It is undated, but must have been written in the 1570's.

hether to me, vij or viij dayes before the begynnyng of the next tearme, you
shall have the best advyse that I can geve you.

Thus havyng this second tyme by letter remembered you of theise matters,
I leave from further troubling you.

It will be noted that Sir Nicholas does not tell Sir Henry that he can
see his situation if he will only tell his steward to produce such and such
an account. We shall also see, when we look at Sir Nicholas's own
affairs, that no formal balances have survived among his papers, though
informal appraisals must have been made at several seasons of the year,
just as one had been made on the eve of Candlemas, when he wrote
this letter. There is, however, a solitary instance of a comparison of
income and expenditure which is sufficiently interesting to be worth
study. This is a single sheet of paper, for the estates of Sir Robert Drury,
of Hawstead, Suffolk, which bears the endorsement, 'A General
Account, 20 January 1609'.[1] A condensed version of this, which
preserves the formal arrangement of the account, is printed in Table 1.
It will be seen that the steward begins in the upper half of the page by
listing the items of income which had fallen due in the last four months,
so as to show the whole amount due, the amount actually received, and
the balance still to be paid. In the lower half, he first listed, on the left-
hand side, the sums spent in a number of categories which were standard
items in the budgets of the period, and then filled the right-hand side
with other expenses, such as payments under bonds or deliveries connected with journeys, and ended by adding the cash in the house. The
account is not formally balanced, but the sum of the expenses, at the
foot of the page, coincides, within a shilling or two, with the income
actually received.

There are obvious problems in this account. If it was intended to
balance, we have to assume that there was no cash on hand at the
beginning of the period, or that what there was was being ignored.
We do not know whether the lady of the house received all her
spending money through the steward, or had her own access to the
money-bags. We know nothing about any income or expenditure
which Sir Robert chose to withhold from the system. Even if we can

Bacon MSS., University of Chicago.

The Wealth of the Gentry, 1540–1660

TABLE I. *An abstract of the Drury 'General Account'*
(22 September 1609 – 20 January 1610)

	Amount due £ s. d.			Amount paid £ s. d.			Unpaid £ s. d.		
Various arrearages (rents and wood sales)	270	7	6	100	0	0	170	7	6
Sale of stock	91	10	0	78	10	0	13	0	0
Sale of oats	1	5	0	1	5	0	—		
Sale of wool	25	4	0	13	0	0	12	4	0
Sale of feed (tithe)	27	0	0	27	0	0	—		
Sale of land	180	0	0	180	0	0	—		
Enfranchising a close	2	10	0	2	10	0	—		
Three fines	5	10	0	5	10	0	—		
Payment on a bond	20	0	0	20	0	0	—		
A rent	1	13	4	1	13	4	—		
The townsmen of Bury	215	1	6	215	1	6	—		
Michaelmas rents (includes eight accounts and £22 in Christmas rents)	555	1	3	478	9	1	76	12	2
	£1395	2	7	£1122	18	11*	£272	3	8

	£ s. d.						£ s. d.		
Household provisions	56	1	2	Sent to various places			13	0	0
Stable charges	54	3	0	To my master on going			40	0	0
Forging (?) charge	2	0	0	to London, etc.					
Bills and workmen's wages	36	2	1	To my lady			12	0	0
Extraordinary charges	37	17	7	To others of the family			23	0	0
Apparel (master, mistress, and daughter)	13	6	2	Payments on five bonds			530	0	0
				More laid out by my lady			31	12	0
Repairs	3	15	8	as per her book					
Household stuff	7	10	2	To myself			40	0	0
Servants' wages	31	19	10	Money in the house			190	10	5
	£242	15	8				£880	2	5

* Unspecified corn rents were received in addition to the cash income. The wool money and the proceeds from land sales were part-payments.

assume that the Michaelmas rents will recur again at Lady Day, we cannot tell what are the profits from farming, and we know nothing about the nature of the bonds or the reasons for selling land. But at least we see a balance being struck, on an estate which cannot have been worth less than £2000 a year at the time, and was probably worth more.[1] A series of these statements would be very illuminating. But we have only one, for four months.

After he has made what he can of the records of income and expenditure, the patient explorer can examine a group of documents which throws some light on the estate at the death of the owner. But by now he is resigned to the fact that it will only be fitful unless the right combination has survived. The will may contain some clues about the solidity of the testator, in the scale of the legacies and the provisions for the discharge of debts, but the materials for an estimate of either the real or the personal estate are usually missing. The disposal of the real estate has usually been arranged by previous conveyances, and in these cases the will may contain nothing but a reference to the various deeds. Details will be given where the testator has preserved a discretion to alter the earlier dispositions, or where these dispositions have not dealt with all the properties; but generally speaking we can only establish the values of the lands at death if we have access to the accounts of bailiffs and receivers. The personal estate is not appraised. Normally, the testator simply indicates his intentions as to legacies, and leaves instructions as to the property which may be realised—a manor, leases, household furnishings and so forth—to pay for the bequests, the debts, the servants' wages, and the funeral expenses.

The Inquisitions Post Mortem were supposed to be valuations of real estate. They were required where land was held under knight service, as a basis for assessing the incidents of this tenure, but their deficiencies are well known. Not all lands were affected, and not all the inquisitions for a particular estate have survived, as one was required for each county in which the deceased held lands. Moreover, the valuations were notoriously low. Letters have survived from the sixteenth century in which advice was given about how to manipulate the juries which reported the particulars,[2] but the assessments had been a farce long before

---

[1] Professor R. C. Bald is of the opinion that the clear annual value approached £3000. He points out that this account does not include the rents from London properties (*Donne and the Drurys* (Cambridge, 1959), p. 65).

[2] British Museum, Add. MS. 39220, f. 44. In this letter, the heir is told how to secure a good jury from the tenants of Sir John Heigham—'the land is to be found of as small value as you can prove, the charge shall be the less'.

this date and they became so again. The values in the inquisitions for the Bacon and Cornwallis Estates can be compared with the real values in the bailiffs' accounts to show the huge discrepancies in the late sixteenth and early seventeenth centuries.[1] It is a puzzle to know on what basis the former were made. Some of them can be shown to have been once real, but only decades earlier when the Court of Augmentations sold the lands. Others might be any nice, low figure, for all the reason that can now be seen in them. By 1625, when Sir Edmund Bacon obtained his special livery for the lands inherited from his father, the first baronet, an 'incrementum' was being added to the value of each manor—presumably as a token concession to the inflation. But it made very little difference. The chief utility of the I.P.M. is in showing us, where we have no other evidence, what property the deceased held and how it descended. It seems to have no other value.

The personal estate can be determined if we are lucky enough to have the executors' accounts, with their record of assets and expenditures. These are firm figures, and the accompanying inventories have been used more than once in this study. Often, however, it is the old story of fragmentary glimpses—an inventory of the possessions in one house when the owner might have had as many as six—a record of plate, or cash in hand, or farm stock, but not of all three.

The documents enumerated so far have not exhausted the evidence, but enough has been said to demonstrate the difficulty of finding out what a man was worth at a particular time and how he fared over the years. If, in addition to these elementary facts, we want to know enough about the spirit in which his estate was managed to form some opinion about the controversies among the historians of the gentry, we are once again beset by lack of evidence. The Audit Houses and Evidence Chambers of a great estate once contained a vast mass of material connected with its administration, and much of this can still be seen in a good collection of estate documents—deeds, recognisances, bonds, acquittances, leases, rentals, surveys, court rolls, and miscel-

---

[1] We know that the Cornwallis lands were bringing in about £1200 a year in 1595; an I.P.M. put their value at £143 (Iveagh MSS., Box 8, no. 23). The Bacon lands were bringing in about £2400 a year in 1575; an I.P.M. of 1579 said £375.

laneous memoranda. But a lot of it is uncommunicative. The purposes behind the document are often indecipherable; the shots are static where we want a moving picture; and the endless repetition of small affairs numbs the hardiest enquirer. Luckily, just as we are tempted to think that all proportion has been lost among a host of particulars, we find that some coherence can be salvaged from this wreckage of meaning. The letters of a lord to his sons, the memoranda of a steward at the end of the audit, the human drama in a piece of litigation, the comments of a surveyor on rising values, the stories that can be wrung from a patient comparison of recurring items in the accounts, all tell us something. But we would be deceiving ourselves if we thought that much would not remain enigmatic after our best efforts have been tried.

In this spirit of blundering enquiry, we have examined the accounts of a few East Anglian gentry, which have happened to come our way. In the study of Nicholas Bacon, the rising lawyer, we have included an outline of his early career which could not be justified by the requirements of an economic biography. The excuse lies in the fact that he is a figure of the first rank, for whom no biography exists, and the reconstruction of a typical success story from the materials at our disposal seemed a useful exercise. An effort was also made to see how his descendants fared. The subject of the second study is Sir Thomas Cullum, the rising merchant, of Gracechurch Street, London, and Hawstead, Suffolk. Though a lesser man than the Springs or Greshams, who rose to great wealth in this region, Cullum has left a notebook which ought to be the envy of every harassed student of accounts. It compresses, into the lucid compass of a stock account, the gains of forty-eight consecutive years, beginning with the end of his apprenticeship in 1619 and ending with his death in 1664. These two types are commonplace enough in English social history, but an attempt to unravel their finances in this detail has not, we believe, been made for this period.

'The Courtier—In and Out of Office' is a study of Sir Thomas Cornwallis, of Brome, Suffolk. He was a trusted servant of Mary Tudor, whose political prospects were ruined by the accession of

Elizabeth. We are not so well supplied with accounts for the years of office as for those of retirement, but there is enough to observe the adjustments that had to be made. We are also able to see how Sir Thomas—a 'mere' landlord after 1559—weathered forty years of inflation. The unusually good series of expense accounts, already referred to, has been an obvious help in this connexion.

Believing that the problems of the 'mere landlord' have been exaggerated, we have attempted to set them in a clearer perspective in the last chapter. One feature is the exploration of a subject which has been the theme of endless comment in the histories of the sixteenth century but very little close study—the profits of sheep farming. Another is an examination of the movement of rents. The Bures estate—a group of small manors on the borders of Essex and Suffolk which first passed from a family of medieval knights into the hands of a rising doctor, Sir William Buttes, and then drifted into the Bacon empire—gives us one opportunity of testing the inflation of agricultural incomes. The Bacon estates themselves, throughout the full length of their recorded history, provide several more.

It will be obvious that the scope of this tentative work is more limited than the range of the controversy which stimulated it. Some questions, such as the supposed trends of land ownership in favour of certain classes, or of estates of a certain size, have been studiously avoided. Anyone who has spent as much time as the author in trying to find out what a few individuals owned is invincibly sceptical about the possibilities of statistical sampling in our present state of knowledge. Other questions, such as the transformation in the character of the great house of Howard, or the economic problems of the bishopric of Norwich, or the continuity of ruling families in each of the three counties between the dissolution of the monasteries and the outbreak of civil war, were considered only to be postponed. But it is hoped that what is here is not without its interest. Most of the generalisations about the fortunes of the gentry have been based on other regions; East Anglia, the most populous and progressive section of the realm, has not yet been heard from. The manuscripts on which these sketches depend have not, for the most part, been used before. If this has deprived the author of valuable correctives, it has also given a spice of novelty to some of the findings. But the chief interest lies in the effort to grapple with the economics of family history. If the arguments over the Rise of the Gentry have demonstrated anything, it is that our present state of knowledge is one of mitigated ignorance. In such situations, the honest enquirer always has one consolation—his blunders may be as instructive as his successes.

CHAPTER II

THE RISING LAWYER
SIR NICHOLAS BACON

DEPARTING GLORY

F UNERALS were taken seriously in Tudor England. When a ritual was appointed for all the ordinary occasions of life there was nothing informal about the manner of leaving it. A decent burial cost a fortune. At the moment of death, embalmers and surgeons, carpenters and masons, drapers and sempstresses, canons and choristers, cooks and butlers, and whole troops of ordinary servants sprang into action, while the poor looked hopefully on, and the wretches in the foulest prisons knew they would get their alms. Over it all a costly authority was wielded by those professionals in punctilio, the College of Heralds. No young nobleman ever squandered in an evening's dice a fraction of what it would cost to bury him. The marriage of a daughter might run it close, but a visit from the Queen, which could devour a hundred pounds a day, had to be cruelly prolonged to enter the same class. It was not until Puritanism laid its icy hand on idle ceremonies that funerals shrank into their modern frugality, and the days receded when a year's income from a dozen manors might vanish in the vault.

On the morning of 9 March 1579 a crowd stood expectantly outside York House, near Charing Cross.[1] It was one of those palaces lining the river which not so long ago had belonged to bishops but were now

[1] The following reconstruction is closely based upon a detailed record of funeral expenses, of which there are two copies. One is entitled 'The whole charges of the funeralles of Sir Nicholas Bacon Knight...a.d. 1578' (MS. Ashm. 836, Bodleian Library). This probably belonged to the eldest son, Nicholas. The other copy, which must have been that of the second son, Nathaniel, was in the Townshend MS. which H. W. Saunders edited in *History Teachers' Miscellany* (Linton, Cambridge, 1927), v, 27, 45, 75. This was an executor's account, kept by Bartholomew Kemp, Treasurer, which began on 10 March 1579 with a list of receipts and then recorded the payment of funeral expenses, legacies, and wages up to 11 May. For supporting documents (warrants, receipts, etc.), see Townshend MSS., Safe 2 (37), Garsett House, Norwich.

The Rising Lawyer

given up to lawyers and noblemen. A generation later, a duke would erect at the foot of its gardens the Buckingham gate which still stands on the embankment. Today the house was swathed in black. Black bays hung all around the outer court; there were black curtains at the windows and black valances on the widow's bed. Maids had strewn the chambers with perfumed rushes. In the chapel the lying in state was at an end. It was seventeen days since two physicians, two surgeons, and the Queen's chandler had done their duties, and by this time the families had mustered from their houses in Essex, Suffolk, Norfolk and Hertfordshire. Across the road, the bells of St Martin-in-the-Fields would toll all day.[1] In old St Paul's, spireless now for over a decade,[2] but still towering above the ancient city, another peal would ring. A tomb had been ordered there two years ago[3] in the best Renaissance fashion—the knightly figure at rest, the columned canopy, the opulent inscription.[4] And a site to stir the fancy had been chosen. His lordship's companion in the choir would be no less than John of Gaunt, duke of Lancaster. If Elizabeth's sense of breeding had withheld a peerage from the sheep-reeve's son, she would hardly censure this consolation. Today the duke's tomb was boarded up—but only to prevent it from being scratched. Blacks, of course, were everywhere. The pulpit, the communion table, the stools where the chief mourners would sit, the arches in the aisles, had each received their quota. The vergers got a fee for all the bays hanging on the west side of John of Gaunt, and the Dean and Chapter for all the bays on the east side. There was a nice punctilio about

[1] 'Item the ixth of March was buryed Sir Nicholas Bacon...the best cloth xx^d, the whole daies knell ij^s iiij^d, vi peales xij^d—v^s' (*A Register of Baptisms, Marriages, and Burials in the Parish of St Martin in the Fields...from 1550 to 1619*, ed. Thomas Mason (Harleian Society Registers, xxv (1898)), 123; *St Martin-in-the-Fields: The Accounts of the Churchwardens, 1525–1603*, ed. John V. Kitto (London, 1901), p. 308).

[2] The Lord Keeper, together with his brother James, had been appointed to a committee to deal with repairs to the spire after it crashed in 1561. The estimates are in the Bacon MSS. (Chicago).

[3] Dean's letter authorising the Lord Keeper's workmen to have access to site of tomb (H.M.C. Rep. IX, Pt. I (Dean and Chapter of St Paul's), 71). Michael Shaller's MS. notebook (St Paul's Cathedral Library) makes it clear that the date was 4 August 1576, not (as in H.M.C. Report) 1574.

[4] A mutilated torso was recovered after the Great Fire and lies now on a stone slab in the crypt. For an engraving of the original tomb, see Sir William Dugdale, *The History of Saint Paul's Cathedral* (London, 1818), p. 50. The inscription, attributed to George Buchanan, was printed in *Biographia Britannica* (London, 1747–63), I, 368–9.

fees. According to their status and function, the Dean, two prebends, ten choristers, twelve petty canons, six vicars, the bell-ringers, the chapter clerk, the keeper of the vestry, the keeper of the pulpit, and two door-keepers, each received a just sum.

Of all the preparations, nothing consumed so much time and money as the organisation of the blacks. The deceased, who had a proper sense of the value of money, had wanted to set some limit to them. He seems to have thought that those who could afford them ought to pay for their own. Nevertheless, exceptions were to be made for certain friends and relations. When we contemplate the acreage bestowed on the exceptions, the mind boggles at the thought of the cloth involved in a reckless funeral. Here again that medieval deity, 'order and degree', ruled everything. The Lord Treasurer got twelve yards for himself at 30s. a yard, seven yards and half for each of two gentlemen at 16s. a yard, and a yard and a half for each of three yeomen at 12s. a yard. He was the principal mourner, but the earls of Leicester and Huntingdon got the same because they were noblemen. Mr Secretary Walsingham came next with eight yards of the top quality and a suitable supply for his yeomen—but nothing for gentlemen. Then came a group which included five sons and three sons-in-law, the Master of the Rolls, the Attorney-General, the Solicitor-General, the Master of the Queen's ·Jewel House, and Sir Thomas Gresham. They all got six yards for themselves at 26s. 8d. a yard, and three yards at 12s. for two yeomen. From them we drop down to £1 a yard for the Dean of St Paul's, who has only one yeoman. Two physicians keep him company, Doctors Huicke and Smith, and two brothers-in-law, Mr William Cooke and Mr Henry Killigrew. After the church, came the city (for Sir Thomas Gresham was in a class by himself). Thomas Audley, skinner, and Hugh Morgan, grocer, had been active in the deceased's affairs—about £2000 was lying at Morgan's when he died. They rated four yards each at 18s. a yard, but no yeomen.

The widow, Lady Anne Bacon, got nine yards of the best quality for herself; thirteen yards at 18s. a yard for four gentlewomen; six yards at 12s. a yard for her chamber-maid; and enough to drape her bedroom. The daughters and daughters-in-law received the same scale as the sons and sons-in-law, not forgetting their gentlewomen, who matched the yeomen. After the family came the household. There were ten senior officers who included the Steward, Seal Bearer, Sergeant at Arms, Treasurer, Auditor, Receiver, and Secretary; five 'gentlemen extraordinary dwelling in London'; eight yeomen officers in charge of the Cellar, Pantry, Kitchen, Wardrobe, Chamber, Hall, and Lodge; fifteen 'yeomen in ordinary'; two 'yeomen extraordinary but lately ordinary'; and fourteen 'grooms in house ordinary'. Here were about seventy servants, all furnished with cloth on a graduated scale. The senior officers, who were themselves gentlemen, were a trifle better equipped than Audley and Morgan—five yards at 18s. a yard, with an allowance for yeomen thrown in. The lowliest usher had a yard and a half at 12s. Needless to say, the Heralds had an adequate allowance. It was not included in the bill for £97 which they submitted for their fees, their expenses in garnishing the hearse, and other perquisites. But elsewhere we read that Clarenceux had five yards and a half at 20s. a yard, with enough for four attendants; York, Windsor, and Richmond had the same quantity each at 12s. 4d. a yard, with enough for two attendants.

Altogether, this thrifty provision had allotted a thousand yards of cloth to 304 mourners at a total cost of £668. 11s. 10d.

Funerals sometimes went to St Paul's by the river, the central highway of Tudor London; but this one went by horse and foot up the Strand and Fleet Street. Sixteen beadles marched in front to clear the way. They were followed by sixty-eight poor men, 'according to the number of years of his Lordships age'.[1] Each had been given three yards of cloth at 6s. 8d. a yard, a shilling to get it made into a gown, and a shilling for his dinner. Next came the yeomen servants of the household, with the standard, followed by the forty-one servants of gentlemen, the twenty-one servants of knights, and the nine servants of lords. Behind them was a company of friends, relatives, and household officers. The emblems of rank—pennon, helm, and crest, sword and target and coat of arms—were borne in front of the hearse, which had

---

[1] This was not an invariable practice. At Sir Thomas Gresham's funeral in the same year, there were simply a hundred poor men and a hundred poor women.

the four Heralds in attendance. Mounted mourners on their draped horses followed, the widow among them. She seems to have been the only woman present. More yeomen brought up the rear, and the parish fell in behind.[1]

Stretched out in a long line of pairs, all moving with the dignity of a society perpetually on parade, the procession represented every respectable element in Elizabethan life—court, nobility, gentry, church, bar and bench, citizenry and yeomanry. The man whom they were honouring had been a central figure, in touch with every side. Lord Burleigh knew him as a mainstay of his party; the group that had soared to the top at Elizabeth's accession and stayed there. There had been moments of anger between them,[2] but on the whole it had been a fast alliance of kindred spirits, upholding the virtues of shrewdness and common sense in an age of dangerous ambitions and violent enthusiasms. They were also brothers-in-law, each having found a congenial wife among the brilliant daughters of Sir Anthony Cooke, the Protestant humanist who had been the governor of Prince Edward. Alexander Nowell, the Dean of St Paul's, who preached the funeral sermon, remembered him as a man who shared his churchmanship and his love of learning, for the Lord Keeper had been an architect of the Elizabethan Settlement and a life-long patron of education. Sir Thomas Gresham, who was to follow him to the grave in this same year, had known him longer than any of them. His memory went back to the clever young lawyer who had made his way into the richest business circles of the 1530's and married the daughter of a London mercer as his first wife. Sir Thomas had married her sister, and in time their children had married; a natural daughter, the result of one of Sir Thomas's many visits to Flanders as the business agent of the English government, had married the Lord Keeper's son Nathaniel. This connexion with the Greshams may stand for all the links with the City of London—the brother James who was a fishmonger and sheriff, the brother Thomas

---

[1] The order of march for funerals of various degrees is given in John Nichols, *Illustrations of the Manners and Expences of Antient Times in England* (London, 1797), pp. 71–4. He also describes the funeral of the earl of Derby in 1572.
[2] See the revealing letter of 21 July 1563, from Cecil to Bacon, quoted by Conyers Read, *Mr Secretary Cecil and Queen Elizabeth* (London, 1955), pp. 281–3.

who was a salter and alderman, the people he could turn to for a lease
or a loan, and who found themselves repaid in good works and good
judgement as well as cash. Then there was his own fraternity, the
lawyers; that closely guarded circle at the top of the profession who
knew, better than anyone else in Tudor England, how a fortune could
be made out of nothing.

Far beyond the range of London's bells others were being tolled in
Essex, Hertfordshire, Suffolk and Norfolk. In each county a mass of
lands and lordships had put the Bacon family on the map. In three of
them stood one of those monuments which were the passion and sometimes the ruin of the Tudor gentry—a new-built mansion. First had
come Redgrave Hall, where the monks of Bury St Edmund's had kept a
hunting lodge; then Gorhambury, where the monks of St Alban's had
owned a group of farms; then Stiffkey, which a son had just begun to
build out of his father's money and under his vigilant eye. Nor was this
all the building that stood to the Lord Keeper's credit. There was a
grammar school in Botesdale for the neighbourhood children; a library
in Gray's Inn, where he had been Treasurer and his five sons had
followed him; an Inn for the Cursitors in Chancery Lane; a campaign
to provide his old college at Cambridge with a new chapel; and a town
house, just commissioned, for this third son Edward.

No one in the procession knew the cost of all this, or the length of
the purse that had paid for it, better than Bartholomew Kemp. He had
been the Lord Keeper's Treasurer for many years. 'I pray you, cosen
Kemp, pay this.... I pray you, cosen Kemp, pay that....' The warrants
from the executors were coming in thick and fast, ordering him to pay the
funeral expenses, the legacies, the wages of servants, and the outstanding
debts. He knew what the Lord Keeper's office was worth, what every
manor, pension, wardship, and stewardship brought in. He knew, what
no one now knows, how much flowed in that was never entered in
his lordship's books; the unsolicited gifts, the sweets of influence.
Knowing all this, he could face today's expenses with a quiet mind. The
funeral was costing a thousand pounds,[1] but there was no cause for alarm.

---

[1] MS. Ashm. 836 puts the total at £919. 12s. 1d. The executor's account says £1000. Sir
Thomas Gresham's burial in December 1579 cost £800. The earl of Leicester's, in 1588 (reflecting

The Wealth of the Gentry, 1540–1660

Successful men usually obtained satisfactory pedigrees for themselves in the sixteenth century. The generations behind the grandfather might have been anybody for all anyone knew, and there was no trouble in finding an expert to say they were somebody. A professor of theology, who had tutored the Bacon children in Geneva, was engaged in this ancient pastime when he dedicated the following passage to the family in a pious number entitled 'A Fruitfull Commentarie upon the Twelve Small Prophets':

> Nowe that your house...is most noble, appeareth both by the English and French histories, in which there is often made honourable mention of the same: and also by this, that even nowe at this day there is remaining a most wealthie village in Normandie, as bigge as a great towne, called Baconvil, in French Bacceville, situated neare unto Dieppe...the which keepeth still the memorie of your name together with the remnants of a most strong castle, and to which both the Frenchmen themselves, and all the inhabitants, and *the thing itself* doth witness and declare to be a monument of your most noble and honorable familie.[1]

The 'thing itself' had great potency. Bacon, a professional judge, was satisfied that an identity of name between himself and a medieval knight was all the evidence that the College of Heralds needed to establish a lineal descent.[2] But he can have had no illusions about his own father. According to tradition,[3] he was the son of a sheep-reeve

---

both a superior status and another decade of inflation) £4000; *D.N.B.* For other details of funeral expenses, see Lawrence Stone, 'The Anatomy of the Elizabethan Aristocracy', *op. cit.* pp. 11–12, and G. Scott Thomson, *Family Background* (London, 1949), p. 139.

[1] Lambert Danaeus, *Commentariorum...in Prophetas Minores*, published in Geneva in 1586, translated under the English title in 1594. This was dedicated to the son, Anthony Bacon; he had previously dedicated a work to Anthony's stepbrother, Edward. Both had visited Geneva. The italics in the quotation are mine.

[2] Canon Cooke, 'Materials for a History of Hessett', *Suff. Arch.* V (1886), 41 ff.

[3] The tradition is probably derived from a note in 'A Book of Pedigrees of the Gentry of Suffolk entitled Drury', B.M. Add. MSS. 5523, f. 98, which reads as follows: 'This Sir Nicholas Bacon, lord Keeper, beinge brought up by his father the Abbotts sheep Reive at schoole at length being sent to be made a prieste and perceivinge that his Crowne must be shaven, rather then he would abide that which he soe much misliked, he ran away and after he had hid himselfe a great while, at the length by an uncle (on the other syde) of his that was a riche tailor he was sente and mayneteyned at the Innes of Coorte from whence he was admitted to the dignity which after he came into.' Internal evidence (see f. 99: 'where the said Nathaniel now liveth anno 1614') suggests the date of composition. The compiler had access to some accurate information, but there

of the monastery of Bury St Edmund's, an official who supervised the shepherds, bought stock, sold wool, meat and skins, and handed over the profits to some steward. It was a responsible occupation for some yeoman who knew the sheep business, could read and write, and had enough substance to guarantee his credit.

Robert Bacon, Nicholas Bacon's father, fulfilled these qualifications, but the tradition is not confirmed by the few gleanings from legal documents which form the sum of our knowledge about him.[1] These show him to have been a yeoman, farming land around the villages of Hessett and Drinkstone, within nine or ten miles of Bury St Edmund's. His will, proved in 1548, mentions a widow, Isabel, who had been an Isabel Cage of Pakenham, in the same district. He had two sons, Thomas and James, besides Nicholas, and we know from other sources that there were daughters. He died when his sons were already successful men, so the good stock of cattle, corn, and furniture which the widow inherited ought not to surprise us. Even so, it was no more than a decent portion for a farmer. Nicholas had joined him at some time in the lease of a little land from the Mayor of Thetford, on which they kept sheep, and he was left these in the will. They were doubtless added to the thousand or more which he already owned in 1548 at the nearby manor of Ingham.

It seems that there was a grandfather, John Bacon, who had left Drinkstone to settle in Hessett. The elaborate deeds in which Nicholas provided, in after years, for the inheritance of his huge estate, never mentioned any ancestor behind this grandfather; probably because he knew of none. John Bacon had died about ten years before Nicholas was born, and we learn from his will that he had left a little property to his children. The eldest son John was left the homestead in Hessett and

is one obvious error in the sixteenth-century pedigree (viz. the marriages of Anne Ferneley), and he credits Nicholas with an elder brother, a 'counsellor of Lincoln's Inn', of whom there is no other record. Nicholas's sisters are probably correctly described, viz. Anne, the elder, who married Robert Blackman of Bury, and Barbara, the younger, who married Robert Sharp of Bury, and had two children, Barbara, wife of Bartholomew Kemp, Bacon's household official, and John, servant to alderman Bacon. At least we know that the Lord Keeper's children referred to the Blackmans and the Kemps as 'cousins'. Nicholas's two brothers, Thomas and James, are described as third and fourth sons of their father.

[1] Gladys Scott Thomson, 'Three Suffolk Figures', *Suff. Arch.* xxv, pt. 2 (1951), 149.

some land in Drinkstone and Tostock. Nicholas's father was left a manor in Barton by Mildenhall (Suffolk manors were often very small), subject to a rent charge for the benefit of the girls. One daughter got £20; a granddaughter whose father had died, the same. A married daughter, who must have already had her portion, got nothing. With its gifts of a few shillings to the altars and the poor in the parishes where he had land, its provision for a trental at Babwell friary and a year's masses somewhere else, it was the will of a pious, self-respecting yeoman.

We also learn that these Bacons had kinsmen in the same village who were distinctly better off. They called themselves gentlemen, and a patient explorer of estate records, content with a fleeting glimpse of his quarry, could find traces of them in more than one West Suffolk and Norfolk village. They counted their sheep in hundreds where Robert Bacon may have counted his in scores. They had been the leading family in Hessett for some time. The visitor to the village church may wonder if the letter B, carved so clearly on its walls, does not commemorate their fifteenth-century benefactions, and there is no doubt about the steady enrichment that lay ahead of them in the sixteenth century. The blood-tie between them and the 'Drinkstone' Bacons was probably remote, but there were other ties. When old John Bacon, Nicholas's grandfather, made his will in 1500, his gentlemanly cousins were given a contingent option to buy parts of his property, and two of them, father and son, acted as witnesses. When the older of these— another John Bacon—died in 1513, a contingent remainder was given to Robert Bacon, Nicholas' father, who was also one of the executors. Whether we have a clue here to the start that Nicholas was given a few years later, it is impossible to say; but at least the connexion was going to be maintained. When Thomas Bacon, gentleman, died in 1547, the young kinsman who had shot up from the humbler branch was one of his executors.[1]

This is almost all that anyone has been able to discover about

---

[1] Extracts from the wills quoted above were printed by Canon Cooke, *op. cit.* pp. 41 ff. See also G. Scott Thomson, *op. cit.* pp. 158–61: 'Thomas Bacon's will (1547) shows one flock of sheep in Thurston and Barton, a second in East Wretham, a third in West Wretham, and a fourth in Culford.'

The Rising Lawyer

Nicholas' origins, and the best evidence for his date of birth is the statement in his funeral expenses that 68 poor men—one for every year of his life—marched to his grave.[1] This means that he was born in 1510 or 1511. The place was probably Hessett, and the chances are that he received his early education from the monks in Bury St Edmund's,[2] where the great abbey which had dominated the countryside for half a millennium was nearing its end.

East Anglia has been a pleasant backwater in English life since the Industrial Revolution mercifully passed it by, but before 1750 it was the wealthiest and most vigorous section of the realm. Ambition was easily stirred where farming thrived, fortunes were made in the woollen industry, towns vied with each other in the erection of splendid churches, and such leaders as Thomas Wolsey, son of an Ipswich butcher, and Stephen Gardiner, son of a Bury clothmaker, cut their path to the top. The first requirement for an able boy who wanted to break out of his class was a good education. It was less than thirty miles from Bury St Edmund's to Cambridge, but it cost money to send a boy there, not to mention the effort of imagination. We shall never know who persuaded Robert Bacon, or who paid the bill; but ability was less easily hid in that neighbourly England than in some of our mass societies, and there was a growing thirst for education in an age that had suddenly discovered how parched it was.

Nicholas was thirteen when he went up to Corpus Christi in 1523 and seventeen when he took his B.A.[3] We can speculate on the influence which two great movements, the Renaissance and the Reformation, must have had on a developing mind, and we can wonder how many of the useful friends of later life were met at college. But we really know nothing of his career at Cambridge beyond the simple fact that he did well. Certain lists survive which recorded the top thirty

[1] The usually accepted date of Bacon's birth is 1509 (e.g. *D.N.B.*), but this seems to have no firm foundation. The date 1510 (or 1511) is suggested not only by the will, but also by the portrait in the National Gallery, which indicates that he was sixty-eight in 1578, and by the remark of his son Francis, quoted p. 33 below.

[2] A probability only. Lord Campbell, citing no evidence, says he was educated 'under his father's roof' before going to Cambridge (*Lives of the Lord Chancellors and Keepers of the Great Seal of England* (7th ed.: New York, 1878), II, 227).

[3] J. and J. A. Venn (eds.), *Alumni Cantabrigienses* (Cambridge, 1922–54), I, 65.

individuals, from the entire university, who took their B.A. in his year. In earlier times such lists may have been determined by questions of precedence, but at this date they are thought to have been based on merit. The first name was that of John Frith, of King's College, who was to be burned at Smithfield six years later as a Protestant martyr. The third was Bacon's.[1]

Between this date and his admission to Gray's Inn in 1532, his biography is almost a blank. These were the five years between seventeen and twenty-two when careers are usually determined. The decision not to enter the church—he had held a Bible clerkship at Corpus—must have been made at this time. It is also reported that he spent part of these years in study and travel abroad, during which time he lived for about a year in Paris; but his journeys have left no trace in the archives.

His friend Matthew Parker, whom he had known at Corpus, chose the church. His brothers chose business. He chose the law. No one climbed so high in this century as the boys who chose law. Cardinal Wolsey, whose spectacular fall occurred as Nicholas was making his choice, was the last churchman to eclipse the lawyers, and the day of the business men was only dawning. The training took place within that 'third university' whose curriculum we know from Chief Justice Fortescue's description in the previous century and from a survey which Bacon himself was ordered to make a few years later, when Henry VIII was playing with the idea of creating a special sort of 'King's Inn' out or the plunder of the monasteries.[2] Henry's Inn would have been a home of *belles-lettres* and a nursery for the foreign office as well as a school for lawyers, but it was the latter only which Bacon encountered at Gray's. The fashionable tastes of the time were doubtless cultivated by the lawyers, but the curriculum was the traditional system for drilling the common law into future practitioners. If not exactly a liberal education, it was a tough and bracing discipline for practical minds. Sons of gentlemen, down from Oxford and Cambridge, were given some exposure to it, but theirs was not the routine of readings, formal

[1] J. R. Tanner (ed.), *The Historical Register of the University of Cambridge* (Cambridge, 1917), p. 367.
[2] The reports, which were drawn up by Nicholas Bacon, Thomas Denton and Robert Cary, were printed in E. Waterhouse, *Fortescutus Illustratus* (London, 1663), pp. 539–46.

pleadings, and scholastic harangues at meal-times that faced the professional. That Bacon was a professional seems clear enough from the baffling speed of his advancement. If the records are not misleading, he seems to have outpaced his ablest contemporaries. He is said to have been admitted to the Inn in 1532, called to the bar in 1533, and made an ancient in 1536.[1]

These years seem to have been spent more in study than in practice. One instance of legal advice to a friend is of interest as the earliest surviving letter from his pen. Matthew Parker, who had been made Dean of Stoke College, near Clare, in 1535, had written for an opinion about some college business connected with the take-over from his predecessor, and Bacon gave it, adding, 'to be more sure of this, I went to Westminster, and there I moved this Question to our Lord Chief Judge, who was of the same mind'.[2] Doubtless his services were often used in this way, but it seems to have been a family belief that he had never engaged in practice before he got his first government job. When his son, the future Lord Chancellor, was angling for the position of Solicitor-General in 1595, he wrote to his uncle, Lord Burleigh, in these words, 'and if her Majesty thinketh that she shall make an adventure in using one that is rather a man of study than of practice and experience, surely I may remember to have heard that my father, an example, I confess, more ready than like, was made solicitor of the augmentations, a court of much business, when he had never practised, and was but twenty-seven years old'.[3]

If a good education was the first prerequisite, the second was 'a good lord'. Who will be a good lord to me? This was a crucial question when all the great men were surrounded by begging faces and no one got anywhere without a nod. It is pleasant to be able to see one gesture which was made on his behalf in these hidden years. Archbishop Cranmer wrote to Thomas Cromwell recommending 'one of Gray's Inn, named Nicholas Bacon, whom I know entirely to be both of such towardness in the law, and of so good judgement touching Christ's religion, that in

---

[1] Joseph Foster, *The Register of Admissions to Gray's Inn* (London, 1889), p. 9; R. C. Fletcher, *The Pension Book of Gray's Inn, 1569–1669* (London, 1901), p. xxvii; *D.N.B.*
[2] John Strype, *The Life and Acts of Matthew Parker* (London, 1711), App. pp. 4–5.
[3] James Spedding (ed.), *The Letters and the Life of Francis Bacon* (London, 1861–74), I, 362.

33

that stead he shall be able to do God and the King right acceptable service'.[1] The position was that of town clerk at Calais, and Bacon must have taken some steps to improve his chances there, as Cranmer was able to inform Cromwell that several of the officials at Calais would look with favour on Bacon's appointment. Had he perhaps stopped there during his travels? Was he able to use the good offices of some of the East Anglian gentry who we know were stationed there? It is immaterial, for nothing came of it; but if Cranmer was able to speak for him, on the basis, we surmise, of his Cambridge record and legal services in London, others would do the same. And there were better places than Calais. The Court of Augmentations, where someone got him the job of solicitor in 1537, was indeed 'a court of much business'.

What else was needed but a good marriage? Here again we move in darkness, but a little light has filtered in. His first bride has been known hitherto as Jane Ferneley, daughter of William Ferneley of West Creeting, Suffolk. But who were the Ferneleys? A complete answer to this question would make a fascinating chapter in the business history of early Tudor England; a revelation, within the folds of a complicated cousinhood, of all sorts of commercial dynasties in London, Norwich, Ipswich, and other East Anglian towns. William Ferneley was no simple squire, but a prominent member of London's leading company, the mercers. Admittedly he never became master, sheriff, or lord mayor; but a scrutiny of the mercers' minutes in the third and fourth decades leaves no doubt about his solidity. He was second warden in 1529; appears often as an assistant; supervises property; stands high in the pageantry; busies himself in the management of St Paul's School; and becomes upper warden in 1539.[2] When assessments were made, he was always in the highest bracket. If his son-in-law wanted £100, 'father Ferneley' could easily produce it.[3] He seems to have retired from the mercers about 1545 and is last mentioned two years later. Doubtless he

---

[1] John E. Cox (ed.), *Miscellaneous Writings and Letters of Thomas Cranmer* (Parker Society, XVI (1846)), p. 384.

[2] Mercers Company Court Minutes, 1527–60 (unpublished), 16B; 30B; 31A; 35B; 36A; 48A; 73A; 77B; 79A; 81B; 99A; 111A; 117B; 135A; 177A; 192A.

[3] Acquittance, 5 April 1546 (Bacon MSS. (Chicago)). There are indications that his father-in-law helped Bacon to buy the manor of Hinderclay, for which the money had originally been paid by his brothers Thomas and James.

had settled in Creeting St Peter's, where the chancel would be paved with his descendants' monuments for the next century and a half, and his home would endure to this day as Creeting Hall Farm. He had taken his wife, Agnes,[1] from a dynasty of Ipswich merchants, the Daundys, who were well established at the end of the fifteenth century and would go on owning manors until the end of the seventeenth.They had three children. We can leave Thomas to set up as a squire in Creeting Hall: we shall return to Jane as Bacon's wife: meanwhile, let us follow Anne.

Anne Ferneley's first husband was a forgotten William Rede. A visitor to the museum of the Public Record Office can inspect a piece of portraiture, on a parchment deed, which shows him kneeling with his wife and children at the feet of King Henry VIII.[2] It was the kind of thing which recipients of royal manors—especially the self-made men —enjoyed commissioning. William Rede was a cadet of a business dynasty which had been launched in Norwich and then settled across the border in Beccles.[3] His father and elder brother were provincial mercers. He himself was admitted to the London mercers in 1531.[4] There is a letter to his 'aunt Toley' which shows that making money was uphill work at first.[5] But he was not alone in the world. 'Aunt Tolcy' was the wife of Henry Tooley, one of the richest merchants in Ipswich. By 1535 William Rede was admitted to the livery of his company. By 1540 he had married Anne Ferneley. He was on the best of terms with the Greshams and he was buying his first estate in the country out of the profits of his trading. But these were days when death struck often and early. By 1543 Nicholas Bacon and Augustine Steward were winding up the Rede estate, under the supervision of Sir Richard Gresham.[6]

---

[1] *The Visitations of Suffolk*, ed. W. C. Metcalfe (Exeter, 1882), p. 29.
[2] C 110-69 (P.R.O.).
[3] Metcalfe, *op. cit.* pp. 59–60; *Suffolk in 1524* ('Suffolk Green Books', no. x; Woodbridge, Suffolk, 1910), p. 378.
[4] Mercers Company Court Minutes, *op. cit.* 46A. See also 53A, 85A, 86A, 87A.
[5] Letter, n.d., Town Correspondence (E.S.R.O.).
[6] The executors' records, including the will, inventories of goods and debts, rents from lands, and acquittances, are among the Bacon MSS. (Chicago). The wardship of William Rede, son and heir, was granted to Bacon 26 April 1544.

The Wealth of the Gentry, 1540–1660

Augustine Steward is a name that leads to Norwich, just as Daundy or Tooley led to Ipswich. William Rede had three sisters; one married to a merchant in King's Lynn, another to a Daundy, the third to Augustine Steward. More than a little is known about Steward. His house still stands on the Tombland, opposite the entrance to Norwich Cathedral. His portrait can be seen in the Council Chamber. His part in the great crisis which overtook his city in 1549, Kett's rebellion, can be read and admired. He was among the best that the second city in the realm produced—an able business-man, a public-spirited citizen, a well-loved master.

But all these families, Stewards, Redes, Daundys, Tooleys, and Ferneleys, were dwarfed by the Gresham connexion, with its shrievalties, mayoralties, masterships, knighthoods, and manors. An alliance with this great and still rising house must have seemed a commanding advantage to the young solicitor. In 1540, if not before, they became his friends; in 1544, his relations. The first date was the year in which he married Jane Ferneley; the second was the year in which Anne Ferneley, widow of William Rede, married Thomas Gresham.[1]

THE RISE TO FAME

As a young man of twenty-seven, in his first political appointment, Nicholas Bacon was helping to administer the greatest social revolution in England's history since the Norman Conquest. No doubt it hardly seemed so while it was happening: a sense of proportion about such things only comes afterwards. Still, it must have been sufficiently stirring. Almost every class in England was involved in the immense, exciting scramble for the confiscated property of the church. Favourites who were being rewarded for their personal attractions, politicians who were being built up as territorial magnates for the better government of the realm, officials who had done a useful bit of work, could all look forward to enjoying the royal bounty. Lands would either be given to

---

[1] John W. Burgon, *The Life and Times of Sir Thomas Gresham* (London, 1839), I, 49–50; Basil Cozens-Hardy and Ernest A. Kent, *The Mayors of Norwich, 1403 to 1835* (Norwich, 1938), pp. 48–9; Frederic W. Russell, *Kett's Rebellion in Norfolk* (London, 1859), pp. 85–6; Mercers Company Court Minutes, *op. cit.* 186 A. The wedding portrait of Sir Thomas Gresham on his marriage to Anne Rede is in the possession of the Mercers Company.

them for nothing or sold on very favourable terms. Outside these privileged circles stood the serried ranks of cash customers; the speculators who would buy in order to sell again; the merchants wanting urban premises or an estate in the country; the stewards, bailiffs and farmers of the monks, who saw a chance to own what they had so long managed; the gentleman whose family had owned one of the two manors in the village for the last hundred years and who could now own the other; the townsfolk who had leased the abbot's fen for more years than anyone could remember and were now eager to make it the town fen. By creating a vacuum in every village, and dozens in every town, Henry VIII had ensured a nation-wide competition for the privilege of filling them. It goes without saying that no feeling of sympathy for the dispossessed, or of dislike for the government, would prevent an individual, a family, or a corporation from feeling that it had a duty to help itself.

Bacon spent nine years on the inside of this business. The job of his department was to take surrenders, administer the estates, adjudicate the disputes, and arrange for the sale or gift of lands. Traces of his activity can be seen in its records, as he toured the country to take surrenders, took his share in the auditing of accounts, and performed his duties as a legal counsel for the crown.[1] Before many years were up he was dabbling in monastic estates himself; buying for friends and relations, buying to sell, and buying for keeps. By the time he moved on, at thirty-six, he owned a group of manors around Redgrave, he was selling off shops and houses in London, he was making money out of wardships and leases, he had entered the sheep business, and he had bought St Saviour's Hospital in Bury to provide himself with stone for a house. He knew that he could find a hundred or two a year for six or seven years to build himself a country seat, and he expected many more hundreds for the plate, tapestries, furniture, clothes and horses. Dissolving monasteries had been a profitable business. Rich, Pope, Williams, Southwell, and the Mildmays had all been his colleagues in

---

[1] He was involved in the surrenders of Christchurch, Canterbury (*L. & P.* xv, 147), the collegiate church of Southwell (*ibid.* p. 490), commanderies in Yorkshire and Lincolnshire (*ibid.* xvi, 358), Wingfield College, Suffolk (*ibid.* xvii, 218), and the chantries in the London area (*ibid.* xxi, pt. 1, 105, 146).

the Court of Augmentations. None of them seems to have had any trouble in augmenting his own income.

The next twelve years were spent as attorney in the Court of Wards.[1] It was a situation where the competitive pressures of interested suitors was no less likely to pour money into the laps of the officers, and where the bargains which the officers could buy for themselves were far from trifling. Wardship and livery were among the incidents of tenure by knight service, a form of land-holding which had lost its military justification but which the crown had preserved and developed as a source of revenue. Reforms in this area had been one of the characteristic interests of Henry VII, the book-keeping Tudor, and Henry VIII had completed his work by ordaining that as much as possible of the property of the church should be sold under this tenure, and by creating a special court to manage the crown's interests. The incidents fell very heavily on the landowning classes. The crown took possession of the lands on the death of a tenant and adult heirs could only redeem them after paying a fine. Minor children became wards of the crown, with only a claim to such part of the revenues as was needed to maintain and educate them. The crown sold the wardship, to which the lucrative right of marriage was attached, to anyone who was ready to buy it. Some idea of the eagerness of substantial owners to keep some sort of control over this licensed plunder may be gathered from Bacon's later request, which was granted in consideration of his services, that if he died with minor children the wardship might pass to his brothers. In a typical situation, the landowner was hardly dead before his friends and relations were hot-footing it to court to get the wardship into safe hands, only to discover, in many cases, that some courtier had got there before them.[2] As for the bargains which the officers could buy, Bacon's

---

[1] On 2 January 1547, he succeeded Richard Goodrich, who became attorney in the court which Bacon was leaving (*ibid.* xxi, pt. 2, 414). Throughout this chapter I have assumed that Bacon left the Court of Wards on his appointment as Lord Keeper of the Great Seal in December 1558 (e.g. pp. 38, 39, 51, 84, 87, etc.). I am reminded, however, by Mr Hurstfield, whose work appeared after this was written, that he only vacated the office of Attorney in 1561 (J. Hurstfield, *The Queen's Wards: Wardship and Marriage under Elizabeth I* (London, 1958), p. 25).

[2] For modern studies of the Court of Wards, see H. E. Bell, *An Introduction to the History and Records of the Court of Wards and Liveries* (Cambridge, 1953); the following articles by J. Hurstfield: 'Lord Burghley as Master of the Court of Wards, 1561–98', *T.R.H.S.* 4th series, xxxi

own history provides one of the rare examples of a precise record of the profits.[1]

For seven of these twelve years—coinciding with the reign of Edward VI—the young lawyer made steady progress in wealth and influence. Though heads were still rolling with the regularity which Henry VIII had taught English politicians to expect, Bacon was not yet in these exposed positions. One thinks of him when one reads Sir John Mason's formula for survival. Sir John was the son of a cowherd whose uncle had sent him to Oxford, and from there his abilities had won him a career as a diplomat. He attributed his success to cultivating 'the exactest lawyer and ablest favourite for the time being', to speaking little and writing less, and to observing such discretion that all parties thought him their own.[2] We are not suggesting that Bacon was as pliant a time-server as the genial Mason is thought to have been; but he was the kind of lawyer Mason depended on (may indeed have been one of them, for they were in the same circle), and there is a record of at least one service performed for the current favourite. On 16 December 1546 Bacon lent 300 marks to the earl of Hertford, to be repaid on 2 February. We have only the receipt which shows that he got his money back.[3] But Henry VIII had wheezed his last breath on 28 January, and these were the weeks in which Hertford was planning the coup which gave him control of the government under Edward VI. Hertford got a dukedom out of this, to appease the ambition which was quenched a few years later on the scaffold. But many of his henchmen lived to enjoy their rewards.

The administrations of this chaotic minority were Protestant and Bacon's ties were with a distinguished group of scholars and humanists who functioned below the dangerous level.[4] His contacts with some of them, like Parker, who was now head of their old college, or Sir John Cheke, the don with political ambitions, may have gone back to his

(1949); 'The Revival of Feudalism in Early Tudor England', *History*, new series, xxxvii (1952); 'Corruption and Reform under Edward VI and Mary', *E.H.R.* lxviii (1953); 'The Profits of Fiscal Feudalism, 1541–1602', *Econ. Hist. Rev.* 2nd series, viii, no. 1 (1955); and J. Hurstfield, *The Queen's Wards: Wardship and Marriage under Elizabeth I* (London, 1958).
[1] See below, pp. 84–8.   [2] *D.N.B.*
[3] Acquittance 7 February 1547, Bacon MSS. (Chicago).
[4] For comments on this coterie, see Conyers Read, *op. cit.* p. 70.

Cambridge days; and long before Henry VIII's death he had been a close friend of Sir William Buttes, the court physician whom John Foxe praised for having befriended Protestants in the dark days of that sovereign. But the nature of his convictions is unknown. He may have already been, what he finally became, a Protestant at heart. But it is just as possible that he was still taking his religious opinions from those in authority, who happened for the time being to be Protestant. It was hardly a layman's business to have a mind of his own when the clergy were divided.

He took one important step in these circles which improved his position while at the same time it increased the risks if the religious tide should ever turn. Wives in these centuries were usually spent after a dozen years of childbirth, and by 1553 he needed another. The last surviving references to Jane Ferneley are in the accounts for the building of Redgrave Hall. In October 1552 the officer in charge of the works gave her 10s. to pay a local tradesman for some gloves—she was presumably on a visit to the almost completed mansion. The next year the same officer was paying a mason for 'sixe days wourke about my Misteris tome'.[1] That marriage had taken Bacon into the world of business. The new one was all intellect and culture; but it was also highly fashionable. Sir Anthony Cooke was said to have the best educated daughters in England—a reputation to which he owed his appointment as the governor of Prince Edward. One of them married William Cecil, the future prime minister who was already a secretary of state. Another married Sir Thomas Hoby, the courtier who introduced Englishmen to the charms of Castiglione. Bacon married a third.[2] Some idea of her accomplishments and convictions may be gained from the fact that when Bishop Jewel, in after years, wrote the standard Latin defence of the Church of England against Rome, she turned it into English with enough style for a modern authority to rate her among the best translators of the century.[3]

---

[1] Redgrave Building Book, Bacon MSS. (Chicago), ff. 132, 207.

[2] The marriage has not been dated hitherto. Bacon's evidences show that the jointure, on the manor of Ingham, Suffolk, was being arranged in an indenture dated 26 January 1553 (Farrer transcripts, E.S.R.O.).

[3] C. S. Lewis, *English Literature in the Sixteenth Century excluding Drama* ('Oxford History of English Literature' (Oxford, 1954), p. 307.

The Rising Lawyer

The prospects must have looked bright enough at the wedding. Bacon's professional eminence had been recognised by the appointment as head of Gray's Inn.[1] His political future was none the worse for the connexion with Cecil. Suffolk was happy enough to welcome the new squire.[2] The ever-growing estate was spreading into Essex, Hertfordshire and Norfolk and there were three boys from the first marriage who might perpetuate his name, not to mention the chance of more from the second. Yet within a matter of months the boy-king wasted away, leaving a desperate regent to fight off the claims of a Catholic successor.

Bacon's role in the events that determined whether England would be governed by Lady Jane Grey or Mary Tudor was not that of a principal. Indeed, almost nothing is known about it. Yet he must have shared all the anxieties of his brother-in-law, who found himself staring at ruin more than once, and the course they took to avoid it must have been planned together. Cecil had managed to transfer his services from the duke of Somerset to the duke of Northumberland, but when that adventurer embarked on his gamble to make Lady Jane Grey queen, his secretary of state found himself, like every other councillor, in real peril. On the one hand, Protestantism was doomed and his own position jeopardised if Mary Tudor succeeded. On the other hand, Northumberland's plot to exclude her was such as to make any prudent man tremble. The judges were unanimously opposed to the alteration of the succession and we can imagine that Bacon's warnings were added to theirs. When Northumberland compelled both judges and councillors to endorse his plans, Cecil expected to suffer death for the opposition which had preceded his own signature, and gave Bacon a farewell letter

[1] Appointed Treasurer, 24 October 1552 (R. J. Fletcher (ed.), *The Pension Book of Gray's Inn* (London, 1901–10), I, App. II, 497). A tribute to Bacon's learning had been paid in November 1548 by Sir William Staunford, in a dedication from Gray's Inn of a standard work, *Exposicion of the Kinges Prerogative*: 'I have always meant this devise unto you,...partly for that I know yourself to have observed the lyke order in your own study, which in a few yeres hath gotten you, above others, the great learning you have, partly also for that I covet your judgment in these matters wherewith you bee dayly...exercised.'

[2] He was made a J.P. for Cambridge and Suffolk on 26 May 1547 (*Cal. Patent Rolls, Edward VI*, I, 81, 89). He was presumably in London during Kett's rebellion, but many of his friends and relations, such as Matthew Parker, Sir John Cheke, and his brother-in-law, Augustine Steward, were prominently involved on the side of law and order. On 3 August 1550 he was appointed a governor of the new grammar school in Bury St Edmund's. Well-to-do neighbours had made the usual offers of assistance in building Redgrave Hall.

41

to be sent to his wife.[1] But Northumberland was far too uncertain of his own future to make any examples. He had quite enough on his hands to make his plan stick when Edward's death, on 6 July 1553, was followed by Mary's appeal to the country.

Cecil's biographer surmises that Cecil was one of the many councillors who were ready enough to see Northumberland fail while continuing to serve him. What no one has noticed is that Mary's route, which ran through Cambridge and Bury St Edmund's to the Duke of Norfolk's house at Kenninghall, and from there to Framlingham, which could stand a siege, took her within a few miles of Redgrave. Every house in the area had to make its decision, and several of their owners, like the Cornwallises, Bedingfields, and Jernegans, made their fortunes by acting promptly. When the two week's reign of Lady Jane Grey was over, and Northumberland under arrest, Cecil, still secretary of state, was sent to Ipswich with some documents for Mary's signature. There he found Bacon's wife with the Queen.[2] She had no doubt jumped on the band-wagon at Redgrave.

It is hard to criticise the brothers-in-law for their conduct in this crisis, Northumberland being what he was; but their decision to con-form under a government which proceeded to restore Catholicism and burn the Protestant heretic poses the kind of question that will always be debated. Many of their circle made a different choice. Everybody knows what happened to Cranmer, Ridley, and Latimer. Matthew Parker went into hiding. Their father-in-law, Sir Anthony Cooke, their brother-in-law, Henry Killigrew, Sir John Cheke, Sir Richard Morison, and the young earl of Bedford—to name only a few—went into exile. Was there anything ignoble about acting as if some things were worth a mass? It would depend, no doubt, on what things, and nobody knows whether Redgrave, or Wimbledon, loomed larger in their minds than some conception of national welfare. It seems clear, however, that England owed much of its stability in this century to the avoidance of extreme decisions by its upper classes, and that the lot of

---

[1] Conyers Read, *op. cit.* p. 96.
[2] P. F. Tytler, *England under the Reigns of Edward VI and Mary* (London, 1839), II, 203; Conyers Read, *op. cit.* p. 101.

the exiles was sensibly alleviated by the people who stayed at home.[1] *Mediocria Firma*—the motto which Bacon inscribed above his porch at Redgrave—would not recommend itself to a Protestant martyr, but it had its social utility.

Bacon had preserved his office in the Court of Wards, his treasurership of Gray's Inn, and his position as a J.P. in Suffolk. His wife was one of the gentlewomen of the Privy Chamber, painful though some of the company must have been.[2] Cecil was employed on more than one official mission, including the embassy which brought Cardinal Pole into England, to absolve the realm from its sins. However, there is no doubt that the reign meant the suspension of political ambitions. They were neither able, nor anxious, to compete with the families that dominated the national and local scene. Cecil spent the last three years in retirement as a country gentleman. Bacon, though still employed, must have felt himself at a standstill. Yet there was one consolation: already rich, he grew richer.

From this frustrated, if prosperous, condition, they both soared to the top on the accession of Elizabeth. And there they stayed; for twenty years in Bacon's case, double that in Cecil's. Bacon made one false move which cost him a year's retirement from the council; otherwise his loyalty and wary moderation, his efficiency and good humour, his learning and eloquence, withstood all emergencies. Among his many accomplishments, one quality stands out. His celebrated son, that complicated, brilliant bundle of talents, seems to have thought his father a simple man: 'plain and honest' is what he called him.[3] It was the simplicity of the self-made man of business, who dominated any company he was in by hard-headed competence.

[1] *Ibid.* pp. 109–13. There is a bond, dated 5 February 1556, among the Bacon MSS. (Chicago) showing that Bacon helped to keep Sir Anthony Cooke in funds by arranging the sale of a manor.
[2] *Cal. Patent Rolls, Philip and Mary,* I, 24, 27; *ibid.* II, 12; Fletcher, *op. cit.* I, App. II, p. 500.
[3] E.g. Spedding, *op. cit.* I, 202–3. Bacon obviously plumed himself on his plain dealing. In a resentful letter of 21 July 1563, Cecil wrote, 'I will never, howsoever you used to nip me with speeches, that you *love plain dealing,* which words I often mark, lack any portion of truth, plainness or honesty that you have'. Conyers Read, *op. cit.* I, 282.

The Wealth of the Gentry, 1540-1660

What did it cost in the sixteenth century to build up a position like Bacon's, and how did he find the money? We pass now from the familiar outlines of a success story to its unfamiliar economics. One difficulty about each question must be admitted at the outset. So far as the first is concerned—what did it cost?—there is far less information in the Bacon records about expenditure than there is about income. All the household books which must have been kept at Redgrave, Gorhambury, and York House, from the master summaries down to the journal books, have disappeared. But we are not prevented from making some attempt to answer the question, though the usual indulgence has to be claimed for this blundering science.

The first thing we can do is to try to show what the lands cost. This is more nearly possible than we have any right to expect, for there is a group of sources which gives us the price of almost every large property bought for keeps and a great many of the small ones. Among these, four stand out: letters patent, receivers' accounts, acquittances and books of evidences. The first usually furnishes the price paid for royal grants, and the bills of sale prepared by the Court of Augmentations, in the form of a 'particular', are additional evidence. The Receivers' Accounts are limited both in time and content; but there is a continuous series of sixteen during the height of his prosperity (1559-75),[1] and if the payments which cannot be found are a painful reminder of the limitations of such records, those which are there help to complete the jigsaw puzzle. The acquittances—receipts for payments made by Bacon's servants—have survived in considerable numbers: the first half of his official life (c. 1540-59) being represented by a transcript of a volume into which his clerks were ordered to copy the receipts, and the whole career by many originals.[2] The books of evidence are in some ways the most valuable of all. There are houses today in which the visitor will still be shown 'the evidence-chamber'. The book of evi-

[1] Bacon MSS. (Chicago).
[2] E. Farrer made the transcript, in 1930, from an important book of evidences which has since disappeared; Bacon Acquittances, S. 929.2 (E.S.R.O.). The originals of many of these, and many others which were not in the book that Farrer copied, are among the Bacon MSS. (Chicago).

44

dence was like a medieval cartulary, and the most impressive of Bacon's volumes which has survived looks as though it had been taken, unused, from some monastic estate-office, and filled with his records. This is the volume in which all the deeds relating to properties in Hertfordshire and Essex have been meticulously copied.[1] It may be surmised that the books were compiled with reference to the future division of the estate. This one dealt with the properties which would pass, after the expiry of the second wife's life interest, to her two sons, Anthony and Francis. There was one which dealt with the eldest son's inheritance (Nicholas's), which was based on Redgrave, and another for Edward, the third son by the first marriage, who would inherit Bramfield. All of these have survived in one form or another;[2] only Nathaniel's (the second son of Jane Ferneley) has disappeared. Among the details frequently preserved in the deeds is, of course, the price.

Table 2 is an incomplete list of the amounts spent yearly on land between Bacon's first appointment at the age of twenty-seven and his death at sixty-eight. As no purchase is known to have been made in his first two years of office, it is a record for thirty-nine years. A few approximations have had to be adopted, such as the assumption that the price of one or two properties can be estimated by multiplying the annual value by the conventional rate of twenty to twenty-two years' purchase. It has also been necessary to make some arbitrary assignments of instalments; a practice which may distort the expenses of a particular year, but does not affect the average. We are sufficiently familiar with Bacon's habit of paying for a property within a very short time to guess that the amount would ordinarily be divided over a two-year period. Mortgages were devices for the desperate at this time, and the occasions when he chose to discharge a capital sum by a rent charge or an annuity were very few. Apart from these approximations, the figures are fairly reliable. But there are several things which have had to be omitted. First, it is possible that some big property has escaped us; but if so it is

[1] MS. xi, 3 (H.R.O.).

[2] The book of evidences dealing with the inheritance of the eldest son is the same referred to p. 44, n. 2, above, as having been examined by E. Farrer, and not seen since. Farrer transcribed many of the deeds on sheets of foolscap, and filed them by parishes in his collections, which are now in W.S.R.O. and E.S.R.O. B.M. Add. MS. 25590 deals with Edward's inheritance.

The Wealth of the Gentry, 1540–1660

TABLE 2. *Expenditure on land, 1540–79* (£)

1540	INGHAM (S)*		489
1541	—		—
1542	MAGNA HOLLAND (E)	1105	
	Site of Babwell Friary, Bury St Edmund's	100	
	Site of White Friars, Norwich	36	
	Foldcourse, Rougham (S)	54	
			1295
1543	INGHAM, A SECOND MANOR (S)	267	
	Site of St Saviour's Hospital, Bury	? 100	
	Wardship of William Rede	67	
	Small purchases	75	
			509
1544	ST MARY'S HOSPITAL, BISHOPSGATE (L)	1315	
	Other London property	200	
	Small purchases	110	
	Wardship of John Coggeshall	20	
			1645
1545	RICKINGHALL ETC. (S and B)	785	
	REDGRAVE (S)—in addition to surrender of Magna Holland	90	
	— redemption of a £10 annuity	200	
	Rent of Frinton (E)	20	
			1095
1546	HARLESTON (S)	274	
	Site of Friars Observant, Southampton	40	
	Rent of Frinton (E)	20	
	Tenths† to crown	17	
			351
1547	STANFORTH (N)—first instalment	500	
	Nayland Chantry (S)	129	
	Wardship of Joan Everingham	40	
	Rent of Frinton and tenths	35	
			704

★ The initial letters are for counties: S, Suffolk; E, Essex; L, London; B, Bedfordshire; D, Derby; Do, Dorset; N, Norfolk; H, Hertfordshire.

† These rents, which the crown reserved on the sale of certain manors, are underrated throughout this table, as no systematic search has been made for all of them.

The Rising Lawyer

TABLE 2 (cont.)

Year	Description		
1548	STANFORTH (N)—balance	600	
	HINDERCLAY, WORTHAM AND BURGATE (S)	1011	
	Rent of Frinton and tenths	35	
			1646
1549	Rent of Frinton, tenths, etc.	40	40
1550	BROOKS WHARF (L)—half interest	200	
	Rent of Frinton, tenths, etc.	40	
	Small purchase	13	
			253
1551	WALSHAM CHURCHHOUSE (S)	? 770	
	Wardship of Edmund Foxe	40	
	Tenths	15	
			825
1552	Tenths, etc.	20	20
1553	CHEDDER (S)—a rent of £30 p.a.	400	
	Copyholds, Gislingham (S)	77	
	REDMERE (N)	? 200	
	Tenths, etc.	20	
			697
1554	TIMWORTH (S)	280	
	MELLIS ST JOHN'S	72	
	BLACKBURN HUNDRED—rent oats	108	
	Hornmill	30	
	Wardship of William Flammok	30	
	Tenths, etc.	20	
			540
1555	DALBURY (D)	200	
	Tenths, etc.	20	
	Small purchase	13	
			233
1556	MARKS (E)—as security for a loan of	666	
	LIBERTY OF BURY ST EDMUND'S (S)	133	
	Tenths, etc.	20	
			819
1557	Rent of Burganny House	13	
	Wardship of Thomas Garneys	134	
	Tenths, etc.	20	
			167
1558	MARKS (E)—bought for a further	300	
	Rent of Burganny House	13	
	Tenths, etc.	25	
			338

47

TABLE 2 (*cont.*)

1559	Tenths, etc.	25	
	Wardship of William Yaxley	50	
	Wardship of Thomas Pleasaunce	18	
		——	93

1560	GORHAMBURY (H)—in addition to an annuity of £50	1200	
	ECCLES (N)	400	
	PLAYFORDS IN BARNHAM (S)	153	
	REDBORNE RECTORY (H)	440	
	Small purchases	125	
	Tenths, etc.	25	
		——	2343

1561	BLACKBURN HUNDRED	280	
	THRAXTON (N)	? 800	
	ASHFIELD (S)	800	
	PARKER'S PLACE, KING'S LANGLEY (H)	500	
	Wardship of George Bacon	20	
	Small purchases	33	
	Tenths, annuities, etc.	100	
		——	2533

1562	TARRAUNT, ETC. (Do)	1172	
	BRISSINGHAM (N)	? 1100	
	Wardship of Robert Pulham★	12	
	Tenths, annuities, etc.	100	
		——	2384

1563	METTINGHAM, ILKETSHALL AND SHEEPMEADOW (S)	3540	
	BRAMFIELD (S)	1256	
	Tenement near Marks	140	
	Small purchases in London	65	
	Tenths, annuities, etc.	100	
		——	5101

1564	BURGATE (S)—a moiety. In addition to the surrender of Tarraunt	60	
	ECCLES—redemption of an annuity	184	
	Tenths, annuities, etc.	100	
		——	344

★ We have made the arbitrary decision to include no wardships after this date, though nearly £300 is known to have been paid by Bacon or his servants between 1563 and 1575. For the complications of this problem, see pp. 86–8 of this chapter.

TABLE 2 (*cont.*)

1565	Small purchases	77	
	Tenths, annuities, etc.	100	
			177

1566	BURSTON (H)—first instalment	300	
	Site of Wyverston Hall (S)	50	
	Purchases near Redgrave (S)	257	
	Purchases near Marks (E)	59	
	Tenths, annuities, etc.	100	
			766

1567	BURSTON (H)—second instalment	400	
	BURGATE (S)—second moiety. First instalment	500	
	Purchases near Marks (E)	433	
	Purchases near Gorhambury (H)	210	
	Purchases near Redgrave (S)	117	
	Tenths, annuities, etc.	100	
			1760

1568	Purchase near Marks (E)	170	
	Childwick mill near Gorhambury	200	
	Purchase near Walsham (S)	117	
	Purchase near Redgrave (S)	67	
	Purchase near Bramfield (S)	45	
	Tenths, annuities, etc.	100	
			699

1569	Small purchases near Redgrave (S)	47	
	Small purchases near Gorhambury (S)	65	
	Tenths, annuities, etc.	100	
			212

1570	STIFFKEY (N)—first instalment	1000	
	Small purchases	55	
	Tenths, annuities, etc.	100	
			1155

1571	BURGATE (S)—second moiety. Second instalment	500	
	STIFFKEY (N)—second instalment	1000	
	Purchases near Redgrave (S)	108	
	Purchases near Gorhambury (H)	56	
	Tenths, annuities, etc.	100	
			1764

TABLE 2 (*cont.*)

1572	BURGATE (S)—second moiety. Last instalment	800	
	STIFFKEY (N)—last instalment	600	
	STODY (N)—first instalment	465	
	Purchases near Redgrave (S)	73	
	Tenths, etc.	50	
		——	1988
1573	STODY (N)—final instalment	1430	
	Purchases near Redgrave (S)	33	
	Tenths, etc.	50	
		——	1513
1574	NETHERHALL IN STIFFKEY (N)	? 700	
	Purchases near Redgrave (S)	40	
	Tenths, etc.	50	
		——	790
1575	WYNDRIDGE (H)	900	
	Purchase near Redgrave (S)	25	
	Tenths, etc.	50	
		——	975
1576	Purchase near Redgrave (S)	45	
	Tenths, etc.	50	
		——	95
1577	—		—
1578	WOOLWICH MARSH	1300	
	Tenths, etc.	50	
		——	1350

likely to have been in the first half of his career and it must have been resold. Secondly, almost no leases are recorded in this table. These would have involved the payment of a fine and then a small annual rent. We do not know, for instance, what York House, his London residence as Lord Keeper, cost him. If he had to pay the fine, it could have run into the hundreds, but the rent is unlikely to have been as much as £50 a year. Thirdly, we do not know what it cost him to buy out the sitting tenant on some of his manors, where he wanted either a higher rent or control of the land. Fourthly, it is certain that some small purchases have eluded us, in spite of the precise records which survive for many of them. Fifthly, Sir Ralph Rowlett, the owner of Gorhambury, is known to have parted with his Hertfordshire manors on favourable terms, and to have acknowledged that he was doing so in consideration of services: if these represented an outlay on Bacon's part, we do not know what it was. Lastly, no legal expenses or gratuities have been included. Redgrave, valued at about £1200, cost him over £60 in this way; but later in his career, when he was more used to receiving gratuities than giving them, the costs of a purchase was unlikely to have been as high as 5 per cent. But of course legal expenses were a continuing necessity, where title had to be cleared and land settled on various heirs. He was in the best position to see that he was well served, but we do not know what his lawyers received. The difficulty of guessing the maximum error involved in these omissions is obvious, but it is possible that the real expenditure was 20 per cent higher than the amounts shown here.

This table is a record of gross expenditure; that is, it includes all sums that Bacon is known to have paid. But of course these included some borrowed money, and some money which was quickly recovered by resale. To form some rough estimate of how much of his own income was being put into land every year, and what the permanent estate cost him, we have removed the loans where they can be identified, and deducted the sums spent on properties which he did not keep. The possibility of error here is again not slight, but the attempt seems worth making.

When this is done, as in Table 3, we see that during the nineteen years that Bacon was in the Court of Augmentations and the Court of Wards, he was able, on the average, to put about £500 a year into land, and about £1150 a year during the twenty years that he was Lord Keeper. If Table 2 requires an upward adjustment of 20 per cent, then averages become £600 a year, and £1380 a year, respectively. There is every reason to suppose that the bulk of his savings went into land after living expenses and extraordinary charges had been met. This was the normal way of disposing of the cash on hand whenever it exceeded a few hundreds. He is said to have bewailed at his death his failure to do more for the children of the second marriage, who are described in his will as his poor orphans. A little more time would have allowed him to scrape together a few more parcels of cash for Francis, like the £1300 which was spent in the last year to buy him Woolwich Marsh. Still, the estate was sufficiently impressive. The manor is a notoriously ambiguous entity, but there were over thirty altogether—about fifteen in Suffolk, ten in Hertfordshire, five in Norfolk, and a very substantial

TABLE 3. *Net expenditure on land, 1540–79* (£)

	Gross expenditure*	Net expenditure		Gross expenditure*	Net expenditure
1540	489	300	1561	2,533	1,263
1541	—	—	1562	2,384	1,000
1542	1,295	1,141	1563	5,101	5,000
1543	509	442	1564	344	344
1544	1,645	375	1565	177	177
1545	1,095	1,095	1566	766	766
1546	351	77	1567	1,760	1,760
1547	704	585	1568	699	699
1548	1,646	1,646	1569	212	211
1549	40	40	1570	1,155	1,155
1550	253	253	1571	1,764	1,764
1551	835	835	1572	1,988	1,988
1552	20	20	1573	1,513	1,513
1553	700	700	1574	790	790
1554	540	510	1575	975	975
1555	233	33	1576	95	95
1556	819	886	1577	—	—
1557	167	33	1578	1,350	1,350
1558	338	338			
1559	93	75	TOTAL	37,721	32,177
1560	2,343	1,943	Average†	967	825

* As in Table 2.

† The average for the nineteen years (1540–58) is 474; for the twenty years (1559–78), 1143.

one in Essex. Over and above these, there was a rectory in Hertfordshire, a block of London property, another block of leases in London and the country, and two franchises, one of them the majestic, if dilapidated, Liberty of Bury St Edmund's, which the abbots had owned from time immemorial. The price of all this, independently of anything spent on improvements, must have run between £35,000 and £40,000.

Next we can isolate the expense of building his houses. A Tudor mansion was built out of income, and the overseer kept an itemised account of the costs, year by year, until the work was finished. More than one of these Building Books has survived. A generation before Nicholas Bacon started, Thomas Kytson, a self-made merchant, built the beautiful Hengrave Hall near Bury St Edmund's which still stands today, and the Hengrave manuscripts at Cambridge show that over £3000 was spent between 1525 and 1539.[1] There is a similar record for Redgrave.

He began in 1545 by clearing the site. We know from the bill of sale that the monks had left some kind of park and 'a mansion-house, sore decayed'. Jocelin de Brakelond described how Abbot Sampson enclosed and stocked many parks and how he used to watch the coursing in some walk of the woods when his guests were hunting. Perhaps this was one of them. Enough survived in the way of a hunting lodge for Bacon to incorporate a little of it in his house and to use the rest as a source of raw material. Workmen were employed at 5d. a day to 'beat down the walls' and the going rate for dismantling 20,000 tiles was 3d. a thousand. Freestone was no problem when monasteries and hospitals had just become surplus stores. At Ixworth today all that remains of the old priory is a fine undercroft in the base of a Victorian house. The following entry tells us what happened to the rest of it. 'To Wright Mr Ashefelds man for taking downe fre stone at Yxworth viii*s* viii*d*. For carreng on lode of ston that was lefte in the waye by cause of a cart that was broken iii*d*. To Franciss wief for brede chese and drynke for the carters that caryed the ston from Yxworth xvii*d*.' Mr Ashfields's man was also kept busy at Saint Saviour's Hospital in Bury St Edmund's, which Bacon had bought with this purpose in mind. 'To Wright and his man for takinge downe fre stone at the hospital iiii*s* iii*d*; for the cariage of vii loods of ston from the hospital of Burye to Redgrave at ii*s* the loode, xiiii*s*.' Other loads were brought in from local priories and nunneries, but the item which makes the most chilling reading is this: 'Paid to Bugg the xxiii of Marche for carienge of iiii Altur-stones, the one from Wurtham at viii the lood, and one from Hinderclay at viii*d*, one from Rekynghall, and one other from Redgrave, at eyther of them vi*d* the lood, ii*s* iiii*d*.' The government of Edward VI had ordered the removal of altars from parish churches, and as patron of Wortham, Hinderclay,

[1] Hengrave MSS. 80 (C.U.L.).

Rickinghall, and Redgrave, Bacon was able to put the altars to a Protestant use. He no doubt paved his hall with them, and one can imagine what the Catholic peasantry had to say about 'that buggar Bugg' as he carted them through the lanes.

The bricks were burnt on the estate and used as required. The timber came out of the woods at Redgrave, Hinderclay, and Rickinghall. The small red tile that was used to roof the house, and is still the mark of an old building today, came from a nearby kiln at Wyken. Many items were manufactured on or near the site—the lead gutters and conduits, the laths, and some of the ironwork. Local craftsmen were used for the jobs within their skills, while experts were brought in from farther afield and boarded. Some free-masons were sent by Edmund Wythe-pool, who was building the Christchurch mansion which is now a museum in Ipswich. Others, together with glaziers and the best of the carpenters, came from Norwich or London. Contracts, or 'bargains' as they were called, were made with the master-craftsmen and the terms meticulously incorporated in legal indentures. We know from his correspondence that the business-like Bacon left nothing to chance when hiring workmen. The overseer must have been carefully picked. For the early years it was a cousin, John Bacon; later a capable Redgrave man from a family of well-to-do yeomen.[1]

Year by year Redgrave Hall began to take shape; the house with its red tiles and tall chimneys, its crow-stepped gables and ogee turret; the pilastered doorway with its sculptured emblem above it; the wainscoted chambers and their mullioned windows—some twenty for the family, as many more for household officers and servants; the thatched stable, preserved, perhaps, from the abbots' days; the dairy, brewery, barns, and mill; the fish-ponds; the extended park with its deer and cattle and its new fence. Today there is only a hint or two of what it once was like. A parchment inventory of 1649—about a century later—which enumerates the rooms and shows that the contents, which included £1000 in cash and jewels and another £1000 in plate, were worth about £6000 at that date.[2] An oil painting, of about the same

---

[1] Redgrave Building Book, Bacon MSS. (Chicago).
[2] Inventory taken at the death of Sir Edmund Bacon, second baronet (Bacon MSS. (Chicago)).

period, more odd than beautiful—this was before Englishmen had learnt how to handle landscape—shows the frontage of the house, with dogs and cows and fashionable ladies posturing in the foreground.[1] After another century, Redgrave succumbed to the fashion which compelled a Tudor home to don a classical toga: a Palladian shell was built around it, concealing all that survived of Bacon's work, but preserving the hall as a kitchen for the Augustans. In 1946, after enduring an ordnance dump in one corner of the park and a camp for prisoners of war in another, the house was totally demolished except for a single doorway, which the wreckers had exposed, and which the owner could not bring himself to pull down. This was Bacon's front door; but it will fall down in a year or two, and the monks will have the last laugh. There will be nothing left but their magnificent oaks.

Lucky in his progeny, Bacon has been unlucky in his buildings. The chapel he promoted at Corpus was pulled down in the nineteenth century. The library at Gray's Inn has long since disappeared. Even his tomb was burnt in the Fire of London, leaving a broken torso to be laid on a slab in the crypt. Only at Stiffkey is there still a mansion where the wings which are not occupied by bats and owls can be let to Americans. His most ambitious building had the shortest life. In 1563, on a site where Geoffrey de Gorham had built a medieval hall, and where a thousand acres of land and 250 of woods offered a suitable outlook, he began his second house. The visitor who drives up to Gorhambury today, past the Roman amphitheatre which lay under the grass in Bacon's time, is first confronted by the eighteenth-century residence of the earls of Verulam. Behind that are the walled gardens of the house which Francis Bacon built in 1601, and next to these graceful ruins is a nettle-bound, rusting, wreck of a porch, which is all that is left of his father's home.

Table 4 records the costs. It will be seen that Redgrave took ten years to complete, with annual expenditures ranging from as little as £17 in the first year, and £28 in 1549, when Kett's rebellion must have suspended the activities, to a maximum of £200. The total for this decade was £1300. The interval between 1554 and 1560 is bare, but

[1] In the possession of John Holt Wilson, Esq., Rickinghall, Suffolk.

that is due to the lack of records. There may have been further expenses at Redgrave, and there were certainly some at Gray's Inn where extensive alterations were carried out during his Treasurership.[1] In 1560 his new status suggested improvements at Redgrave, and an investment of over £400 was spread over the next three years. Gorhambury consumed £3176 in six years, with an outlay of £952 in one of them. Unfortunately, we have no details for this house, beyond the annual expenses.[2] To this we have to add further sums for the last decade—

TABLE 4. *Building expenses** (£)

1545	Redgrave Hall	17	1566	Gorhambury Hall	952
1546	Redgrave Hall	104	1567	Gorhambury Hall	571
1547	Redgrave Hall	268	1568	Gorhambury Hall	296
1548	Redgrave Hall	101	1568	Redgrave Hall	10
1549	Redgrave Hall	28	1569	Redgrave Hall	155
1550	Redgrave Hall	171	1570	Redgrave Hall	27
1551	Redgrave Hall	200	1574	Gorhambury Hall (?)	200
1552	Redgrave Hall	195		(Gallery)	
1553	Redgrave Hall	113	1574–9	Stiffkey Hall	500
1554	Redgrave Hall	103†	1579	Corpus Christi College	200
1555–9	?	?	1579	Gorhambury Hall	100
1560	Redgrave Hall	172	1579	London House	80
1561	Redgrave Hall	202		(Fetter Lane)	
1562	Redgrave Hall	47			
1563	Gorhambury Hall	315		TOTAL	6167
1564	Gorhambury Hall	463		Average (1545–54)	130
1565	Gorhambury Hall	577		Average (1560–79)	244

* These figures are derived from building books, receivers' and bailiffs' accounts, executors' records, and correspondence.

† Includes £50 known to have been spent on lead but not included in the Building Book (12 tons had been bought from the Court of Augmentations for £48). Some glass and iron was bought outside the framework of these accounts, but the amounts were probably small.

about £200 on Redgrave, about £500 on Stiffkey, £200 for a chapel at Cambridge, perhaps another £300 at Gorhambury (including the expenses of a gallery) and £80 which he is known to have spent on a

[1] The rebuilding of the Hall was undertaken while Bacon and Gerrard were Treasurers. It took four years to finish and cost £863. 10s. 8d. Fletcher, *op. cit.* 1, xxxi.

[2] Lambeth MS. 647, 5: 'A Briefe of the whole charges of the money bestowed upon the buylding of Gorhambury betwene the first day of March a.d. 1563 and the last day of September 1568.'

town house for his son Edward. This brings the total to £6167. If we knew all the facts—the unrecorded outlays on houses in London and the country, and the possible contributions to Gray's Inn and to the Cursitors' Inn (which he organised in Chancery Lane)—another £1000 might well be involved. Still, we have every reason to be surprised by the moderation of this bill. Spread over the years between the beginning of Redgrave and his death, it cannot have averaged more than £130 a year before he became Lord Keeper or much more than twice that sum afterwards. The Queen seems to have registered some of this surprise when she visited him at Gorhambury. 'My Lord,' she said, 'what a little house have you gotten.' He replied, 'Madam, my house is well, but it is you that have made me too great for my house'.[1] Perhaps this was the incentive to the new gallery; but his buildings, like so much else in his career, seem to have been governed by the principles ot '*Mediocria firma.*'

In addition to lands and buildings, there are some other matters whose cost we know. Next in order of expense was probably the settlement of his children. Nicholas and Nathaniel, and three daughters, Elizabeth, Ann, and a third who was also called Elizabeth, were married in his lifetime—between 1561 and 1572. The marriage of the eldest son to a carefully chosen heiress involved the compensation of two uncles for the fact that she would inherit all their property as well as her parents'. This cost £800.[2] The three daughters received portions of £800, 1000 marks, and 1300 marks, respectively;[3] making a total in this area of £3133.

---

[1] Spedding, *op. cit.* VII, 114. This anecdote, which was included in Francis Bacon's *Apophthegmes New and Old*, was referred to Redgrave in the first edition, and then by a later correction to Gorhambury.

[2] See below, pp. 91–3.

[3] As the marriages of the daughters are not discussed in the final section of this chapter, they may be summarised here. Ann, the second daughter, married Henry Woodhouse of Waxham, son of Sir William Woodhouse, head of a prominent Norfolk family. This family was friendly with, but apparently not related to, the Wodehouses of Kimberley (see John, earl of Kimberley, *The Wodehouses of Kimberley* (privately printed, 1887)). Acquittances in the Bacon MSS. (Chicago) of 25 October 1565 (£400), 28 October 1565 (£200), and 1 November 1566 (£200) show that £800 was paid under an indenture of 2 June 1564, between Bacon on the one part, and the brothers, Sir Thomas and Sir William Woodhouse, on the other. It is presumed that this was the marriage indenture. For Woodhouse pedigrees, see *The Visitations of Norfolk, 1563, 1589, and 1613*, ed. Walter Rye (Harleian Society, XXXII (1891)), and no. 3410, Clayton MSS. (N.C.L.).

Elizabeth, the eldest daughter, married the courtier Sir Robert Doyley, of Berkshire (see *The Visitations of the County of Oxford, 1566, 1574, 1634*, ed. William H. Turner (Harleian Society, v

The Wealth of the Gentry, 1540–1660

Another expense was the entertainment of the Queen. This was a notorious financial ordeal, and there are signs that the sheep-reeve's son may have found it a social one. The following letter from Gorhambury in 1572 was probably addressed to his brother-in-law, Cecil. 'Understanding by comen speche, that the Quenes Majestie meanes to come to my howse, And knowyng no certenties of the tyme of her comyng nor of her aboade, I have thowght good to praye you that this bearer my servaunt, might understond what you knowe therin, And yf it be trewe, Then that I might understond your advise what you thinke to be the best waye for me to deale in this matter ffor in very deede, no man is more Rawe in such a matter then myselfe.'[1] She is thought to have visited him three or four times in the course of those progresses which were such a deft demonstration of public relations at the public's expense. The amenities called for gifts as well as entertainment; on one occasion a gold steeple-cup, on another a salt in the shape of a turkey-cock decked with cupids and pearls, on a third a cup, garnished with 'iij Emerodes iij rubyes and vj perles upon the bryme of the Cover and six rubyes aboutes the bodye and rope of smale perles about the toppe and a table rubye'.[2] Perhaps trifles like these could be kept under a hundred pounds, but the great question was 'her aboade'—how long would she stay? In 1577 she arrived at Gorhambury on 18 May and stayed till 22 May—a long week-end. After the guests had gone, and

(1871), 226). An acquittance of 9 May 1571 (Bacon MSS. (Chicago)), shows that Robert Doyley, then of Greenland, Bucks, received £200 in full payment of 100 marks for the marriage money of his wife, Elizabeth, eldest daughter of Sir Nicholas Bacon. This Elizabeth later married Sir Henry Neville, of Berkshire, and Sir William Perient, Lord Chief Justice of the Common Pleas (Metcalfe, *op. cit.* p. 109).

Elizabeth, the youngest daughter, married Sir Francis Wyndham, the recorder of Norwich who was made a judge of Common Pleas in 1579 (*D.N.B.*). He was the younger brother of Sir Roger Wyndham, the litigious tyrant of Felbrigge, Norfolk (see H. A. Wyndham, *A Family History, 1410–1688: The Wyndhams of Norfolk and Somerset* (London, 1939, I, 112 ff.). An acquittance of 27 May 1571 (Bacon MSS. (Chicago)) shows that Francis Wyndham, esquire, of the city of Norwich, received £400 in full payment of 1300 marks, given as a marriage portion with Elizabeth, youngest daughter, etc. She later married Robert Mansell, the vice-admiral who took a prominent part in the development of glass manufacture in England.

Premier gentry at the end of Bacon's life seem to have expected to pay between 1000 marks and £1000 for their daughters' portions. Sir William Drury of Hawstead, Suffolk, a courtier who died in 1590, wanted his eldest daughter to have £1000 and the other, 1000 marks (Bacon MSS. (Chicago)). For the Cornwallises and Kytsons—Suffolk gentry of the same class—see below, chapter IV, pp. 170–1.   [1] B.M. Lansdowne MSS. XIV, 79.

[2] A. J. Collins, *Jewels and Plate of Queen Elizabeth I* (London, 1955), pp. 543, 563.

everyone had praised the portrait, and the gate through which her expensive foot had trod was being locked against further use by any other mortal, the servants had time to count the silver and add up the bills. The cost was nearly £600, without including Bacon's gift.[1]

Finally, we know that the office of vice-admiral of Suffolk, which he bought from his son-in-law Sir Henry Woodhouse in 1578, cost £310;[2] that an investment in the Society of Mineral and Battery Works may have run to £100; and that at the time of his death there was about £2000 worth of plate,[3] much of it no doubt given, but he must also have made gifts himself. The Receivers' Accounts supply more details of extraordinary expenses, such as wages to schoolmasters and gifts to the local poor, but as these were only in tens of pounds, we can ignore them for our present purposes.

How much further can we go? All we have done so far is to isolate the cost of land, buildings, marriage settlements, and a few extra-ordinary expenses. Beyond this we have no specific information, though we know what were the various categories of expenditure in a magnate's budget. The basic items were household provisions in the broadest sense of the word—i.e. diet, stores, plate, and furnishings; apparel; a wage-bill made up of wages, liveries, fees to household officers and pensions to relatives; gratuities, in a society where high and low expected presents; equipment for the home farms; stable and riding charges; law-suits; taxes; charities; and official missions. Some assumptions may perhaps be made about Bacon's scale of living. As he was the last man in the world to 'pour his substance down the privy', we can rule out one sort of conventional extravagance; as a lawyer at the head of his profession, we can rule out another—the ruinous law-suit; as a courtier, he must have shouldered his share of entertainment, but if there had been many bills like the entertainment of the Queen at Gorhambury, some rumour of the feastings would probably have come

---

[1] *Ibid.* p. 563; Lambeth MSS. 647, 9. Stays of a few days seem to have cost others about the same amount. The longer visits to Lord Burleigh's house at Theobalds were said to run as high as £2000–£3000, and a visit to the earl of Leicester at Kenilworth in 1575 was rated (on what evidence is not clear) at £6000. Lawrence Stone, 'The Anatomy of the Elizabethan Aristocracy' *op. cit.* p. 6.

[2] Acquittance, 29 September 1578, Bacon MSS. (Chicago).

[3] For commercial investments, and the estate at death, see pp. 88–9 below.

down to us, as they have in other cases. Lastly, it is obvious to the student of the period that a lot of satisfactions could be obtained for sums like £100.

Beyond this all is guess-work, within a few limits which are suggested by our slender knowledge of other budgets. At one level, we know that premier gentry of Suffolk, like Sir Thomas Cornwallis of Brome, or Sir Thomas Kytson of Hengrave, were spending over £1000 a year during the period when Bacon was Lord Keeper.[1] At the highest level of landed society, the earl of Northumberland inherited about £3000 a year in 1585.[2] But in all three cases we are talking about 'mere' landlords, without incomes from office or proportionate expenses. The closest case to Bacon's that we know anything about was that of Matthew Parker. His period as archbishop (1558–75) coincided with Bacon's Lord Keepership and some of their responsibilities were similar. His son, who was anxious to vindicate his father's reputation for liberality, put his income at £3428 a year. Of this £2400 was consumed annually in certain basic expenses; £1300 in household fare (this was exclusive of furnishings and plate), £300 in household wages and liveries, £400 in annuities and fees, and another £400 in pensions to curates and contributions to two hospitals. This left £1028 a year for all the other expenses. The son isolated as many of the extraordinary expenses as he could, for the whole term of the office, in much the same way as we have isolated some of Bacon's. In Parker's case these were as follows: £2270 in entertaining the Queen, £2400 in benefactions at Cambridge, £500 in buying land at Cambridge, a few hundreds to authors, £2600 in buildings (Canterbury Palace had been burnt in Cranmer's time) and £1100 in marriage portions for three nieces. If these sums are added they are found to account for over a half of the annual surplus of £1028 a year, and we are left to infer that the balance was consumed by ordinary charges which were not included in the fixed basic expenses—i.e. by furnishings, plate, books, travel, litigation and so forth.[3]

---

[1] See chapter IV, Table 15 below.

[2] Gordon R. Batho, 'The Finances of an Elizabethan Nobleman: Henry Percy, Ninth Earl of Northumberland (1564–1632)', *Econ. Hist. Rev.* 2nd series, IX, no. 3 (1957), 436.

[3] *Correspondence of Matthew Parker*, ed. J. Bruce and T. T. Perowne (Parker Society 1853), XII–XIII; J. Strype, *Life and Acts of Matthew Parker* (1711), p. 425.

The Rising Lawyer

We can speculate on the ways in which Parker's position would differ from Bacon's. His income would be stabler (for Bacon's rose with the steady enlargement of his estate) and less enriched by gratuities. Some of his outlays would be higher. The bill for annuities, fees, curates' pensions and hospitals (£800 a year in all) would be far in excess of anything Bacon was paying; the benefactions are bigger than anything that can be traced to Bacon; the cost of entertaining the Queen may have been higher. On the other hand, his expenditure on land was trifling compared with Bacon's average of over £1150 a year, and the amounts spent on buildings and marriage settlements was only about one-third of Bacon's. It seems certain that the Lord Keeper's levels were higher—if not at the time of their appointments at least thereafterwards. How much higher, we can only venture to guess after we have examined his recorded income.

HOW WAS THE MONEY FOUND?

How was the money found? We began the section on expenses with one admission of ignorance and here we must make another. The Bacon manuscripts have almost nothing to say about the most fascinating of all the enigmas—the size of the gratuities. There is a tantalising glimpse of the system on a single sheet of paper[1] upon which Bacon jotted down what it cost him to buy Redgrave over and above the amount paid to the crown. This little bill came to £65, some of which consisted of fees to surveyors and clerks, but about £40 was paid as follows: Sir Thomas Darcy £10, Mr Butts £6. 13s. 4d., Mr Chancellor £24, Sir Anthony Wingfield £10. In the case of Sir Anthony Wingfield, a powerful Suffolk figure whom it would be useful for any purchaser of Redgrave to cultivate, it is possible, though not likely, that Bacon was simply buying out a legal interest. We happen to know that Sir Anthony had been using Redgrave park. But the other three sums are unmistakably gifts. Mr Chancellor was the chancellor of the Court of Augmentations, who had undertaken a personal suit to the King on Bacon's

---

[1] 'The charges of myne exchange for Redgrave besydes the recompence to the kynges grace made by me' (Bacon MSS. (Chicago)).

behalf;[1] Darcy and Butts (whose names come first in this account) were favourites. All the officers of the court must have received gifts. Suitors complained that 'the serche from auditor to auditor, from clerke to clerke' lightened the purse like the Pope's purgatory,[2] and where the underling got his shilling it is unlikely that the superior missed his pound. But there is no record of what Bacon got, either in this job or his other two. His son, who was impeached for accepting gifts as Lord Chancellor, and who defended himself on the grounds that he had never allowed them to influence his judgement, made an interesting remark on that occasion, but hardly one that lightens the obscurity. He protested that he was the most upright judge the country had had since his father![3] In the final analysis, the only basis for a guess at the unofficial rewards is the difference between the best estimate of his total expenses and the whole recorded income.

The recorded income from office in the first two appointments makes it sufficiently clear that the crown expected its servants to support themselves by other means than direct fees. Bacon began with £10 a year, payable in quarterly instalments of 50s.[4] By the time he left the Court of Augmentations, he had £70 a year, and a pension of 50s. as 'a student at the lawes'.[5] His salary in the Court of Wards was only £90 a year.[6] The remuneration of the Lord Keeper, who performed the duties of the Lord Chancellor, was on an altogether different scale, and we have precise records[7] of the fees collected by Bacon's receivers. These are shown in Table 5 B. The 'certainties' only varied with the leap year, which added another day's diet at 23s. a day: the other items, which brought this category up to £960 a year, were £200 for attendance in the Star Chamber, an annuity of £300, and an allowance for robes of £40. The 'casualties' were based on fixed fees for different

[1] See the 'Particular' for the exchange of Great Holland, Essex, with Redgrave, Suffolk (Bacon MSS. (Chicago)).

[2] Letter to Lord Lisle, 17 February 1540, quoted Joyce Youings, *Devon Monastic Lands: Calender of Particulars for Grants, 1536–1558* (Devon and Cornwall Record Society, new series, I (1955)), p. viii.

[3] Spedding, *op. cit.* VII, 559–60.   [4] *L. & P.* XIV, pt. 2, 311.

[5] *Ibid.* XXI, pt. 1, 311; *ibid.* pt. 2, 445; *ibid.* XX, pt. 1, 516.

[6] *Ibid.* XXI, pt. 2, 414.

[7] Acquittances, 11 October 1559, 16 November, 16 December 1560, 28 October 1562 Receivers' Accounts, 1559–75 (Bacon MSS. (Chicago)).

classes of deeds; perpetuities at 13s. 4d. each, patents at 2s. each, exemplifications at 6s. 8d. each. In the first year of office, which produced the richest harvest, twenty-nine perpetuities, 3360 patents, and six exemplifications yielded £357. 6s. 8d. The Office of Dispensations and Faculties was a branch of the Chancery where certain grants made by the archbishop of Canterbury were confirmed by the great seal. Finally, there was a wax allowance of £16. In all, the office produced between £1200 and £1300 a year, against which certain costs would have to be offset in the way of robes, wax, and diet, but the dimensions of these are unknown. To this substantial sum we may add the Queen's annuity of £100 per annum. It was probably not regarded as part of the office, but it represents the remaining fee, of any size, which Bacon received from the crown.

The best effort we can make to show the income from the ever-growing lands is presented in Table 5 A, sections I (Suffolk), II (Norfolk), III (Essex), IV (Herts.), V (London and Middlesex), VI (Somerset), VII (Leases), and IX (Foreign Receipts). These figures, which are based on receivers' accounts, furnish a fairly firm guide to the revenue in the most prosperous years, from Michaelmas 1559 to Michaelmas 1575. The curve may be projected over the last three years of his life, 1575–9, with reasonable plausibility, but all we can say at the moment of the first half of his career is that the income must have risen from a few pounds in 1540 to the neighbourhood of £1000 in 1559. We have included some figures for 1556–9, but these are based on bailiffs' accounts, which for various reasons prevent us from seeing anything like the normal deliveries. Unusually big sums were being detained by the bailiffs as 'arrears' in 1556 and 1558, and their accounts do not include four classes of income which were someone else's responsibility at the time—urban rents, rents from leasehold property, foreign receipts, and the profits of at least six flocks of sheep. The actual income may have been twice as big as the incomplete returns. However, we attach less importance to this guess-work for the last years of Mary's reign, than to the picture, for 1559–75, of a net income expanding from just under a thousand a year to close on £2500.

What sort of a landlord was this 'new man'? This is a question which requires some attention in view of the legends which have circulated about the robber-barons of the Reformation and the bourgeois rationalists of the agrarian revolution, and in view of the genuine uncertainty which the professional feels about many aspects of the subject. It is hoped to publish a study in which the acquisition and management of the Bacon estates will be reviewed in detail.[1] Meanwhile it may be enough to consider him briefly under the aspects of farmer, purchaser, speculator, and rentier.

Sheep-farming was in the Bacon blood. The champion country where he was brought up was one vast sheep-walk; every village had its flocks; his father, uncle, brothers, and cousins were all in the business. The pastoral customs of the region, which hinged on the fold-course privileges of the lords of manors, and the economics of the industry are sketched in a later chapter. There is not the slightest doubt that the young lawyer expected to deal in foldcourses and flocks the moment that he started to buy property, but the absence of accounts before 1556, and the fact that he became a rentier shortly afterwards, means that we have only fitful glimpses of this enterprise. However, he never seems to have become more than a middle-sized flock-master. His first purchase in 1540 was the manor of Ingham, which had been a sheep-farm of the monastery, and within a year or two he enlarged the pasturage there by buying another lordship, with its foldcourse, from Sir Clement Heigham.[2] Eventually, he was able to keep three flocks there. Other foldcourses passed through his hands in the forties, but two of them, on the heath outside Norwich where Kett's companions were to roast no small number of sheep in 1549, were surrendered to his brother Thomas long before that date,[3] and a third was only bought from Sir Arthur Darcy in order to pass it on to Sir Thomas Jermyn.[4] He started a flock at Redgrave, but as the abbot had not kept more than 360 on those limited grounds, it must have been small. Stanford, a Breckland manor which he bought in 1546, was a different proposition;

---

[1] This will be entitled, *The Estates of Nicholas Bacon, 1540–1580.* Part I will be a General Introduction, Part II a Review of the Individual Properties, Part III Appendices.

[2] Acquittance, 4 May 1547 (Bacon MSS. (Chicago)).

[3] *L. & P.* XVII, 704; *ibid.* XVIII, 557; *Cal. Patent Rolls, Edward VI,* I, 113.

[4] *L. & P.* XX, 496; Acquittance, 14 August 1542 (Bacon MSS. (Chicago)).

he had two flocks there of 800 ewes and 400 hoggs. He held a moiety of Redmere, where sheep were kept, and Eccles, another Breckland manor, which he leased in 1557 before he bought it in 1560, had a capacity for 1000 ewes; but it is not clear that he kept a lot of his own sheep on either of these manors. All we know definitely is the statement in a bailiffs' account of 1556 that six flocks were being kept at that time: Redgrave (1), Ingham (3), Stanford (2). This would point to a limit of about 4000 sheep. He could have been renting courses or enjoying interests in flocks, of which we know nothing; but he obviously fell far short of the real giants in the region, like the Fermours or the Southwells, whose flocks might range from 12,000 to 20,000.[1]

The income from 4000 sheep at this date could be of the order of £150[2] a year, but by the time our table starts, the courses and stocks were leased; Ingham and Stanford about 1559, Eccles by 1561 at the latest. When Stody was bought in 1572, with grounds for 1000 wethers, it was leased with a stock, and the same practice was followed with Stiffkey. It is possible that some sheep were kept in the park at Redgrave (though the foldcourse there was leased) and at Gorhambury, and Nathaniel had a flock at Stiffkey at the time of his father's death. But these were all home farms. On no other manor is there any indication that Bacon was engaged in sheep farming in the second half of his career. Either the industry had lost some of the attractions which it had during the booming days of the first half of the century, or he had withdrawn for some other reason which is not clear. The fact that his responsibilities had increased on becoming Lord Keeper is in itself no reason why competent servants should not have continued to run this business for him.

A word must be said about the home farms. We have seen how it was common for their profits to be recorded in the foreign receipts. When the receivers began their accounts in 1559, this category was a catch-all which included, among other items, the sale of farm produce around Redgrave. In 1561, for instance, some £75 was entered from the miscellaneous sales of steers, grain, wool, sheep, and skins, each item being precisely itemised. But a year or two later the clerks changed

[1] See chapter v, pp. 182–4 below.   *Ibid.* pp. 188–9, 194.

their practice, and the sale of produce virtually disappeared. It had obviously become the separate responsibility of a bailiff of husbandry, whose accounts are lost. The same policy must have been adopted for Gorhambury and Stiffkey when they came into use. We therefore know almost nothing about them, and our picture of the income in the peak years includes nothing from this source apart from the early sales at Redgrave. There is no reason to suppose that any large business was going on, as the purpose of these farms was to supply the household, but it is quite possible that we are undervaluing the income, on this account, by some scores of pounds.

When we consider Bacon as a purchaser of land, two questions are in our minds: firstly, how good were his bargains, and especially his purchases from the crown; secondly, does his career lend any support to the idea of a rising gentry who throve at the expense of the thriftless?

Bacon can be shown to have paid the crown about £10,000 for various parcels of property, all of it formerly in the hands of the church and the bulk of it in Suffolk, though there were important tracts in London, Norfolk, Hertfordshire, and Dorset. Over £6500 was paid between 1540 and 1548, after which there were only small purchases until 1560–2, when a commission to sell crown lands, of which he himself was a member, led to an expenditure of over £2500. No purchase has been found after this date. Only one instance of an outright gift has been traced—the grant, 'for services', of the manors of Wyverston and Walsham Willows in 1559,[1] which together were worth just under £90 a year at that time.

Historians have always been interested in determining how far the monastic lands were sold at hard prices.[2] So far as Bacon is concerned, we know from his correspondence that he regarded a twenty-years' purchase of a property that would hold its annual value as a sound investment.[3] By these standards, all the purchases of the period 1540–8

---

[1] *Cal. Patent Rolls, Elizabeth*, I, 86–7.

[2] For the most recent study of this complicated subject, see H. J. Habakkuk, 'The Market for Monastic Property, 1539–1603', *Econ. Hist. Rev.* 2nd series, x, no. 3 (1958).

[3] E.g. letters of 16 April 1569, 23 February 1570 (Bacon MSS. (Chicago), included in E. R. Sandeen (ed.), 'Correspondence of Nicholas Bacon, Lord Keeper' (unpublished M.A. thesis, University of Chicago, 1955).

were sound, to say the least, for the 'rate' of twenty years remained constant and the values steadily improved. Assuming that the different items in the manorial income—rents of assise, leases, profits of court, and woods—were accurately appraised at the time of the sale, rents of assise was the only item that would remain more or less fixed. Leases would be worth more as they fell in. Profits of court, in which the potentially important element was the fine on the transfer of copyholds, might be trifling at the time of the dissolution, but the pressures which were to make them soar by the end of the century were already being felt in Bacon's lifetime. And the biggest inflation of all would occur in wood sales. It was hard to do badly under these conditions. But we can go further and suggest that in some respects, not sensational but substantial, the valuations made at the time of the sale were less than those which the purchaser himself could immediately realise. In the first place, it is unlikely that the surveys made by the Court of Augmentations, with the best will in the world, could be as thorough as those of an owner whose agents could dig out all the rights. There is more than one mention in the Bacon papers of the elusive roods and shrinking tenures which were pulled into the open after the new lord had settled in. But far more important than this were the possibilities that lay in leases. In its appraisal of a manor, the court of these years seems to have made no attempt to go behind the face value of a lease, regardless of its length. This practice was only realistic in the case of very long leases, but in all the manors bought by Bacon only one instance of such a lease has been found—a ninety-nine-year term pinned by Thetford Priory, in return, no doubt, for a consideration, on the small manor of Playfords in Barnham, during the feverish eve of the dissolution. Otherwise the leases were for twenty-one years or less, and one cannot help observing that the typical history of a Bacon purchase from the crown was a big jump in income, in the early years, followed by only a moderate improvement later, or none at all if there was not time before his death for another renewal.

Unfortunately, the records are scantiest where we need them most, and there is always the possibility that the jump is due to purchases of surrounding land. In the case of Ingham, there are not enough records

5-2

for an opinion. In the case of Redgrave, considerable sums were spent to recover the demesnes which the abbey had sold as copyholds when its end was in sight.[1] In the case of Hinderclay, the leasehold income was more than doubled in the early years, but we cannot be sure that there were no purchases, even though they have left no trace. However, there are two other instances which clearly show the opportunities for profit. One is simply an example of what the court would tolerate. Bacon bought the manor of Magna Holland, Essex, in 1542. Less than three years later he exchanged it with the crown for Redgrave, at the same value at which he had bought it, but in the interval he had pinned an eighty-year lease on the demesnes in favour of his brother at the same rent which the previous farmer had been paying.[2] The fact that this had obviously decreased the value of the property seems to have concerned nobody.

The other example is more material. In November 1544 he bought Rickinghall—yet another manor in the same area. A certain John Morris seems to have got a forty-year lease out of the abbey in 1535 at £18 a year, but after the court had made its surveys in 1542 this was reduced to twenty-one years at the lower figure of £15. 4s., which was made the basis for Bacon's purchase. But we are lucky enough to know what Bacon's agents thought of these values, for a survey has survived which he ordered in his first year as lord (2 September 1545). We learn from this that the farmer held 356 acres of pasture worth £26. 3s. 6d. a year (1s. to 1s. 8d. an acre), 20 acres of meadow worth £2. 11s. 4d. (2s. to 3s. 4d. an acre), and 101 acres of arable worth £5. 4s. 6d. (8d. to 1s. 8d. an acre). Moreover—those elusive roods!—there was said to be another 21 acres 'not shewed by the farmer' but by one, John Dowe, worth 15s. 8d. When these items are added, it appears that John Morris, in the opinion of Bacon's surveyors, was enjoying lands worth £34. 15s. for his rent of £15. 4s. They further reported that while keeping 329 acres for himself he was subletting 169 for £12. 7s. 4d., and thus very nearly enjoying his own farm for nothing. Bacon got rid

[1] K. M. Dodd, 'A History of the Manor of Redgrave in the County of Suffolk, 1538–1700', (unpublished Ph.D. thesis, University of Chicago, 1958).
[2] 'Particular' for the exchange of Magna Holland, Essex, and Redgrave (Bacon MSS. (Chicago)).

of this farmer within a year of the survey and relet the manor for another twenty-one-year term at £28. 10s. 8d. We do not know what it cost him to alter the lease, but a manor bought on these terms was clearly a bargain.[1]

The possibilities of profit in an urban purchase of 1544 will be examined when we consider Bacon as a speculator, but meanwhile let us continue the scrutiny of the terms on which he bought the permanent estate. The purchases of 1553–4 were not large, but three of them are interesting. By this time the crown had raised 'the rate' from twenty- to twenty-two- or twenty-four-years' purchase, in recognition of the inflation. The first case occurred in 1553 when he bought about 100 acres of land in Gislingham which had belonged to the Knights of St John of Jerusalem. It consisted of seven copyholds, paying the usual fixed rents, which amounted in all to £3. 4s. a year. As the rate was 24, the price was £76. 16s. Within six months he had realised £242 by selling about 90 of these acres to the two yeomen who held them. The next case occurred in 1554 when he bought a mill near Creeting St Peter's, where the Ferneleys lived, for less than £30, on the basis of a lease of 1539 (twenty-one years) which had fixed the rent at £1. 6s. 8d. The tenant at this time was said to be subletting the mill for £7 a year, and making over £8 out of the property altogether. Three years later, as the lease was nearing its end, Bacon let the mill for £6 a year under a twenty-one-year term. In 1573, when he was getting rid of non-essentials in order to invest heavily in Norfolk, he sold it for £200: assuming the standard rate, it was then worth £10 a year. Finally, to complete the tale of these juicy morsels, he bought a portion of Blackburn Hundred in 1554 which consisted of rent oats, and a capon or two, valued at just under £5 a year, and costing him about £108 at a rate of 22. There was a certain amount of rubbish in Hundreds, and the good rents must have taken somebody's time to collect; but it was difficult to lose when the oats had been priced at 10d. a comb. The accounts show that he was often paid double that in the first few years, with several cases of 2s. a

[1] L. & P. XVIII, pt. 1, 554; ibid. XIX, pt. 2, 412; Lilian J. Redstone (ed.), '"First Ministers Account" of the Abbey of St Edmund', Suff. Arch. XIII (1909), 338–9; B.M. Add. MS. 40063; Breviate of Leases, 1562 (Bacon MSS. (Chicago)).

comb, and an eventual lease to one of his own bailiffs at 2*s*. 4*d*. a comb. It seems likely that over the years the property brought in at least twice its presumed value.[1]

Most interesting of all are the purchases which Bacon made when he himself was in charge of the sales. One of them, Playfords in Barnham, has already been mentioned. It was a little manor, in a town where he and his father had once kept a flock of sheep. The priory had leased it to the Croft family for ninety-nine years, but as the rate was twenty years' purchase, it fulfilled Bacon's idea of a sound investment. He paid about £150, and when his son sold it in 1585, with the lease only half expired, he was able to realise a few more pounds. Another item in the same parcel was the rectory of Redborne, close to his Gorhambury estate. It was valued at £22 a year, on the basis of a forty-one-year lease which was due to expire in five years. Bacon knew all about this property, as he had once held an interest in it. He bought at a rate of 20, and was able in 1565 to find a new tenant who would pay exactly treble the rent—i.e. 100 marks a year. Finally, there was Eccles, a manor close to Redgrave, on the Norfolk side of the border. A certain John Reynolds, who was a bailiff of the duchess of Norfolk, had been given, as a reward for his services, a beneficial lease of this manor which represented a clear profit of £23 a year, i.e. he was to pay the crown £9 for demesnes leased at £32. Within a month of the grant—this was the spring of 1557—Bacon bought up this thirty-year lease under terms which look very favourable; after paying the £9 rent to the crown, and an annuity of £16 a year to Reynolds, he would have £7 a year to himself. However, as his relations with Reynolds are unknown, we attach less importance to this than to the sequel. When he was in a position to buy this manor in 1560, he did so at a twenty-year rate of the values involved in the beneficial lease. In other words, a property currently producing just under £50 a year was sold on the assumption that it was worth about £20 (i.e. the rent of £9, which was taken to be the value of the demesnes, and a further £12 in rents of assise, which had not been included in the original lease to Reynolds). The only charge on the

---

[1] These three cases have been worked out from a comparison of 'particulars' with bailiffs' accounts, receiver's accounts, and other notes among the Bacon MSS. (Chicago).

clear profit of nearly £30 a year was the annuity of £16 to Reynolds, which ran for about a dozen years.[1]

There is nothing in all these examples to convict the government of great laxity in its disposal of crown lands, and still less to convict Bacon of fraud. No state has ever been able to unload masses of property on to the market without leaving opportunities for the big buyers, and the more cynical among us may feel, after reading this story, that Bacon had every right to be astonished by his own moderation. However, he was obviously doing well enough out of his purchases from the crown. As for his luck with other sellers, we will only say that while we have found no sensational bargains, we do not doubt that there were some good ones, and we only know of two in which he complained that he was hardly treated. These last cases are very well documented by his instructions to his sons, Nicholas and Nathaniel.[2] One involved a moiety of the manor of Burgate, near Redgrave, which he bought from Robert Rookwood; the other was Stody, near Thornage in Norfolk, which he bought from Robert Bosom. Both were so strategically placed that he could not bring himself, at the height of his prosperity, to let them escape, so he ground his teeth and paid. 'A much worse penny-worth than Rookwoods, which was ill enough' was his final comment on Stody, after all the resources of relatives, stewards and surveyors had been exhausted. But the returns, though below his hopes, were really not so bad. If the truth were known about all his purchases, one might find them conforming fairly closely to his idea of a sound investment—a twenty-year purchase of a firm annual value. Certainly there are many instances, especially among his smaller deals, where he bought at this rate and then immediately rented the land at the assessed value.

Who did he buy from, and how many declining peers or gentry can we find among the sellers? Here we must be content with very rough estimates of the sums paid to different classes of sellers,[3] and incomplete

---

[1] Same comment as on p. 70, n. 1. Precise documentation for the history of individual properties will appear in Part II of the projected study of the Bacon estates.

[2] Those to Nicholas are included in E. R. Sandeen, *op. cit.*; those to Nathaniel are among the MSS. of the Norwich City Library. See n. 1 above.

[3] The gross figures which follow, amounting to £38,000, are based on Table 2, and are therefore an understatement.

knowledge of the individuals. We have already said that he paid about £10,000 to the crown. The next group consisted of office-holders and their families, and about £11,000 may have been paid to them. Of this nearly £5000 was paid to Henry Denny, the son of Henry VIII's favourite, Sir Anthony Denny, for the Mettingham College estate and the manor of Bramfield. Though no attempt has been made to examine the Denny fortunes, the chance that the second generation was embarrassed is not likely when we recall that Henry's son, Edward, was sheriff of Hertford in 1603, Baron Denny in 1604, and earl of Norwich in 1626. The next biggest sum went to Sir Ralph Rowlett, of Gorhambury, the childless heir of a merchant office-holder—about £1700 that we know of, and probably more, as Sir Ralph acknowledged in deeds that he had received many services and benefits from Bacon and left him four more manors in his will. They were brothers-in-law, Sir Ralph having taken his second wife from the daughters of Sir Anthony Cooke. It is also clear, from the estate left to nephews and others, that Sir Ralph died a wealthy man. Three others received sums in the neighbourhood of £1000; Sir Richard Wingfield, from a Suffolk clan that held all sorts of offices under the Tudors; Sir Robert Rochester's heirs—he was the comptroller of Queen Mary's household; and Lord Willoughby of Parham (the nephew of a wealthy office-holder, and the first cousin of Katherine, duchess of Suffolk) who was given a barony at the coronation of Edward VI. From these purchases we drop down to others, of £300 or less, which involved such courtiers as Viscount Lisle, who later became duke of Northumberland, Sir Arthur Darcy, a younger son of the early Tudor courtier, Sir Thomas, Lord Darcy, and Sir Clement Heigham, the Suffolk lawyer who became Speaker of the House of Commons in Mary's reign and a baron of the Exchequer.

The next group was composed of over a dozen gentry, some of whom may have held minor offices for all we know, but most of whom were probably local country gentry. Some £15,000 may have been paid to them. Then came the yeomanry, several of whom can be identified as thriving local figures, from whom land was steadily bought in small parcels to build up the estates around Redgrave, Gorhambury, and

Marks. No attempt has been made to work out this total precisely, but it cannot have been less than £2000 and may have been more.

It is apparent at a glance that the peerage hardly comes into this picture. There was one transaction involving the duke of Norfolk, in which the manor of Brissingham, bought from gentry, was exchanged for £1000 and some lands around Mettingham, which Bacon wanted, valued at a thirty-year purchase of a £10 annual value. Lord Willoughby may have got £1000 or so for some rent charges valued at £60 a year. Otherwise, there was only £274 paid to Viscount Lisle for the manor of Harleston, and £133 to Lord Darcy for the liberty of Bury St Edmund's. As for thriftless sellers, only three cases have been identified, and one of them may have been more a case of bad luck than improvidence. The first was Bacon's own son-in-law, Sir Henry Woodhouse, of the premier Norfolk family that lived at Waxham. The letter in which Bacon gave this young man a simple lesson in book-keeping has already been quoted, but it may have been as ineffective as such advice often is. One of the little problems in the Bacon accounts is to explain how the manor of West Somerton happens to appear there for six months in 1576, the local historians being of the opinion that it passed from Sir Henry that year to a London alderman. Putting a few bits and pieces of evidence together, the best guess seems to be that Woodhouse mortgaged it to Roger Townshend, and then came to his father-in-law, together with Townshend, to get him out of his troubles; that Bacon lent him enough money to pay off Townshend and had the manor conveyed to himself; and that after taking the profits for six months he found that the only way to recover his loan was to have the manor sold off. Further proof of Sir Henry's problems may perhaps be seen in the fact that he sold his office of vice-admiral to Bacon in 1578; but we are in no position to say how serious they were.

The second case was a clear-cut example of declining gentry. The Banyards, from whom Bacon bought Stiffkey in 1570, had been tottering into bankruptcy for some years. Their foldcourse had been mortgaged in 1560, well-to-do friends had lent money, and their credit was exhausted. Judging from a few begging letters that have survived, the father and son-in-law were a sorry, quarrelsome pair. Bacon agreed to pay £2600, of which £1000 would go to the father's creditors. The price seems to have been the standard one, from his point of view, as he proceeded to let the manor for £130 a year; but he had some difficulty in collecting the rent. The third case also involved debts, but they were probably more honourably contracted. Thomas and Elizabeth Hales were neighbours of the Cookes in the Romford area of Essex. Elizabeth had inherited Marks and the Red Lion (the present Golden Lion) from her father, Richard Eton, who came from a family of London mercers; but Thomas had spent six costly years in the courts trying to clear the title. Bacon was one of several people from whom he borrowed money. The debt—which must have been about 1000 marks—was first secured by an annuity, then a mortgage in which Hales was given three years to pay part of it off, with the condition that if he failed to do so, the manor became Bacon's on the payment of a further £300. Judged by the contemporary law of mortgages, this was gentlemanly treatment. Hales failed to meet his payments, with the result that first the manor, and then the Red Lion, became Bacon's. There seems to be nothing in these cases[1] to Bacon's discredit, and very little to give comfort to the sponsors of the theories which suggested our questions.

While we have discussed the values at which Bacon bought his lands, and touched on one or two sales, we have made no judgement of the extent to which speculative buying entered into his plans. How does the expenditure on land which was bought to be sold again compare with the investment in the permanent estate? On the whole we are inclined to think that speculative buying was of no great consequence after the early years when the monastic estate was first being unloaded, and there are at least two difficulties about this period. First, how do we know when he *was* buying? The letters patent often conceal the identity of the real buyer, and it is only our knowledge of the household officers who acted for him in later life which enables us to be sure of some of his purchases. We happen to know that when his brothers bought Hinderclay they were buying it for him, but nobody can be sure

---

[1] See footnotes on pp. 70, 71. These three cases will be documented under the manors, West Somerton, Stiffkey, and Marks.

that they know all the transactions in which he was involved. Secondly, how can we be sure, when his name does appear in a grant, that he was not simply performing a service for friends or relatives? Sometimes the question is answered by the acquittances. He spends £43 on monastic lands in Lancashire in 1544, and then sells them to his servant, William Bretton, at cost price a few months later.[1] Several of the small purchases of this period may have been in this category—£11 for two mills in Worcestershire, £17 for a messuage in Devonshire, £11 for lands in Nottinghamshire[2]—and more substantial grants must have been passed on to his officers as part payment for their services. But there are several cases in which the relative, or friend, may have offered some consideration for the service that was being performed. The standard history of Suffolk manors knows nothing about Bacon's ownership of Harleston, which he bought from Viscount Lisle in 1545,[3] but it does know that it was held by a certain William Page.[4] We happen to know that William Page, of Bury St Edmund's, had married Bacon's aunt Margery in 1539.[5] Did he get Harleston at cost price, or was there something in it for Bacon? The Franciscan friary at Babwell was bought in 1542 and then passed on to a widowed friend, Elizabeth Coggeshall, whose son John became Bacon's ward.[6] Was there any profit here? Finally, in 1544 Nicholas Bacon and a certain Thomas Skipwith bought the manor of Burston, in Hertfordshire, for £700. This was a property which Bacon himself was to own in later years, but the grant of 1544 was made in favour of Skipwith and his heirs.[7] What did he get out of it?

These questions are insoluble, but if we set all these doubtful cases aside, we are still left with one large purchase which was made at this time for speculative purposes. In 1544 he bought a parcel of valuable property in the city of London which had belonged to St Mary's

[1] Acquittances, 24 March and 12 December 1544 (Bacon MSS. (Chicago)).
[2] *Ibid.* 18 July, 1 August 1543, 17 May 1544.
[3] *Ibid.* 22 December 1545.
[4] Walter A. Copinger, *The Manors of Suffolk* (London, 1905–11), VI, 193.
[5] Margery Bacon was the widow of John Bacon, of Hessett, who had died in 1536 (Cooke, *Suff. Arch.* v, 78).
[6] *L. & P.* XVII, 163, 257; *ibid.* XIX, pt. 1, 373.
[7] *Ibid.* XIX, pt. 1, 370.

The Wealth of the Gentry, 1540–1660

Hospital without Bishopsgate.[1] It consisted of residential dwellings, business premises, and a few inns, scattered over more than twenty parishes, most of which had been leased for terms ranging from forty to ninety-nine years in the decade before the dissolution. The clear annual value of the rents came to £167 and the rate was an eight-years' purchase. Bacon and his two servants, William Bretton and Henry Ashfield, paid £1315 in cash. There is almost no indication that he still held any of this purchase when his receivers' accounts begin in 1559. The only property at that date which can be clearly assigned to this source was a tenement with a gate-house and garden in St Giles without Cripplegate which had been leased for ninety-nine years at 18s. a year in 1537. Bacon paid £7. 4s. for it in 1544, and his son sold it forty years later, with the lease less than half finished, for £20. The bulk of the purchase was probably sold off within the first few years and we are lucky enough to have two clear indications of what he made out of it.

John Rollisley was a tenant who occupied 'the Gonnepowder house', in St Botolph's parish, which he had leased from the hospital in 1536 for ninety-nine years at £3. 6s. 8d. a year. His first step may have been to buy his own premises, but of that we know nothing. However, within three months of Bacon's purchase, he contracted to buy adjacent property, 'now or late' in the tenure of fourteen individuals whom he names, for £278. 16s. and the Michaelmas rents; £100 to be paid down and the rest the following summer. Receipts show that the bargain was completed, and the only problem is to see if the grant to Bacon, with its itemisation of tenements and rents, enables us to determine the profit. This shows thirty tenants in St Botolph's paying about £45 a year, the biggest single rent being £6. 15s. and the majority a pound or less. Ten of the fourteen tenements can be clearly identified, with a total rent of £17. 9s. 4d. The remaining four must have brought the total to some figure between £20 and £25. If we assume £20, Bacon paid £160 and obtained, within a year, £299; if £25, the figures are £200 and £304.

Richard Hodge was a baker who had taken in 1538 an eighty-year lease of some premises on Cornhill for which he paid the hospital

[1] L. & P. XIX, pt. I, 500–1. The other materials relating to this case—the 'particular', acquittances, indentures—are in the Bacon MSS. (Chicago).

£1. 13s. 4d. a year. This was part of a block that Bacon bought, and before long Hodge had acquired the lease of another part—two messuages and a warehouse rented at £4. 13s. 4d. under a ninety-nine-year lease of the same date as the other. Bacon had paid £50. 13s. 4d. for these properties, and he sold them to Hodge in January 1547 for £70, while still reserving for himself a rent of £3 a year—which was almost half their annual value.

Hodge cannot have been more than a little man. After a down payment of £30 he was given over two years to pay off the balance in instalments of £5. But by 1549 he was ready to buy three more tenements in the Cornhill block, and this time with no rents reserved. In the same year Robert Jens, a poulterer, bought another two next to these. However, in none of these five sales do we know anything about the price. We can see from the abutments of the grant to Jens that Bacon still held at least one of the Cornhill properties in May 1549, five years after the original purchase, but we do not know how fast the whole parcel moved.

This is the only recorded case of a large speculative purchase in London. He is known to have spent a few more hundreds on urban property at this time, some of which was certainly turned over, but in view of his life-long connexions with the City we may be surprised that there was not more. The examples we have just cited suggest that the profits in urban monastic estate were at least as good as those in the country, but it may have involved the kind of petty business that lost its appeal as his fees from office rose. At all events, there is no evidence of serious speculation in the good records from 1559 to 1578. The London property which passed into his hands seems to be more the result of family and official needs than anything else—a few tenements from the Chamber or a city company, a few tithes, a site for Edward's house, and a substantial block in Chancery Lane to accommodate Chancery officials and household dependents. It was only at the end of this second period that his rental income in London rose as high as £150.[1]

No doubt there were occasions, after the excitements of the early years, when he bought a rural property with no intention of keeping it.

[1] See Table 5 A, sections V and VII.

There is no reason why he should have turned down a good bargain which thrust itself upon him, and a man of his means and connexions would often be pressed to buy. But the recorded cases are not numerous; Thraxton, Norfolk, which he bought from Sir Christopher Heydon and quickly turned over to Sir Richard Southwell; Parker's Place, in King's Langley, Herts, which he agreed to take from a courtier's heir for £500, if the title was good, and promptly sold to the Cheyneys of Chesham Bois. Doubtless there were more: but the income from the sale of lands during the Lord Keepership is more the result of the management of the permanent estate than anything else—the sale of fringe lands, the substitution of more desirable properties, and the accommodation of dependents with small sales.

Finally, what of Bacon the rentier? Anyone who approaches this question with the conventional image of the improving landlord in mind is bound to encounter some surprises. So far from radical innovation being the key-note of this history, the predominant impression is conservatism—the traditionalism of all the accounting procedures, the preoccupation with a multitude of ancient and often petty rights, the absence of anything which can be described as 'rationalisation'. If others were remaking the face of rural England, this man, one is inclined to feel, was not. Yet there was nothing whatever of the casual in his make-up. The spirit of businesslike determination is stamped on every estate letter, in the marginal comments on his medieval rolls, and in the minds of all his officials who knew very well that the great man would be counting roods and capons in the interludes of mightier affairs. When we have looked at a few adjustments that were suggested by new conditions, we shall still believe that the best description of his spirit is nothing more sensational than immemorial shrewdness.

The main features of his management are as follows. (1) Thorough surveys of the demesnes and every precaution to attract the best bids. If the survey did not precede the purchase, as at Stody, where we know all about the pains taken by John Le Hunt to expose Robert Bosom's wiles, it soon followed. Bacon wanted to know exactly how many acres of arable, pasture, meadows, and woods he was buying, and what were the going prices; and if his sons dawdled in getting them properly let by Michaelmas or Lady Day, they heard all about it. If he was buying a foldcourse, he wanted to know how many hundred sheep it would feed, how many lambs they got from a hundred ewes, how much wool, and what the local farmers were paying for 'tath' (that is, for the benefit of having the flock fold over their acres). But he must have learnt all this in his cradle. (2) Thorough surveys of the rents and suits owed by copyholders and freeholders. This was a typical field for administrative vigilance. It not only established the small fixed sums that were usually due in the shape of annual rents, but the nature of fines, the rights to cut timber, the right to sell a copyhold at some future date, and the right to that intangible but satisfying commodity, the 'command' over tenants. (3) The enlargement of the property by suitable purchases as opportunity offered, and the provision of a stock of sheep or cattle if that was indicated. (4) A moderate pressure to get a higher income from copyhold fines as land values rose. (5) A growing interest in rents in kind; and (6) a growing income from woods. As the last three features reflect the impact of inflationary conditions, we may pause a moment over the two that can be relatively easily explained—the pressure on copyhold fines and on rents in kind.

Though custom varied as to the fixity of copyhold fines, and distinctions were made between different kinds of estate and different kinds of transfer, there was a common tendency in East Anglia, at the time of the dissolution, to charge two shillings an acre. When the last abbot of Bury St Edmund's was raising money on the eve of the dissolution by creating copyholds out of demesne, this was the fine which he asked from a group of yeomen to whom he sold over two hundred acres in Redgrave.[1] As their rents were to range between 8*d*. and 1*s*. an acre, it seems likely that the two shillings fine was thought of as twice the annual value. The abbot's idea of the price of an acre may already have been a little low—after all, he was not going to collect these rents—but it was not indecently so. However, by the time Bacon died in 1579, it had risen two- or threefold. This naturally produced a campaign for higher fines. Where they were arbitrable, they were raised. Where there

[1] Indenture of 29 October 1537, between John Melford, abbot, and John Harvey *et al.* (Bacon MSS. (Chicago)).

was doubt as to whether they were adjustable or not (and they could have seemed fixed in recent memory, without fulfilling a lawyer's idea of 'certainty') every effort was made by a vigilant steward to show that they were 'uncertain'. If this was difficult, it was still possible for the lord to urge a readjustment on his tenants and procure it by one means or another. His case had obvious merits, but after such compositions it was not uncommon for a later generation of tenants to report, 'For our fynes, they were certeyn; but nowe, by what meanes we know not, our custom is so broken that they are arbitrable'.[1] By the time Bacon died, it was common for the lords of the region to get four shillings an acre, and sometimes more.

What evidence there is for the early years suggests that Bacon was taking the standard 2s. an acre. In some cases it was no doubt less, and a very interesting report has survived of the steps he took to raise the fine at Walsham. Some well-to-do yeomen here brought an action in the Chancery against the Lord Keeper's son, in 1584, accusing him of levying outrageous fines. They said that in the good old days tenants at Walsham had never paid more than a shilling an acre, until the late Lord Keeper pointed out that this fine was 'very small in respect of the goodness of their landes'. But seeing that the custom was such that 'by compulsion he could not dryve them to paye any greater unlesse the tenants [of their] voluntary accorde woulde yealde thereunto, his honour thought it better by faire meanes to wyne them then otherwise by extremity to enforce them...and thereupon...delte with certen of the tenants...to compounde...that they would raise their fynes to a greater rate'. These tenants agreed, the complaint continued, 'partly for that they durst not incurr his Lordshipps displeasure for he was of such greate power and authority they were altogether unfitt and unhable to stande in contencon of suyte with him if he shoulde have taken that course against them: and partly also for that he did promyse them, that they shoulde never after that tyme paye any greater fine then...two shillings for every acre'. But then the younger Nicholas succeeded, and 'perceyvinge the custome aforesaid to be in some part violated by

---

[1] Verdict of a Methwold jury in reply to the royal inquest of 1606 (Townshend MSS., Safe 2 (16), Garsett House, Norwich).

certen of the tenants...in the lyef tyme...of his father, and therby the
fitter opportunity ministered unto him to bringe the same further in
question; never respectinge his fathers said promyses...hath of late
exacted very greate and grievous fynes...farr above the rate demanded
and taken by the saide late Lord Keeper...and doth daily labor to have
the said fynes arbitrable, and to be assessed and rated at his own will
and pleasure'.

The son had various things to say in reply: that these substantial
complainants—one of them owned as much land in the village as the
lord himself—were posing as champions of little men; that the court
rolls showed that the fines at Walsham had always been arbitrable; that
he had heard some talk about his father's willingness to consider a fixed
fine of two shillings but that no agreement had been reached; and that
even if it had been reached, the action of one life-tenant (i.e. his father)
would not bind his successors.[1] What the story shows is Bacon's belief
in the reasonableness of a two-shilling fine at some such date as 1560, and
his apparent willingness to settle for that at Walsham. When we
examine the court rolls on other manors—and of course the data are
often incomplete—we sometimes find that there is no discernible trend,
and in other cases that there is a tendency to take four shillings an acre
in the seventies where he had previously taken two. On the whole, this
seems to be an unsensational history. The big pressure on fines only
came when land values really spiralled upwards after his death.

The attractions of taking rents in kind in a period of rising grain
prices are obvious. However, inflation or no inflation, it had always
made sense, unless the resources of the home farms were very ample, to
take some rents in kind in order to provision the households. How far
beyond this did Bacon go? The record is fairly quickly summarised. At
Ingham, a stock-and-land lease which was renewed in 1562 provided
for a rent of £93 and 133 combs of barley and rye with an option to
pay 5s. a comb. This was obviously made with an eye on the inflation.
The going price was about 4s. a comb; if it rose another shilling, Bacon
would still have his grain; if higher, the farmers—who incidentally were
his own servants—could settle for cash. They seem, for some years at

---

[1] C/2 Eliz./P 12/48 (P.R.O.).

least, to have paid in grain. At Rickinghall, where the chance came in 1570 to renew a lease of 1546, he raised the previous rent of £29 by 60 combs of white wheat. At Hinderclay, an earlier opportunity (before 1556) seems to have enabled him to add 68 combs of grain to a previous rent of £13. At Burgate, the leases of 1571 included about 26 combs of wheat. We have already referred to Blackburn Hundred, where 100 combs of rent oats, bought in 1554, at 10d. a comb, could be sold for two or three times that value. All these properties were in the neighbourhood of Redgrave, and it was in this same area that he bought a crown lease of Mildenhall, in the early 1560's, which brought in about 200 combs of malt. At Gorhambury, we know of at least one lease where the farmer was required to pay, in addition to a money rent, a third of his crop; and when Redborne Rectory was leased in 1565, at treble its previous money rent, there was a prudent little clause requiring the farmer to sell the household 40 combs of oats at 2s. 6d. the comb. Finally, when Stody was bought in 1572, Bacon expressed the hope that his son could find a farmer who would pay his rent either wholly or partly in kind; but he was disappointed, because we know that the rents were paid in cash. Taken in all, this record suggests that Bacon was well aware of the advantages of little wind-breaks against inflation, but the needs of his growing households were probably uppermost in his mind, and it is obvious that if his rents in kind are converted at as high an average rate as 5s. a comb they were not worth much more than £150 a year.

If to these three matters—somewhat bigger fines on copyholds, a somewhat keener interest in grain rents, and a small harvest from woods—we add a moderate improvement in leases, then we seem to have exhausted the impact of the inflation on the management of the Bacon estates. There is no evidence that he ever thought of reorganising his properties in any radical way. Here and there a copyhold might fall into his hands and be turned into a leasehold, with a modest improvement in rent, but the occasions are too few to have any significance. Some properties, like Wyverston, would be built up into more attractive propositions, but this was done by intelligent purchases. As for enclosures, none can be attributed to him with any confidence, though it may be that there was some parking around Redgrave and Gorhambury out of various lands that he had bought.

There were, of course, reasons why a landholder in the open-field regions of East Anglia, where so much of his property lay, should have no strong interest in enclosure. The foldcourse privileges were a leignorial monopoly, and any enclosure of open-field arable within the area of the privilege (which was often co-extensive with the village) interfered with its enjoyment. Though some ancient enclosures might be immune, and some new ones might become immune by composition, the general tendency of the pastoral customs was to discourage enclosure, or to permit it only on the understanding that the closes would be opened for the flock, between harvest and sowing, and in the fallow season. Thus when the abbot of Bury St Edmund's stopped keeping sheep at Redgrave at the time of the dissolution, there was a spurt of enclosures among the tenants;[1] but the restoration of seignorias authority on such properties must have applied the brakes once again. When Bacon was asked by a tenant at Timworth to sanction an enclosure, he made it clear that consent would only be given if he, Bacon, got 'easement for his sheep'.[2] Of course, the lord needed some enclosures for his sheep and other cattle, and there are examples, like Stody, where Robert Bosom and his father had created a number of closes out of heath and demesne arable in the generation before Bacon bought their manor.[3] But we have the word of Nicholas, Junior, in a dispute that occurred at the end of the century, that neither he nor his father had enclosed there.[4] As for his properties outside the foldcourse region, we can only say that the records, which are not meagre, have furnished no evidence.

The curve in Bacon's income from land in Table 5 A is obviously due far more to new purchases than to the improvement of old rents. There had undoubtedly been improvement before 1560, and there was somewhat more in this period than meets the eye, as some matters, like wood sales, might be carried in the foreign account or elsewhere. There was

[1] Redgrave Court Rolls (Bacon MSS. (Chicago)).
[2] Compotus Roll, 2 and 3/3 and 4 Philip and Mary (Bacon MSS. (Chicago)).
[3] Survey of Stody by John Le Hunt, August 1572, B.M. Add. MS. 14850.
[4] B.M. Add. MS. 39221, f. 93 ff.

also, we may surmise, a keen interest in improving leases as they fell in after this period. Towards the end of his life, his surveyors were closely examining the manors which he had inherited from Sir Ralph Rowlett to show the huge gap between current values and one old lease,[1] and there was more to be expected at Mettingham, which had been leased just before he bought it. However, we return to the observation with which we began: there was nothing in all this which a shrewd peasant, brought up in the old ways, could not have seen for himself.

After this necessary digression on land management, there are still one or two other sources of income to be considered. We have referred earlier to the fact that the Bacon manuscripts provide one of the few precise examples of the profits which officials were allowed to make out of wardships. In the summer of 1559, a few months after he had left the Court of Wards for the Chancery, Bacon bought the wardship and marriage of a certain William Yaxley for £50.[2] William's great-grandfather, John Yaxley, had been a distinguished lawyer in the reign of Henry VII. His grandfather, Anthony, and his father, Richard, had both died in 1558. Bacon seems to have known them well; the grandfather as another lawyer, the father as a friend and neighbour. A cousin, Francis, who owned Yaxley Hall in Mellis, was a courtier who was about to come under suspicion as a Catholic conspirator. William's widowed mother lived in Norfolk and depended heavily on an octogenarian uncle, Dr Miles Spencer, a chancellor of Norwich Cathedral, who had done well out of the dissolution. Bacon brought the boy up in his own household and was ready to marry him, when he came of age, to his youngest daughter Elizabeth—less because of the size of his fortune, which, though respectable, could easily have been bettered, than from reasons of friendship and neighbourhood. The boy would have about £100 a year from his father's lands, and another £200–£250 a year from his mother and Dr Spencer. He could buy two properties from Bacon, on very reasonable terms, which would set him up in Mellis—the Bacon manor already mentioned, and Yaxley

[1] Survey of Napsbury, 3 September 1577 (MS. XI, 2 (H.R.O.)).
[2] For the following paragraph, see *Cal. Patent Rolls, Elizabeth* I, 24; *D.N.B.* (Francis Yaxley); Edmund Farrer, 'Yaxley Hall: Its Owners and Occupiers', *Suff. Arch.* XVI, pt. I (1916), 1–28; Sandeen, *op. cit.*, Letters 7–27.

Hall, over which Bacon acquired some sort of control after the death of Francis Yaxley in 1565.[1] When we add to these prospects the reflection that a son-in-law of the Lord Keeper would not be alone in the world, we may wonder why William upset the plans of the matchmakers at the very last moment by refusing to marry Elizabeth. The best guess is his religion. He took a bride from the circle of Catholic families that had dominated Suffolk politics in Mary's reign—Eva Bedingfield—and was more than once in trouble as a recusant.

There is a manuscript[2] in the Bacon collection which shows that the clear annual value of William Yaxley's lands (that is, those left by his father) was thought to be £94 in 1561, and that the following sums were paid into Bacon's account during the eight years of the wardship: 1559, £97; 1560, £55; 1561, £106; 1562, £121; 1563, £93; 1564, £72; 1565, £72; 1566, £127. The total of £743 corresponds closely with the receipts which also appear in the Receivers' Accounts. When it came time to marry William Yaxley, Bacon explained that he had been offered 1000 marks for the marriage, and all the negotiations were conducted on that basis. It was this sum which provided the basis for his objections to the smallness of the jointure originally proposed by the widow and Doctor Spencer, and when these difficulties were overcome, only to have the agreement wrecked by the boy's decision, it was this sum which Spencer and his niece had to make good. The gross receipts for the rights of wardship and marriage, which had cost Bacon £50, were therefore £1410. However, against this we must offset not only the unknown cost of the boy's maintenance and education (which may have run to a couple of hundred for the whole period) but also a very large sum which Bacon was prepared to relinquish at the final

[1] Francis Yaxley, the conspirator, had provided, in a will of 1561, that Yaxley Hall should pass to his father, Richard, and then to this cousin, William. It seems to have been inherited by Richard, who died in 1566, and then to have passed to Bacon, just before the wardship expired in the spring of 1567. However, the negotiations between Bacon and the family imply that Bacon was not obliged to relinquish Yaxley Hall, though he was willing to do so for a consideration. It was not included in the settlement of the wardship in 1567. Bacon received its rent in 1567 and 1568 (£45 in all) and must then have handed it over to William, who is known to have been in possession before 1570. The modern Yaxley Hall is supposed to have been rebuilt by William for his Bedingfield bride (*ibid.*).

[2] 'A rental of Mr Yaxley's Lands'. The main property was the manor of Pountney Hall, in Mellis. There were other lands in Thrandeston, Blowfield, Rickinghall, Wortham, Barton, and Lynn.

accounting for the revenues he had received. Dr Spencer and the widow obviously counted on this when they bound themselves to pay the 'huge sum' of 1000 marks if the boy declined to marry Elizabeth, and the amount of the rebate was eventually fixed at £400. We have naturally scanned the manuscripts to discover the explanation for this, but the only clue, apart from the general assumption of all parties that there was a surplus to be restored, over and above Bacon's 'reasonable allowances', is a single reference by Dr Spencer to the ward's 'socage lands'.[1] The appraisal of the estates in 1561 hardly suggests that these could have amounted to half the value of the properties, but there the figure is. Either the estate included lands to this value which were immune from wardship, or Bacon was being very generous with his friends, or there were angles which we do not understand. Nevertheless, on the most conservative estimate, he had cleared between £700 and £800.

This was a pretty profit, but there are great difficulties in discovering how many wardships a courtier received and what he got out of them. Twenty-one[2] have been discovered which were granted either to

[1] 'I perceyve your Lordship is contented to allowe iiijc of the profyghtes of my nephewes socage landes towardes the payment of the thowsand markes': letter no. 24, Correspondence of Nicholas Bacon (Sandeen op. cit.).

[2] The wardships were as follows:

1543	William Rede, to Nicholas Bacon, for £66. 13s. 4d.	
1544	John Coggeshall, to Nicholas Bacon, for £20.	
1547	Joan Everingham, to Nicholas Bacon, for £40.	
1551	Edmund Foxe, to Nicholas Bacon, for £40.	
1554	William Flammok, to Nicholas Bacon, for £30.	
1557	Thomas Garneys, to Nicholas Bacon, for £133. 6s. 8d.	
1559	William Yaxley, to Thomas Andrews and William Phillips, for £50.	
1559	Thomas Pleasaunce, to Francis Boldero, for £18.	
1560	George Bacon, to Thomas Andrews and William Phillips, for £20.	
1561	Richard Cresswell, to William Phillips, for £20.	
1562	Robert Pulham, to Edmund Wiseman, for £12.	
1563	Thomas Gray, to Bartholomew Kemp, for £75. 6s. 8d.	
1563–75	William Bacon, to Edmund Wiseman, for £3. 3s. 4d.	
	Nicholas Reignberd, to Edmund Wiseman, for £3. 12s. 4d.	
	John Sheldrake, to Edmund Wiseman, for £4. 6s. 8d.	
	John Fyson, to Edmund Wiseman, for £15.	
	Edmund Bacon, to Francis Boldero, for £50.	
	Roger Heigham, to Thomas Andrews, for £33. 6s. 8d.	
	Edward Bacon, to Edmund Wiseman, for £26. 13s. 4d.	
	Thomas Gawsell, to Robert Blackman, for £17.	
	John Broke, to Sir Nicholas Bacon, for £66. 13s. 4d.	

(These details have been taken from the published Letters Patent and from PRO/Wards/Index/ 10217.)

The Rising Lawyer

Bacon by name or to one of the servants, such as Bartholomew Kemp, William Phillips, Edmund Wiseman, Thomas Andrews, and Francis Boldero, who regularly acted for him. Of these, two were granted while he was in the Court of Augmentations, four only while he was in the Court of Wards, and fifteen while he was Lord Keeper. The number was almost certainly larger, for none has been traced to servants during the twelve years that he was Attorney of the Wards, and the four taken out in his name can hardly have been the whole story. However, this gross figure is meaningless as a guide to his own profits. Some of the grants may have been enjoyed (and even paid for) by the servants. Some, like one whose visible receipts are trifling, may have been obtained as a kindness to relations or neighbours.[1] Others may have been of little value. There is one which arose because the estate in question was held by a sub-tenant (who left a minor heir) of a property whose wardship Bacon already held; the visible receipts from this grant, which cost £12, were only £25.[2] We must also observe that only a few of the twenty-one have left any trace in Bacon's private records. The acquittances and other documents which survive for the first half of his career throw very little light on wardships, and the receivers' accounts, covering the period when fifteen were granted, record receipts from only three of them; Yaxley's, and the two little ones just mentioned. Another so-called wardship[3] is credited in these accounts with receipts of £156, but it seems to have been only an annuity which the real guardian transferred to Bacon in consideration of the fact that he, Bacon, was bringing up the heir in his household.[4]

Here, then, we have another enigma. His grants must certainly have

[1] Grant to Thomas Andrewes and William Philipps of the wardship and marriage of George Bacon, son and heir of John Bacon, 17 May 1560 (*Cal. Patent Rolls, Elizabeth*, I, 426). The receivers' accounts show receipts of £8 and £3 for 1560 and 1561.

[2] Grant to Edmund Wiseman of the wardship and marriage of Robert Pulham, son and heir of Christopher Pulham, who held of the crown by reason of the minority of William Yaxley (*Cal. Patent Rolls, Elizabeth*, II, 265). The foreign receipts in the receivers' accounts show that this produced £25.

[3] The so-called wardship is that of Edward Tyrrell, which Sir Valentine Brown procured through his servant, Christopher Cocker, for £196. A bill of 12 March 1571 (Bacon MSS. (Chicago)) shows that the annuity, or maintenance allowance, of £20 a year was transferred by Brown to Bacon for the reason mentioned above.

[4] Table 5A, section VIII, shows receipts from the wardships of George Bacon, William Yaxley and Edward Tyrrell. Those from Robert Pulham are included in the foreign receipts in section IX.

included other plums like Yaxley's. One wonders, for example, what he made out of a wardship of 1557, taken in his own name as Attorney, for which he paid the highest of all these presumably nominal prices— £133. 6s. 8d. But the record is silent.

Stewardships—those coveted symbols of prestige—produced an income of about £100 a year while he was Lord Keeper, besides their indirect benefits. A dozen show up in the Receivers' Accounts, and there may have been more which he gave away to dependents. Those for the archbishopric of Canterbury (£40 a year), the Honour of Clare (£20), the Queen's lands in Norfolk (£10), and Trinity College, Cambridge (£10), were the best paid. Five other bishoprics, the town of St Alban's (which owed its incorporation to Bacon), Rochford Hundred, Essex, and Twickenham Park, made up the total. In one or two cases, like Trinity College, he may have been obliged to pay a pound or two to an under-steward.

Lastly, we may wonder whether this Tudor magnate, with his numerous City connexions, had a stake in industry or commerce. We once thought that it might have been an important one. The historian[1] of the Muscovy Company believed that Bacon was exporting cloth in the forties and fifties, and there were acquittances in the Bacon manuscripts showing that he rented cellars on the quayside, where soap-ashes were stored, and settled various bills for imports from the Baltic.[2] However, this turned out to be a will-o'-the-wisp. The chance discovery of a law-case,[3] in which Nicholas Bacon, Lord Keeper, was sitting in judgement on Nicholas Bacon, mercer, suggested that the export of cloth was more likely to have been the work of his namesake, and the acquittances were part of the settlement of William Rede's estate, in which Bacon acted as executor. His position at court must have obliged him to invest a little money in one or two companies. His membership of the Muscovy Company may have cost him some-

---

[1] Thomas S. Willan, *The Muscovy Merchants of 1555* (Manchester, 1953), p. 77.
[2] Acquittances, 17 November 1543, 2 July 1546 (Bacon MSS. (Chicago)).
[3] C 3 27/43 (P.R.O.). The unpublished Mercers' Company Court Minutes (1527–62) contain several references to Bacon's namesake, who must have been about the same age as the Lord Keeper. As a young member in 1536 he received a loan of £50 from the company: by 1553 he was second warden, and by 1561 upper warden (MS. 1527–60, 100A, 266B: MS. 1561–, 31A).

thing, and we know that he was a shareholder in the Society of Mineral and Battery Works, which was founded in 1565 as a sister company to another manufacturing enterprise, the Society of Mines Royal.[1] But this second investment—a half-share among thirty-six shares—must have been trifling, for the first four assessments on the shareholders, which were levied between 1566 and 1568, only amounted to £36. 10s. in his case,[2] and there are suggestions that the capital called up before 1597 (a date long after his death) did not exceed £200 per share. He seems to have made no money out of either company, so far as we can see.[3] Beyond this, the only other enterprise we have come across was the construction of a little quay at Stiffkey, which he supervised with his usual vigilance from far-away London. It made quite a stir in the village when the first ship sailed in, but it cannot have done much for his income. He got a small rent from the building and may have made a pound or two out of an occasional cargo of fish or tar; but it was his farmer, and not he, who is known to have owned the ships there.[4]

Table 5 c shows the total recorded income, from all sources, between 1560 and 1575. It rises from about £2600 in the first year to about £3800 in the last, and would presumably have run over £4000 by the time he died in February 1579. There are several reasons for thinking that this is an understatement, as the profits of home farms are not included, and some properties, such as lands bought for a term of years, and wardships, have certainly escaped us. But the biggest deficiency is in the impenetrable area of gratuities. In 1601, a contemporary thought that the office of Lord Keeper was 'better worth than £3000 a year'.[5] In these accounts its recorded value was about £1400. How much of

---

[1] H. Hamilton, *The English Brass and Copper Industries to 1800* (London, 1926), p. 18.

[2] There were four collections—'certen charges abowte a Licence of Batteryes of Myneralles'—of £10, £12. 10s., £10, and £4. A note of these, by Bartholomew Kemp, his treasurer, is preserved in Holt Wilson MS. S 1/11 (Box 89) (E.S.R.O.).

[3] W. R. Scott, *The Constitution and Finance of English, Scottish and Irish Joint-Stock Companies to 1720* (Cambridge, 1910–12), II, 416–17. I am informed by Professor M. B. Donald, of University College, London, who is collecting materials for a history of the Mineral and Battery Works, that no money seems to have been made by this company before Bacon's death in 1579, as the brass was unsatisfactory. By about 1596 the manufacture of ironwire was estimated to make £1689 per annum, and each share was valued at £25 per annum.

[4] Correspondence between the Lord Keeper and his son Nathaniel, Bacon MSS., Garsett House, Norwich.

[5] John Manningham, *Diary* (Camden Society), p. 19.

the difference was due to gratuities, and how far had they risen in value by 1601? Precision is impossible, but it would not surprise us, after taking every source of understatement into consideration, and after recalling what we have previously discovered about his expenses, if his real income exceeded the recorded income by another £1000 a year.

There is some information about the value of his estate at the time of his death.[1] An inventory compiled for the executors on 1 March 1579 shows £2450 in cash, £860 in debts (almost all of this being sums due from his lands) and about £2000 in plate (6500 ounces valued at 6s. an ounce).[2] The funeral expenses, the legacies, and the quarterly wages of household servants must have consumed most of the cash. It is curious that this document, and another, prepared ten days later, should have so little to say about debts. We are prepared to learn that his own debts were small, though people in his position were frequently involved in short-term loans and it would not have been surprising to find trades-men's bills of some size. All we do find is less than £200 owing on building expenses at Gorhambury and London, and less than £100 in small debts. The scale of one modest pleasure seems typical: 28s. 'for my Lordes playing at Cardes'. If this record is complete, he must have lived up to an undertaking which he once gave to a seller—'no one will pay you earlier than I'. More remarkable is the absence of any record of sums lent to friends under bonds. We know that he had lent money at earlier stages in his career, and it would have been natural enough to find considerable sums listed among his assets. But apart from £96 due from the bishop of Norwich and £25 from Sir Chris-topher Hatton, the record is bare. It may be that death caught him at a moment when he was bent on accumulating cash. The thought that no adequate purchase of land had been made for his youngest and brightest child seems to have ruffled his peace of mind.

[1] For the will, see an abstract in H.M.C. Rep. XI, App., pt. 4 (Townshend MSS.), pp. 4–7. There is a copy among the Bacon MSS. (Chicago).

[2] See p. 22, n. 1.

The Rising Lawyer

Success stories have a universal likeness, but they take their personality from time and place. Among the upper classes of these centuries it was the dynastic dream that warmed the ambition. They hoped their names would last for ever. But contemporaries were well aware of some of the obstacles, and historians have speculated about the possibility of others. In the first class were the gloomy verdicts of the chromosomes, the sudden hand of death, the hazards of personal character, and the chances of bad luck in business or litigation. In the second class are the theories about the struggles of mere landlords in a period of inflation, and about the importance of office as a means of survival.

What was Bacon able to do for his children, and how did they fare?

We can allow ourselves no more than a rapid reconnaissance of this history. The eldest son, Nicholas, was born about 1540. In 1559 an elaborate entail was arranged—with the duke of Norfolk, Sir William Cecil, the heads of all the superior courts, and several other eminent personages as trustees—which gave Nicholas a life interest in the manors of Redgrave, Wortham, Rickinghall, Westhall, Hinderclay, Wyverston, and Walsham. Within a year or two the time was ripe for a suitable marriage. The girl selected for this purpose, Anne Butts, had the kind of ancestry which provided one commentary on the hopes of the dynasts. On the floor of Acton Church, beside the splendid brasses of Sir Robert de Bures, who lived in Edward I's reign, and Dame Alice de Bryene, whose widowhood in Acton Hall began in Richard II's reign and ended in Henry VI's, lies the diminutive figure of Henry Bures, the last of his line. With ordinary luck, the family might have endured. They owned six manors on the thriving borders of Essex and Suffolk; they were well connected; and the Reformation lay ahead, with its windfalls for high and low. But everything turned on a son. Henry had a daughter, Jane, in 1524, another, Bridget, in 1526, a third, Anne, in 1527, and a fourth, Mary, in 1529. He died in that year, at the age of twenty-six, and the wardships of the four girls were bought by a rising man whom we have met before—the court physician, William Butts. This enterprising doctor did everything in his power to make his

91

mark. He had the best of practices, a safe place at the sovereign's elbow, a wary, solid wife who attended the princess Mary, a portrait by Holbein, an epitaph by Cheke. What else was needed? Only landed property and male descendants. The first was easily achieved. He began with a little manor in Whersted, Suffolk, which had tumbled out of Wolsey's lap; plucked Thornage, Thornham, and Melton Constable from the loot that Henry VIII had seized from the bishopric of Norwich; bought Great and Little Riborough out of the estate of Walsingham Priory, Edgefield out of the lands of Binham Priory, parcels of Carmelite and White Friars' property in London, and a useful assortment of leases. The second prospect also looked hopeful. He had three sons, William, Thomas, and Edmund, whom he married to three of the wards, Jane, Bridget, and Anne Bures, giving each of them an estate to add to their share of the Bures' manors; William became the lord of Thornage, Thomas of Riborough, Edmund of Thornham. But a strange irony overtook him. While the fourth ward, whose marriage he had sold to Thomas Barrow, bestowed five sons (including the founder of Congregationalism) and four daughters on her husband, the three he had kept in the family produced only one girl among them. This was Anne Butts, daughter of Edmund Butts and Anne Bures. It was her lot to carry the whole of the Butts estate and half the Bures estate into the Bacon empire.

The relations between the young solicitor in the Court of Augmentations, and the trusted favourite, must have been close. Without making anything of the coincidence of names—the doctor's wife was a Margaret Bacon of Cambridgeshire—we know that they exchanged favours. The lands of the younger Butts were well placed, and the background of the heiress—a wedding of new blood with ancient gentility—must have appealed to the philosopher of 'mediocrity'. The marriage treaties, involving six principals and three different estates, and accompanied by the usual precaution that, if Nicholas died before the ceremony, his place would be taken by his brother Nathaniel, were successfully negotiated in 1561. Sir Robert Catlin, the Chief Justice, and the heads of the Cecil and Russell dynasties were happy to act as feoffees. The details were naturally complicated, and it might take half a century before the expiry of all the life interests enabled the last manor to drift home; but in essence Bacon paid £800, in compensation to the two uncles, Sir William and Thomas Butts, to secure an estate which, when added to his own entail of Redgrave *et alia*, would give his eldest son just under £1000 a year.[1]

This was according to the values of 1561. But the boy's expectations were steadily enlarged during his father's lifetime by new purchases (Mettingham and Burgate being the biggest) and the money values had soared before his own death in 1624. He was obviously one of the richest landowners in Suffolk. He built himself a second mansion at Culford, was sheriff and M.P. for the county, and became the premier baronet of England when James I created that order—an honour which cost him over £1000.[2] It was rumoured that he could have had a barony through his brother, in 1618, at £1000 less than the retail price, 'which he will not accept: mindful perhaps of his father's motto or posy, mediocria firma'.[3] He left a personal estate of over £6000,[4] and his numerous children were handsomely provided for. The multiplication of landed branches, which his father had begun, was carried several steps further. Besides Edmund, who succeeded him as second baronet of Redgrave, there was Robert, who was given an estate around Riborough, in Norfolk; Butts, who was created baronet of Mildenhall in 1627; Nicholas, whose son of the same name became baronet of Gillingham in 1662;[5] and Nathaniel, who was left Culford, with lands which are said to have been worth £1000 a year.[6] Anne, the eldest daughter, was married to a rich ward, Sir Robert Drury, at

[1] This history has been worked out from the Bacon MSS. at Chicago, the E. R. Wodehouse MSS. (H.M.C. Rep. XIII, App., pt. 4, now in the British Museum (Add. MSS. 39218–39252, Add. Ch. 59797–61129)), and other sources, in Mr K. J. Appel's M.A. thesis, 'The Bures Estate in the Sixteenth Century' (University of Chicago, 1956). See also F. W. Steer, 'The Butts Family of Norfolk', *Norfolk Arch.* XXIX (1946), 187–200.

[2] Sheriff of Suffolk 1581–2 and of Norfolk 1597–8; M.P. for Beverley 1563–7 and for Suffolk 1572–83. Knighted by Elizabeth at Norwich 22 May 1578. Baronet 22 May 1611. G. E. C[okayne], *Complete Baronetage* (Exeter, 1900), I, 1–2. The baronetcy cost him £1095 (Bond, 1612, Bacon MSS. (Chicago)).

[3] Spedding, *op. cit.* VI, 287.

[4] The amount was put at £6400 by the executors (Bacon MSS. (Chicago)). A so-called debt to the crown, for revenues said to have been improperly collected from the liberty of Bury St Edmund's, was compounded in 1628 for £3100 (Bacon MSS. (Chicago)).

[5] C[okayne], *op. cit.* II, 32; *ibid.* III, 241.

[6] Copinger, *op. cit.* I, 283.

a cost of nearly £2000.[1] Sir Nicholas' estate, at its height, must have been worth over £4000 a year.[2] So far as is known, office played no part in this picture. There are many signs in the correspondence with his father that the eldest son, though doubtless worthy, never came up to the parental standards of efficiency. He sought a fitting resting-place, not in St Paul's, but in the parish church of Redgrave.

The accidents of age and temperament were to prevent the Bacons of Redgrave from playing any considerable part in the great convulsions of the mid-century. Sir Edmund, the second baronet, must have been about seventy when the Civil War started. As an intimate friend of Sir Edward Wotton[3] and the patron, in his time, of Bishop Hall and Bishop Bedell, he cannot have felt much sympathy with the passions which stirred the Long Parliament and he had long shown that politics was not his mistress. For years he had lived the life of a cultivated dilettante, turning Redgrave into 'a Philosophical Cell', charming the visitor from the great world, and tingeing stones in his laboratory—he left one of them, which had been picked up in Botesdale Street and 'agatised' by

---

[1] The dowry was £1600, jewels and clothes £200, and Sir Nicholas was to pay for the marriage feast. The Drurys were fifteenth-century squires who had risen through law and politics to the top stratum of Suffolk families. Sir Robert (1575–1614), a soldier, man of fashion, knight of the shire, and patron of the poet Donne, owned houses at Hawstead, Hardwicke, Snareshill, and Drury House, London, and enjoyed an income in 1610 of about £3000 a year. R. C. Bald, *Donne and the Drurys* (Cambridge, 1958).

[2] When the executors were obliged to consider what lands of Sir Nicholas, which had been inherited by his sons, were liable for the payment of the debt to the crown (see p. 93, n. 4), they listed Sir Edmund Bacon's lands (i.e. the second baronet) to the value of £390 per annum; the Lady Bacon's lands (i.e. the widow of the son Nathaniel, who had just died)—£900 per annum; Sir Nicholas Bacon's—£360 per annum; and Bacqueville Bacon's—£250. This amounts to £1900 a year. But they went on to say 'the rest of the lands are not lyable in regarde that parte of them are of ancient intayle, parte estated before the debte, and parte are the lands which came by the Lady Anne Bacon late wife of the said Sir Nicholas Bacon'. The entail can only refer to the entail of Redgrave *cum aliis*, a supposition which is strengthened by the fact that the eldest son's inheritance must have greatly exceeded £390 a year and his younger brother's £900 a year. The 'estated' part must have gone to another child: the executors do not mention the lands of either Robert Bacon or Butts Bacon. The third part (brought into the family by Lady Anne Bacon, wife of the first baronet) must refer to what remained of the old Bures–Butts estate, i.e. Foxearth, Thornage, Riborough, etc., which were still held in 1627. It is obvious that the exempt estate must have been bigger than the liable estate, which suggests an income of over £4000 a year. The bailiffs' accounts show that Sir Nicholas was receiving about £4000 a year in the three years, 1617–19, exclusive of the proceeds of home farms and any other sources.

[3] Sir Edmund had married Wotton's niece and was the recipient of many letters (L. P. Smith, *The Life and Letters of Sir Henry Wotton* (2 vols.: Oxford, 1907)). (For a biographical note, see II, 461.) A few family letters were printed in *The Private Correspondence of Jane Lady Cornwallis, 1613–1644* (London, 1842).

his process, as a jewel in his will.[1] Any confidant of the accomplished Wotton must have been a man of parts, but the heir to £3000 a year had less incentive to use his gifts, in a gainful way, than the ambassador who had begun life with an annuity of £100 marks.[2] Sir Edmund had sat in Parliament in 1588 and 1593. He visited the Continent with Joseph Hall in 1605 and may have been at the Synod of Dort in 1618,[3] where his old travelling companion was one of the English representatives. When he succeeded to the baronetcy in 1624, he took his seat as member for Suffolk in the Parliament of 1625. But this was the limit of his sacrifices to public life. Hall had written in one of his Epistles—*Of the Benefits of Retiredness and Secrecy*[4]—'I no where know so excellent parts shrouded in such willing secrecie. The world knowes you, and wants you; and yet you are voluntarily hid.'

He seems to have remained more or less 'hid' until the outbreak of the Civil War, when a few duties must have fallen his way. We know from his will that old Sir Edmund was the captain of a Parliamentary company in Hartismere Hundred and the donor of a lectureship in Botesdale. As a deputy lieutenant he must have been involved in the activities of the County Committee until the course of the revolution began to displace the authority of the leading families. But it cannot have been a very martial role, or, we imagine, a happy one—the friend of Wotton must have had too many friends on the other side. However, there was one security in this bewildering world; a rent roll which kept its lordly level, and a personal estate, when he died in 1649, as big as his father's—about £6000.[5]

He was succeeded by his brother, Sir Robert, of Riborough, who may have had some difficulties before he inherited, but they seemed manageable enough when he settled the estate in 1650 to provide for the marriage of the future heir, another Edmund.[6] Wyverston, valued at

---

[1] *Wills and Inventories from...Bury St Edmunds*, ed. Samuel Tymms (Camden Society, XLIX (1850)), 216; L. P. Smith, *op. cit.* II, 396, n. 3.

[2] *Ibid.* I, 7.

[3] Tymms, *op. cit.* p. 217. Delegates to the synod were presented with a gold medal. Sir Edmund possessed one.

[4] *The Works of Joseph Hall* (London, 1634), 271.

[5] Inventory of Sir Edmund Bacon, 1649 (Bacon MSS. (Chicago)).

[6] Indenture, 5 July 1650 (Bacon MSS. (Chicago)).

£2000, was alienated to provide a portion for a daughter; lands in Norfolk were offered as security for an old mortgage of £2000; but this still left a handsome entail. Though no serious attempt has been made to penetrate this later history, it seems likely that the status of the Bacons was secure enough, as a premier county family, when the Edmund of this settlement took his turn as sheriff of Suffolk in 1665. Nor is it clear what significance should be attached to the mounting mortgages which led to the sale of Redgrave to the family of Chief Justice Holt after the turn of the century. They were probably raised in the first instance to provide portions for the daughters of Sir Edmund, who died without any surviving son in 1685, and the cousin who succeeded, and decided to sell, was able to continue the family career at Garboldisham. There have been other migrations since, but it would have been a source of solid satisfaction to the Lord Keeper to know that his lineal descendant would be the present Lord Lieutenant of Norfolk.[1]

Having planted his eldest son among the first families of Suffolk, the Lord Keeper launched his second son among their counterparts in Norfolk. Born in 1546, Nathaniel passed through Cambridge and Gray's Inn and was married at the age of twenty-three to Anne Gresham, the natural daughter of the great Sir Thomas. The seat chosen for this branch of the family was Stiffkey, on the northern coast, where Sir Thomas was a neighbouring landowner and the control of the town could be bought from the bankrupt Banyards. Sir Thomas settled the manors of Langham and Merston, Hemsby, and Combs (Suffolk) on the young couple; the Lord Keeper bought the Stiffkey estate for them, and added the Norfolk manors of Stanford and Eccles.[2] For some years Nathaniel had the benefit of his father's vigilant supervision—an education in land management, house building, harbour improvement, and the duties of a justice of the peace, conveyed through the usual business-like letters. He seems to have had something of his father's

---

[1] Sir Edmund Bacon, of Raveningham Hall, Norfolk, baronet of Redgrave and Mildenhall, is descended from Sir Butts Bacon, who was first baronet of Mildenhall and younger son of Sir Nicholas Bacon, first baronet of Redgrave (C[okayne], *op. cit.* I, 2–3).

[2] Francis Blomefield, *An Essay towards a Topographical History...of Norfolk* (London, 1805–10) IX, 409, 426; *ibid.* XI, 167. See also MS. correspondence between Nathaniel and his father (Garsett House, Norwich).

industry and sense of responsibility; *The Stiffkey Papers*[1]—a selection from his official correspondence as a Norfolk magistrate—are a monument to the unobtrusive and indispensable labours of the leaders who formed the backbone of provincial life.

His estate seems to have grown with the years, without any new infusion from office, unless a stewardship or two is to be counted. Before his father died, the neighbouring manor of Netherhall had been added to the Stiffkey complex. At some later date, he leased the manor of Methwold from the Duchy of Lancaster. About 1597 he took a wealthy widow as his second wife—Dorothy, daughter of Arthur Hopton, who had outlived a rich Mr Smith. This gave him a handsome property at Irmingland, where he built himself a second mansion, and he also got control of the inheritance designed for the sons of his wife's first marriage, who became his wards.[2] He was among the many Bacons who held seats in Parliament as a result of the Lord Keeper's rise to fame, and his standing in his county is signified by the fact that he held the second seat in 1584 and 1593, the office of sheriff in 1599, and the first seat in 1604.[3] He got his knighthood at the coronation of James I. There are no figures for his income, but his status would suggest a rent roll of the order of £2000 a year.[4] His will shows that he thought his children, though quarrelsome, had nothing to complain of, and the only debts which weighed on him arose from an unsettled account with the Smith children.[5]

However, there was one irreparable loss. The Stiffkey Bacons, so

---

[1] *The Official Papers of Sir Nathaniel Bacon of Stiffkey, Norfolk*, ed. H. W. Saunders (Camden Society, 3rd series, XXVI (1915)); 'Supplementary Stiffkey Papers', *Camden Miscellany* (Camden Society, 3rd series, LII (1936)).

[2] Nathaniel's will, 10 May 1614, refers to problems created by Mr Gwen Smith 'in regard of my receipts of the profits of his lands duringe his minoryty'. For an account of Nathaniel's receipts and expenses on behalf of Mr William Smith, 1597–1609, see MS. 126 X 6: 20384, 20396, Norwich City Library.

[3] In a letter to Henry Gawdy, 29 December 1603, Nathaniel wrote, 'I am not like to serve often hereafter in anie parliament And having served twice already in the second place, I hope that no man shall have just cause to judge amisse of me though now I seek the first': Bacon MSS., uncatalogued (Folger Library).

[4] The Townshends, a leading family with whom Nathaniel was allied, had more than £2000 a year. A steward's account of 1618–19 (not necessarily a complete statement) shows receipts of £2243 a year, of which about £1100 was made up of rents and farms. As they were big flockmasters, much of the difference may have been due to receipts from stock and wool.

[5] A copy of the will, dated 4 June 1614, is in the Folger Library.

hopefully launched by the Lord Keeper, had foundered on a reef of daughters. Nathaniel married three of them into the best Norfolk families—a Townshend, a Knivett, and a Gaudy—and resigned himself to the thought that the heirloom of his house—a silver cup which his father had made out of his predecessor's Great Seal and given to Stiffkey Hall to match the other two at Redgrave and Gorhambury—would probaby find a resting-place at Rainham.[1]

Edward Bacon, the last son by the first marriage, seems to have been born about 1548.[2] He followed his brothers at Cambridge and Gray's Inn, being admitted to the latter in 1566. He was on good terms with his brother Nathaniel, whose study in London he shared, and to whose home in Norfolk he wrote regularly both from London and abroad. Over twenty of these letters have survived, most of them from the decade 1574–85.[3] During the early 1570's he seems to have been living in Gray's Inn. There is gossip about a robbery and a death and a report of an attempt on the part of the Star Chamber to discipline these vigorous institutions. He then left on a prolonged tour of the Continent. The Lord Keeper, who believed in foreign travel for the young, seems to have made some difficulties about the company and the route. It looks as though he wanted him to go with Francis in the train of Sir Amias Paulett, the ambassador to Paris. But Edward told Nathaniel, with some satisfaction, that he had managed to evade this. Perhaps the idea of exploring on his own appealed to him. He got to Germany, Geneva, Vienna, Padua, Ravenna and Paris—and wondered what his friends at home would think about his exposure to the vices of the Latin world. They must have distrusted Italy, not simply in the ordinary English way, but also as Puritans. A strong strain of sympathy with dissent runs through his letters, and one of his longest halts was at Geneva, where he lived in Beza's house and met the well-known

[1] For sketches of Stiffkey Hall, see *Norfolk Archaeology*, VIII, 143–66; XXIII, 308–40, and 'The Building Activities of Sir Nicholas Bacon, Lord Keeper', an unpublished Ph.D. thesis (Chicago) by Ernest Sandeen. It is to be regretted that Percy Millican, Esquire, of Sprowston Court East, Norwich, who owns the manuscript 'building book' for Stiffkey Hall, is unwilling to have it examined. Descriptions of the Lord Keeper's three cups, and an illustration of the Redgrave one, are in Collins, *op. cit.* p. 587.

[2] According to the monument at Barham, he died 8 September 1618, aged seventy.

[3] Bacon MSS., uncatalogued (Folger Library).

Protestant theologian, Lambert Danaeus, who dedicated a book to him.[1]

Edward cannot have been back long before his father died, and his absence abroad may have something to do with the fact that the old man never got him married. There had been talk of a match with the daughter of Sir Harry Gates, but nothing came of it. It may be, of course, that the Lord Keeper had opened the negotiations for the marriage which eventually occurred, but none of the future in-laws were given blacks at the funeral in 1579. Probably Edward was left to make his own decision.

From all we can learn, it seems to have been a good and happy choice. He became the founder of another Bacon house at Shrubland Hall, near the villages of Coddenham and Barham, in delightful country a few miles from Ipswich. His father must have known both villages well enough; his friends the Gosnolds were settled in Coddenham, and John Southwell, who had served in his household, lived at Barham Hall. Shrubland Manor in Barham had been changing hands through a succession of heiresses: a Booth heiress had carried it to Sir Robert Lytton of Knebworth, Hertfordshire; a Lytton heiress carried it to Thomas Little, of Bray, Berkshire; and Helen Little, their only child, brought it to Edward Bacon.[2] They seem to have been married about 1581.[3] Edward had been left a house in Fetter Lane, an estate at Bramfield, and a legacy of 500 marks. We are told that they moved to Shrubland Hall when Helen was expecting her first son, Nicholas, who was born in February 1588.[4]

The Lord Keeper could have taken a decent pride in the Shrubland Bacons. Edward lived out his days on an income of about £1800 a year,[5] a rich respected squire. His distinction in the county was recognised in the usual ways—a county seat in 1592–3 (he had held several borough ones before), the sheriffdom in 1601, a knighthood

[1] See p. 28, n. 1.   [2] Copinger, *op. cit.* II, 244.
[3] Helen's monument says she had thirty-seven years of married life with Edward, who died 1618. Copinger records a licence to alienate Bramfield in 1580—he was probably settling the estate for the marriage (*op. cit.* II, 22).
[4] Coddenham Parish Register (E.S.R.O.).
[5] The estimate of the anonymous contemporary cited below. See p. 100, n. 1.

in 1603. His wife Helen presented him with thirteen boys and six girls and outlived him by thirty years; a rare achievement. This second generation made a lasting impression on the neighbourhood. It was said of Nicholas, the Lord Keeper's namesake, 'He has been the greatest friend to pious ministers in all these parts of the country and a great housekeeper. He died much lamented at the age of 69. His family came to live at Shrubland Hall when his mother was great with child of him, and from that time for these 69 years that house hath been famous for religion and hospitality.'[1] Two young brothers, Nathaniel and Francis, had been helping Shrubland's reputation. They had thrown themselves into the Parliamentary cause, entered the Long Parliament as members for Ipswich and Cambridge University, and served Cromwell as Masters of Requests.[2] Nathaniel was of the same stamp as his Suffolk neighbour Sir Simonds D'Ewes, though more practical—a lawyer, Puritan, and antiquarian, who defended the claims of Parliament with a historical discourse and compiled the annals of Ipswich during his years as recorder.

In the third generation, deeds of valour were added to these laurels. Captain Philip Bacon, the second son of Nicholas, was fighting with the royalists at Dunkirk while his uncles were upholding the Cromwellian government. There, in the action against the Ironsides, he caught the eye of the duke of York, who helped to advance him after the Restoration. When the Dutch war broke out he won the command of bigger and bigger frigates until he boarded the 58-gun Dutch flagship, from his 38-gun frigate, and carried off its colours to Shrubland Hall. For this he was given the 52-gun *Bristol* which was the first to discover the Dutch fleet on 1 June 1666. The story of his death in action, and of the ceremonies that accompanied the burial of a hero at Shrubland, is told on a mural tablet in the church at Coddenham, where the later Bacons built their family vault. Not far from it is the affectionate

---

[1] A contemporary observer, believed by Suffolk antiquarians to have been the Rev. Matthias Candler, vicar of Coddenham, who died 1663. The author obviously lived in the neighbourhood and knew Mrs Helen Bacon. Copinger, *op. cit.* II, 284, n. 1. A transcript by E. S. Farrer is in the E.S.R.O. Also quoted by W. S. Fitch, 'MS. Collections for the History of Bosmere and Claydon Hundreds' (E.S.R.O.).

[2] D. Brunton and D. H. Pennington, *Members of the Long Parliament* (Cambridge, Mass., 1954), pp. 104–5.

tribute to the last of his line, the Reverend Nicholas Bacon, 'of the ancient house of Bacons of Redgrave', who died in 1796.[1]

Office seems to have played no significant part in any of these main lines,[2] though it may have been sought by some of the cadets, like Nathaniel, Francis and Philip. But the two sons of the second marriage were made of different mettle. Both played for the highest stakes. Both lived in a flutter of bills. And each, in spite of magnificent talents, died in debt.

If Anthony had been so minded, he could have looked forward to a life at Gorhambury not unlike that of his stepbrothers in Suffolk and Norfolk. He was born in 1558, and entered Trinity College, Cambridge, with his brother Francis, in 1573, where he studied under John Whitgift, the future archbishop, and proved himself a gifted, delicate, child. Within two years, when he was still only sixteen, his father planned a marriage for him which gives us some idea of his prospects at that time. The agreement[3] was with James Paget, of Grove Place, Southampton, on behalf of his daughter Dowsabell. The children would have an allowance of £75 a year for the next three years. Nicholas guaranteed an estate of £100 a year, and leases to about the same value, after the lapse of the allowance, and a further inheritance of £300 a year, after the expiry of the Lady Bacon's jointure; in other words, about £500 a year. James Paget, in return for £565 which Nicholas would pay him, guaranteed an estate of £314 a year, after the death of himself and his wife. Under this treaty, which contemplated a marriage in May 1575, Anthony could have looked forward to about £800 a year, which would have quickly passed the £1000 mark, when we recall the conservatism of these legal estimates and the prospects of inflation. But for reasons unknown, the treaty failed.

When the Lord Keeper died in 1579, Anthony was immediately furnished with an assortment of Hertfordshire manors and leases which

---

[1] Bacon inscriptions in this area were printed in *East Anglian Notes and Queries*, new series, IV, 49.

[2] This statement is naturally made with diffidence, as it is not easy to make an exhaustive check. Small positions may have been held. The *D.N.B.* article on Anthony Bacon refers to an attempt to secure a small position for Edward Bacon, of Shrubland.

[3] Indentures, 5 December 16 Elizabeth (Evidence Book, MS. XI, 3 (H.R.O.)).

brought him £360 a year,[1] and we know that in the three years between 1580 and 1583 his receipts averaged £500 a year.[2] Given a suitable marriage, and the prospect of the whole of the Hertfordshire estate on the death of his mother, the life of a country gentleman on £1000 a year might still have been his. But he chose otherwise.

At the suggestion of his uncle, Lord Burleigh, he left London at the end of 1579 in search of political intelligence on the Continent, and stayed there for over a decade. The ambition was to provide the kind of service which would earn its reward from a grateful government, but the cost was prohibitive. His uncle grumbled that he was spending money more like a prince than a squire. His steward,[3] an old servant trained in his father's school, begged him to study the balances he was sending annually, and to come home. His mother—renowned for a frantic zeal which eventually unhinged her mind—coaxed, threatened, expostulated with the ministers, and furiously sold her jewels to keep him supplied.[4] Baffled by the Cecils—he complained that Lord Burleigh had 'inned my ten years harvest without any halfpenny charge'[5]—he transferred his fortunes to the earl of Essex in 1593, promising him better intelligence than the Queen's ministers could ever get. But this was a service which lived on hope, as his brother Francis, already committed and deeply in debt, could have told him. His first act on joining the earl was to sell his Barley manors to a London alderman for £3500[6]—the under-rented manors which his father had inherited from Sir Ralph Rowlett—and those that have studied his career believe that so far from getting richer in Essex's household, he got poorer and poorer, in spite of heroic labours. By 1600, though his brother's fortunes were at last turning, his own credit was exhausted. A year later, within a month or two of his patron's death on the scaffold,

---

[1] Rental of the lands of Anthony Bacon, 22 March 1579 (Lambeth MSS.). The manors were those in Barley—Abbotsbury, Minchenbury, and Hores; Colney Chapel was also held in fee; the leases were in Middlesex and Hertfordshire.

[2] Hugh Mantell's letter of 13 December 1583, and enclosed account (ibid.).

[3] Hugh Mantell. Evidence of his earlier work can be seen in the meticulous surveys of the Gorhambury estates in 1569 (MS. XI, 2 (H.R.O.)).

[4] For a sample of Lady Bacon's concern, see Lambeth MS. 647, fol. 111, quoted in Spedding, op. cit. II, 111.

[5] Quoted D.N.B. (Anthony Bacon).

[6] Anthony asked £4000 from Alderman Martin, and settled for £3500 (Lambeth MSS.).

he died himself at the age of forty-three. Lame and always sickly—Sir Henry Wotton called him the man with the nimble head and impotent feet—the shock of Essex's death finished him.

Francis, his partner in hope and the child of destiny, was the only son of the Lord Keeper who was left to fend for himself. His biographer reports a story, on the authority of a Dr Rawley who was Francis's chaplain in later life and the editor of his works—that the Lord Keeper had laid by a considerable sum of money, to buy his youngest son an estate, but was prevented by death, with the result that Francis got 'only a fifth part of the fortune intended for him'.[1] It may have been so; but we know that the Lord Keeper had only about £2500 on hand at his death; so it is possible that 'the considerable sum' was not yet collected. His will shows that the fear of leaving too little for the last two boys was very much in his mind, and £1300 was scraped together in the last year of his life to buy Woolwich Marsh for Francis. But that was little enough. We do not know precisely what he inherited, apart from this property, and the manor of Marks, and a share of some leases; but it cannot have been more than two or three hundred a year.

He was eighteen when the news of his father's death forced him to return from Paris and make his home in Gray's Inn. In spite of his slender estate, he might well have been hopeful. He was already at home in the world of scholarship, law, and fashion. The accident of birth had made him an 'ancient' of Gray's Inn. More than one judge owed his position to the Lord Keeper, and there was nothing except the pull of wider intellectual interests to prevent the son from making his mark at the bar. With Lord Burleigh as his uncle, and the memory of the Queen's playful compliment to her 'little lord keeper', when he left for Paris in 1576, office must have seemed a certainty. He and Anthony were fast friends. They could pool their credit as well as their talents. It was only necessary for one to succeed, to ensure the success of the other. Small wonder if he was confident, not to say arrogant. Yet no man of his powers and connexions would ever take so long to reach the top.

[1] Spedding, *op. cit.* I, 8.

The Wealth of the Gentry, 1540–1660

The first decade passed with nothing more substantial than a reputation in Parliament and a reversion to a clerkship in the Star Chamber which Lord Burleigh got for him in 1589.[1] He called this Cecil boon 'the fairest flower in my poor estate', but it would be twenty years before he enjoyed its profits. In the second decade, with Essex impetuously pressing his claims, the door seemed always about to open, only to bang in his face. He missed the Attorney-Generalship in 1594, the Solicitor-Generalship in 1595, the Mastership of the Rolls in 1597. Even rich widows eluded him. Before his fortunes began to turn in 1601, he had nothing to offset the mounting load of debt except a modest practice,[2] a small gift of land from the fuming Essex,[3] and some occasional employment as one of the Queen's 'learned counsel'. Even then, his fortunes turned only slowly. The reward for his part in the prosecution of his patron was only £1200.[4] If he got Gorhambury, after Anthony's death, he also got his debts. The alderman's daughter, whom he married in 1605, was no millionairess.[5] And the Solicitor-Generalship, which might have put some fat on his bones in 1595, looked lean enough when he got it in 1607. It was valued at £1000 a year.[6] The long-awaited death in 1608 of Mr Mills, who had been drawing twice that amount from the clerkship in the Star Chamber, not to mention a few rackets which had got him into trouble, was worth as

[1] Spedding, *op. cit.* I, 102–3.

[2] As late as 1608, after his appointment as Solicitor-General, he valued his practice at only £1200 a year (Spedding, *op. cit.* IV, 86). Many of his earlier applications for office had been made in the hope of improving it. No figures are available before 1608, but the statement in the text seems reasonable, when applied to the period before the trial of Essex. One of his problems about making money out of law was, of course, the competition of other interests.

[3] *Ibid.* I, 371. Essex enfeoffed him with a piece of land which he later sold (for less, as he thought, than its value) for £1800.

[4] *Ibid.* III, 14. He was granted this sum out of Catesby's fine.

[5] His wife was Alice Barnham, daughter of Benedict Barnham, silk merchant, who had died in 1598. In a letter of 3 July 1603, when a large number of knights were to be made at the coronation of James I, Francis told his cousin, Sir Robert Cecil, that he would be content to have one, 'without charge', because 'I have three Knights in my mess at Gray's Inn Commons, and because I have found out an Alderman's daughter, an handsome maiden to my liking'. Her portion is not known, but when he was recording his assets three years later, £1200 was still unexpended, and she was credited with £120 a year in possession, and about £100 in reversion after her mother's death. He guaranteed a jointure of £500 a year. His will seems to imply that her inheritance of £120 a year had been bought out of her portion; if so, it may have run over £3000. This would be a substantial relief, but not a fortune. Spedding, *op. cit.* III, 80; *ibid.* IV, 82, 86; *ibid.* VII, 541.

[6] *Ibid.* III, 362.

much as the Solicitor-Generalship and Bacon's private practice combined.[1]

These thirty years in the wilderness had cost the brothers, their mother, and their friends, a pretty penny. The creditors were eager enough to lend when the prospects looked bright; but they closed in, after the repeated failure of his ship to reach home, in spite of its splendid sails, became a jest. In 1598, when he was leaving the Tower after a session with the legal counsel, a money-lender who held his bond for £300 had him arrested for debt.[2] The sheriff did his best to make the confinement as comfortable as possible, but this was only one of a dozen embarrassments. Needless to say, the carefully garnered fruits of their father's industry were fast consumed by sons who had inherited no part of his business sense. Of all the Hertfordshire properties, only Gorhambury survived, and Anthony was just prevented from losing that before he died. Francis put its value at £300 a year in 1603.[3] The rectory of Redborne, the manors of Burston, Windridge, Apsebury, Michenbury, Abbotsbury, and Hores were all gone, not to mention the fringe lands. The manor of Marks was mortgaged to the Herveys and lost in 1593, just as Thomas Hales had lost it to Nicholas Bacon in 1558.[4] Woolwich Marsh, which the Lord Keeper had bought for £1300 in 1578, was mortgaged for £1000 in the 1590's, and only a timely loan prevented the whole property—then valued at £1700—from being seized by the mortgager. It seems to have been sold, with the proceeds divided between the creditors.[5] The gift from Essex was sold for £1800. Twickenham Lodge, where the Lord Keeper had been warden of the Park, and Francis had his home when he was not in Gray's Inn, was repeatedly mortgaged though usually to friends who would not foreclose.[6] More than one record of his debts has survived in Francis's papers. Like others we have known, he could bring himself

---

[1] The clerkship was originally said to have been worth £1600 a year, and in a letter to the King in 1621, reminding him that he had given it up when he became Lord Chancellor, Bacon said £1200. There was no doubt a difference between its nominal and its real value, and Mr Mills had been in trouble for overcharging. The best estimate would seem to be the one in Bacon's private memorandum of 1608—£2000. *Ibid.* IV, 86.

[2] *Ibid.* II, 106–8.

[3] *Ibid.* III, 80; IV, 81.

[4] *Ibid.* I, 243–6; J. G. O'Leary, *The Book of Dagenham* (Dagenham, 1949), p. 48.

[5] Spedding, *op. cit.* II, 27–8; *ibid.* III, 42.

[6] *Ibid.* III, 42.

to look at his situation from time to time, and then forget it again. Dissipation, in the conventional sense, seems to have played no part in this history. He and Anthony were simply above—or below—the care of money.

Between the age of forty-eight and sixty, Francis knew what it was to be wealthy. He put his income in 1608 at £5000 a year.[1] Five years later, when the death of his cousin, the earl of Salisbury, removed the man who had suavely strangled him for so many years, he became Attorney-General. In 1616, he was admitted to the Privy Council. In 1617, a Bacon was once again Lord Keeper. In 1618, he topped his father's achievement by becoming Lord Chancellor and Baron Verulam. In 1620, he was Viscount St Alban's. These were the years which he and Anthony had toiled for, though there were still indignities in having to flatter the latest favourite. An account of receipts and disbursements, for a three-month period in 1618 (24 June–29 September), shows £4160 received, £302 paid out in gifts and rewards, and £3711 in other payments, including interest on loans amounting to £2400, and instalments on a medley of unpaid bills.[2] Perhaps some steward had a rough idea of what he was worth, but we may be sure that he never did. The account just quoted,[3] if it could be safely multiplied by four, would suggest an income of £16,000 a year. An admission of his own, after his fall, that he had lost £6000 a year by his offices, would suggest a minimum of about £10,000; for at that time he still thought that he had an annuity of £1200 a year, a farm of the petty writs worth £600 a year, and his own and his wife's land which may have approached £1000 a year;[4] and when he said he had lost £6000 a year, he added, 'besides caps and courtesies'. What he thought these were worth is not clear; but he confessed at his trial that he had accepted over £7000 from litigants in a period of two or three years, not to mention an interest-free loan of £1000,[5] and as the confession only

---

[1] Spedding, *op. cit.* IV, 86.　　　　[2] *Ibid.* VI, 327–36.

[3] It is worth noting that this quarterly statement seems to have contained no receipts from land. They would normally have come in at other times, i.e. after Lady Day and Michaelmas. If the estimate in his will is reliable, these would have approached £1000, viz. about £700 from Gorhambury, and over £200 from his wife's inheritance (*ibid.* VII, 541).

[4] *Ibid.* VII, 328, 387.　　　　[5] *Ibid.* VII, 252 ff.

dealt with gratuities known to his enemies, there must certainly have been others. Whatever the income, he always lived above it. Where his father had saved, he spent. We may assume that the fees and gratuities were often equal to his needs; that where they fell short, he borrowed; and that what the servants got was nobody's business.

When the crash came, he plummeted back into poverty. During the five years between his conviction in 1621 and his death in 1626, he had nothing but Gorhambury[1] and his chambers in the Inn, the remnants of former splendour in furnishings and plate, a pension which was usually in arrears, and a host of creditors. Optimistic almost to the last, he left a will under which his widow would have a competent portion for a viscountess (he believed it would run to £1500 a year, besides furniture and plate), and substantial sums were bestowed on friends and dependents.[2] But when he died, the duke of Buckingham, on whom he had obviously counted, was being impeached himself; the executors showed no enthusiasm for their duties; and it was only after fifteen months' delay that letters of administration were granted to two of his creditors. He was found to have assets of £7000 and debts of £22,371. Gorhambury, where he had built the idyllic Verulam House at a cost of nine or ten thousand pounds, went to a friend and creditor, Sir Thomas Meautys, who had married Anne, the only surviving daughter of Sir Nathaniel Bacon of Culford.[3] Francis himself was childless. The brilliant Bacons had lasted only one generation.

The history of one family, even when its branches are as numerous as the Bacons, does not allow us to dogmatise about the fortunes of the gentry; but it has its points of interest. We see the patterns which the demographic factor could produce—the possibilities of subdivision where there were too many children, of consolidation when some lines

---

[1] This included Verulam House, which he had built next to his father's mansion. York House, London, which his father had occupied and to which he, Francis, returned on becoming Lord Keeper, was lost in 1621. He seems to have been obliged to surrender the lease to Lionel Cranfield, in return for permission to live once again in London (*ibid.* VII, 334).

[2] *Ibid.* VII, 541. However, in a codicil he later revoked his grants to his wife 'for just and great causes', leaving her only her legal rights. Spedding could discover nothing specific about her offence, except rumours of infidelity and inferences drawn from her later marriage with her gentleman-usher: *ibid.* VII, 539, 545.

[3] *Ibid.* VII, 551–2.

failed, and of extinction if there was no male heir. We learn something of the expenses as well as the profits of office; if the founder of the family owed everything to a career at court, the children of the second marriage knew all about its hazards. Finally, we discover the capacity of landed estates to weather the inflation. We shall see later why the 'mere landlord' of this region could face the future with a fair amount of equanimity.

TABLE 5. A. Income from Bacon lands, 1556–78 (£)

I. SUFFOLK

	1556	1558	1559	1560	1561	1562	1563	1564	1565	1566	1567	1568	1569	1570	1571	1572	1573	1574	1575	1576	1577	1578
Redgrave and Wortham	94	90	184	133	158	153	147	106	135	163	166	145	136	155	149	169	178	136	164	148	160	156
Hinderclay	38	—	56	77	76	80	93	92	87	13	4	18	278	39	159	20	60	58	118	34	115	122
Rickinghall	48	—	64	62	65	55	60	72	61	64	62	93	57	55	77	80	71	82	101	84	73	92
Walsham Church-House	10	—	37	40	38	35	38	31	18	49	30	22	53	27	26	49	33	36	31	38	37	34
Walsham Willows	—	—	—	—	56	69	67	46	67	58	57	52	40	56	68	52	55	67	49	57	49	60
Lands and stocks	71	—	—	—	—	—	—	—	—	—	—	—	—	—	—	—	—	—	—	—	—	—
Mellis St John's	10	—	4	4	5	8	—	11	—	3	16	—	13	—	2	24	2	2	11	—	18	7
Hornmill	—	—	6	6	6	6	6	6	6	6	6	6	6	6	3	—	—	—	—	—	—	—
Ingham	61	—	124	129	152	110	108	103	171	150	106	87	136	109	131	142	49	230	65	160	116	143
Wyverston	—	—	—	55	36	37	37	36	37	36	20	77	71	35	34	29	37	37	33	39	33	32
Talbots in Timworth	12	—	14	11	13	10	12	25	13	13	5	10	19	11	13	16	13	—	—	39	24	19
Playfords in Barnham	—	—	—	8	8	7	7	7	7	11	7	7	7	7	7	7	7	7	7	7	7	7
Ashfield	—	—	—	—	—	—	32	31	44	42	47	53	48	46	42	52	36	48	52	38	41	76
Mettingham	—	—	—	—	34	63	83	110	138	172	177	193	192	188	197	180	153	152	147	151	164	106
Bramfield	—	—	—	—	—	—	24	64	65	64	73	67	67	59	75	78	90	66	87	69	68	68
Wenhaston	—	—	—	—	—	—	14	13	—	—	—	—	—	—	—	—	—	—	—	—	—	—
Blackburn Hundred	9	?	10	14	19	28	12	11	37	30	23	22	19	14	19	31	23	18	22	3	36	16
Yaxley Hall	—	—	—	—	—	—	—	—	—	—	16	29	—	—	—	—	—	—	—	—	—	—
Liberty of Bury	—	—	—	—	20	—	—	—	—	28	13	—	72	—	—	40	—	—	—	—	—	—
Parham	—	—	30	40	30	30	30	30	30	30	30	30	30	30	30	30	—	—	—	—	—	—
Chedworth (Lincs)	—	—	30	30	—	—	—	—	—	—	—	—	—	—	—	—	—	—	—	—	—	—
Mannock's land	—	—	—	—	—	—	3	2	9	—	—	—	—	—	—	—	—	—	—	—	—	—
Burgate	—	—	—	—	—	—	—	—	32	34	47	43	42	44	58	106	139	91	122	108	100	101
TOTAL	353	90	559	609	716	691	773	796	957	966	905	954	1286	881	1090	1105	946	1030	1009	975	1041	1039

A. Income from Bacon lands, 1556–78 (£) (cont.)

II. NORFOLK

	1556	1558	1559	1560	1561	1562	1563	1564	1565	1566	1567	1568	1569	1570	1571	1572	1573	1574	1575	1576	1577	1578
Stanford	11	85	75	108	90	85	90	82	95	69	64	73	90	103	94	68	90	90	90	90	90	90
Moiety of Redmere	—	—	—	—	—	—	—	—	—	—	—	—	—	—	—	—	—	—	—	—	—	—
Eccles	—	—	—	25	35	83	14	118	15	123	65	74	75	73	75	71	76	73	78	75	73	74
Thraxton	—	—	—	—	26	15	—	—	—	—	—	—	—	—	—	—	—	—	—	—	—	—
Brisingham	—	—	—	—	—	77	54	35	—	—	—	—	—	—	—	—	—	—	—	—	—	—
Stiffkey	—	—	—	—	—	—	—	—	—	—	—	—	—	—	—	163	—	91	317	146	139	—
Netherhall in Stiffkey	—	—	—	—	—	—	—	—	—	—	—	—	—	—	—	—	—	—	80	43	43	—
Stody	—	—	—	—	—	—	—	—	—	—	—	—	—	—	—	—	68	116	90	90	40	—
West Somerton	—	—	—	—	—	—	—	—	—	—	—	—	—	—	—	—	—	—	—	42	—	—
TOTAL	11	85	75	133	151	260	158	235	110	192	129	147	165	176	169	302	234	370	655	486	385	164

III. ESSEX

	1556	1558	1559	1560	1561	1562	1563	1564	1565	1566	1567	1568	1569	1570	1571	1572	1573	1574	1575	1576	1577	1578
Manor of Marks	—	—	—	40	70	50	50	50	50	50	50	53	53	53	53	53	53	53	53	53	53	53
Red Lion, Romford	—	—	—	9	9	9	9	9	9	9	9	9	9	9	9	18	18	18	18	—	—	—
Tenement—Adamers	—	—	—	—	—	—	3	7	7	7	7	7	7	27	7	7	7	7	7	—	—	—
Tenement—Messengers	—	—	—	—	—	—	—	—	—	—	3	3	3	4	2	3	3	3	3	—	—	—
Tenement—Arneways	—	—	—	—	—	—	—	—	—	—	5	5	5	5	5	5	5	5	5	—	—	—
Tenement—Harrells	—	—	—	—	—	—	—	—	—	—	5	10	10	10	10	14	14	14	14	—	—	—
Tenement—Copt Hall	—	—	—	—	—	—	—	—	—	—	—	—	—	8	8	8	8	8	8	—	—	—
Tenement—Roses	—	—	—	—	—	—	—	—	—	—	—	—	—	—	1	3	3	3	3	—	—	—
TOTAL	—	—	—	49	79	59	62	66	66	66	79	87	87	116	95	111	111	111	111	53	53	53

IV. HERTFORDSHIRE

Property																					
Gorhambury, West-wick, Pray	—	20	90	94	94	94	94	94	110	120	130	157	150	150	150	150	150	150	150	150	150
Redborne Rectory	—	22	22	22	22	22	22	22	67	67	67	67	67	67	67	67	67	67	67	67	67
Burston	—	—	—	—	—	—	—	—	36	36	36	36	36	36	36	36	36	36	36	36	36
Minchenbury	—	—	—	—	—	—	—	—	—	—	—	—	—	—	21	21	21	21	21	21	21
Abbotsbury	—	—	—	—	—	—	—	—	—	—	—	—	—	—	20	20	20	20	20	20	20
Hores	—	—	—	—	—	—	—	—	—	—	—	—	—	—	6	6	6	6	6	6	6
Apsebury	—	—	—	—	—	—	—	—	—	—	—	—	—	—	16	16	16	16	16	16	16
Windridge	—	—	—	—	—	—	—	—	—	—	—	—	—	—	—	—	—	50	50	50	50
Quillets	—	—	—	—	—	—	—	—	—	—	—	40	40	40	40	40	40	40	40	40	40
TOTAL	—	42	112	116	116	116	116	116	213	223	233	300	293	293	356	356	356	406	406	406	406

V. LONDON AND MIDDLESEX

Property																					
Tenement, Cheapside	—	—	—	5	5	5	5	5	5	5	5	5	5	—	—	—	—	—	—	—	—
Tenement, Houndsditch	—	—	—	2	2	2	2	2	2	2	2	2	2	2	—	—	—	—	—	—	—
Tenement, Barbican	—	—	—	½	½	½	½	½	½	½	½	½	—	—	—	—	—	—	—	—	—
St Giles Wood, Middlesex	—	—	—	½	½	½	½	½	½	½	½	½	—	—	—	—	—	—	—	—	—
St Giles Close, Middlesex	—	—	—	—	—	—	—	—	—	1	1	1	—	—	—	—	—	—	—	—	—
Tenement, Middlesex	—	—	—	—	—	—	—	—	—	1	1	1	—	—	—	—	—	—	—	—	—
Tithes, Bloomsbury	—	—	—	—	—	—	—	—	—	—	3	7	—	3	3	3	3	—	—	—	—
Tenements, Silver Street	—	—	—	—	—	—	—	—	—	—	—	—	—	3	6	22	22	22	22	22	22
Tithes, St Egidius' parish	—	—	—	—	—	—	—	—	—	—	—	—	—	2	2	2	2	2	—	—	—
Tenements, Chancery Lane	—	—	—	—	—	—	—	—	—	—	—	—	—	9	27	27	25	57	109	109	109
Gardens, Fetter Lane	—	—	—	—	—	—	—	—	—	—	—	—	—	—	—	—	—	5	9	8	8
TOTAL	—	—	—	8	8	8	8	8	8	10	13	17	7	24	58	58	55	90	141	140	140

A. Income from Bacon lands, 1556–78 (£) (cont.)

VI. SOMERSET

	1556	1558	1559	1560	1561	1562	1563	1564	1565	1566	1567	1568	1569	1570	1571	1572	1573	1574	1575	1576	1577	1578
Chedder	—	—	—	30	30	30	30	30	30	30	30	30	30	30	30	30	30	30	30	30	—	—

VII. LEASES

	1556	1558	1559	1560	1561	1562	1563	1564	1565	1566	1567	1568	1569	1570	1571	1572	1573	1574	1575	1576	1577	1578
Brookswharf, London	—	—	—	34	34	34	34	34	34	34	34	—	—	—	—	—	—	—	—	—	—	—
Holland, Essex	—	—	—	30	30	20	—	—	—	—	—	—	—	—	—	—	—	—	—	—	—	—
Playfords, Thelnetham Suffolk	—	—	—	8	8	8	9	6	11	6	8	5	5	5	—	—	9	—	—	—	—	—
Osteler, Timworth Suffolk	—	—	—	—	2	4	3	—	7	—	9	—	6	2	4	5	4	—	—	—	—	—
Burgate, Suffolk	—	—	—	—	27	22	22	22	—	—	—	—	—	—	—	—	—	—	—	—	—	—
Sandhills Close, Middlesex	—	—	—	—	—	3	—	—	—	—	—	—	—	—	—	7	—	15	8	—	—	—
Abbotshall	—	—	—	—	—	—	—	—	5	8	7	8	10	6	7	8	11	11	7	—	—	—
Oxlease Meadow, Essex	—	—	—	—	—	—	—	—	—	27	8	8	8	8	10	10	10	10	10	—	—	—
Mildenhall, Suffolk	—	—	—	—	—	—	—	—	—	—	83	40	40	40	40	40	82	52	52	—	—	—
Tithes in Harrow	—	—	—	—	—	—	—	—	—	—	—	—	—	19	4	11	11	11	11	—	—	—
Twickenham Park	—	—	—	—	—	—	—	—	—	—	—	—	—	—	—	—	—	—	22	—	—	—
TOTAL	—	—	—	72	101	91	68	62	57	75	149	61	69	80	65	81	127	99	110	—	—	—

VIII. WARDSHIPS

	1556	1558	1559	1560	1561	1562	1563	1564	1565	1566	1567	1568	1569	1570	1571	1572	1573	1574	1575	1576	1577	1578
George Bacon	—	—	—	8	3	—	—	—	—	—	—	—	—	—	—	—	—	—	—	—	—	—
William Yaxley	—	—	—	76	74	124	96	75	76	130	—	—	—	—	—	—	—	—	—	—	—	—
Edward Tyrrell	—	—	—	—	—	—	—	—	—	—	—	—	—	76	30	20	20	10	—	—	—	—
TOTAL	—	—	—	84	77	124	96	75	76	130	—	—	—	76	30	20	20	10	—	—	—	—

IX. FOREIGN RECEIPTS

X. SUMMARY

Suffolk	353	—	559	609	716	691	773	796	957	966	905	954	1286	881	1090	1105	946	1030	1009	975	1041	1039
Norfolk	11	85	75	133	151	260	158	235	110	192	129	147	165	176	169	302	234	370	655	486	385	—
Essex	—	—	—	49	79	59	62	66	66	66	79	87	87	116	95	111	111	111	111	—	—	—
Hertfordshire	—	—	—	42	112	116	116	116	116	213	223	233	300	293	293	356	356	356	406	406	406	406
London and Middlesex	—	—	—	—	8	8	8	8	8	10	13	17	24	30	55	58	58	90	—	141	140	140
Somerset	—	—	—	30	30	30	30	30	30	30	30	30	30	30	30	30	30	30	30	30	30	30
Leases	—	—	—	72	101	91	68	62	57	75	149	30	80	65	81	99	127	99	30	30	30	30
Wardships	—	—	—	84	77	124	96	75	76	130	—	61	65	81	20	20	20	10	110	110	110	110
Foreign receipts	—	—	—	47	104	164	392	286	475	240	137	44	53	—	214	16	300	110	110	—	—	—
TOTAL INCOME	—	—	—	1066	1378	1543	1703	1674	1895	1920	1662	1569	2007	1659	2010	2079	2182	2171	2521	—	—	—
Allowances:																						
Tenths	—	—	—	15	15	15	15	15	15	15	15	15	15	15	15	15	15	15	15	—	—	—
Annuity paid for land	—	—	—	—	—	—	—	50	67	50	50	50	50	6	5	5	5	—	—	—	—	—
Foreign payments	—	—	—	16	10	5	—	—	—	—	15	30	10	6	5	30	3	—	27	—	—	—
Exonerations	—	—	—	—	—	39	—	50	142	—	5	—	5	—	3	30	—	—	42	—	—	—
TOTAL	—	—	—	31	25	59	15	115	249	65	85	95	80	71	73	50	25	15	42	—	—	—
NET INCOME	—	—	—	1035	1353	1484	1688	1559	1646	1855	1577	1474	1927	1588	1937	2029	2157	2156	2479	—	—	—

B. Income from office, fees and annuities (£)

	1559	1560	1561	1562	1563	1564	1565	1566	1567	1568	1569	1570	1571	1572	1573	1574	1575
Office of the Lord Keeper:																	
Certainties	960	961	960	960	960	961	960	960	960	961	960	960	960	961	960	960	960
Casualties	357	261	162	237	146	137	144	144	155	153	270	153	166	159	163	188	165
Office of faculties	—	152	161	124	25	88	55	94	71	65	34	51	91	49	47	61	49
Wax allowance	—	16	16	16	16	16	16	16	16	16	16	16	16	16	16	16	16
TOTAL	—	1390	1299	1337	1147	1202	1175	1214	1202	1195	1280	1180	1233	1185	1186	1225	1190
Queen's Annuity		100	100	100	100	100	100	100	100	100	100	100	100	100	100	100	100
High Steward, archbishopric of Canterbury		40	40	40	40	40	40	40	40	40	40	40	40	40	40	40	40
High Steward, bishopric of Ely		7	7	7	7	7	7	7	7	7	7	7	7	7	7	7	7
High Steward, bishopric of Gloucester		2	2	2	2	2	2	2	2	2	2	2	2	2	2	2	2
High Steward, bishopric of Bristol		3	3	3	3	3	3	3	3	3	3	3	3	3	3	3	3
High Steward, bishopric of Winchester		3	3	3	3	3	3	3	3	3	3	3	3	3	3	3	3
High Steward, bishopric of Chester		2	2	2	2	2	2	2	2	2	2	2	2	2	2	2	2
High Steward, Trinity, Cambridge		10	10	10	10	10	10	10	10	10	10	10	10	10	10	10	10
High Steward, Honour of Clare		20	20	20	20	20	20	20	20	20	20	20	20	20	20	20	20
High Steward, Queen's lands, Norfolk (late bishopric of Ely)		10	10	10	10	10	10	10	10	10	10	10	10	10	10	10	10
High Steward, St Alban's		4	4	4	4	4	4	4	4	4	4	4	4	4	4	4	4
Warden of Twickenham Park		5	5	5	5	5	5	5	5	5	5	5	5	5	5	5	5
High Steward, Rochford Hundred, Essex		6	6	6	6	6	6	6	6	6	6	6	6	6	6	6	6
Swanmark, Lincoln		1	1	1	1	1	1	1	1	1	1	1	1	1	1	1	1
Lord North				(£3. 6s. 8d. per annum.		Arrears exonerated, 1572)											
Framingham				(£1. 6s. 8d. per annum.		Arrears exonerated, 1572)											
Richard Freyston, esquire				(£2. 0s. 0d. per annum.		Arrears exonerated, 1572)											
TOTAL	—	1603	1512	1550	1360	1415	1388	1427	1415	1408	1493	1393	1446	1398	1399	1438	1403

C. Income from lands, office, fees and annuities, 1560–75 (£)

	1560	1561	1562	1563	1564	1565	1566	1567
Lands	1035	1353	1484	1688	1559	1646	1855	1577
Office, etc.	1603	1512	1550	1360	1415	1388	1427	1415

	1568	1569	1570	1571	1572	1573	1574	1575
Lands	1474	1927	1588	1937	2029	2157	2156	2479
Office, etc.	1408	1493	1393	1446	1398	1399	1438	1403

CHAPTER III

THE RISING MERCHANT

SIR THOMAS CULLUM

WE are sufficiently ignorant of the careers of big merchants who lived through the English Revolution to welcome any addition to our knowledge. The following sketch[1] of Thomas Cullum, draper, alderman, sheriff, and Restoration baronet, has been made possible by the discovery of an account-book[2] in which he kept an annual record of his stock between the end of his apprenticeship in 1616 and his death in 1664. Brief and tantalising though it is, it gives us the outline of an economic biography; and to this we may add the fainter outlines of his party connexions as he weathered the storms of civil war.

Little is known of his ancestry, in spite of the efforts of antiquarian descendants who were closer to family traditions than we are. He was the second son of a John Cullum of Stanhill in Thorndon, Suffolk, and his mother was Rebecca, daughter of Thomas Smith of Bacton in the same county. The Cullums had been settled in Thorndon a long time. The heralds said four generations; the antiquarian descendant found evidence that went back to the middle of the fifteenth century,[3] and there is a record of a Thorndon Cullum who had sat on a jury to try the rebels in 1381.[4] From about 1400 to 1550 they were village smiths,

---

[1] A shorter version of this chapter appeared in the *Economic History Review*, second series, vol. XI, no. 1, August 1958, pp. 19–33.

[2] Brief references to the account-book will be found in Rev. Sir John Cullum, Bart., *History...of Hawsted*, 2nd edn. (1813), p. 180; John Gage, *History of...Thingoe Hundred* (1838), p. 479, n. x; and *Suffolk Archaeology*, XIV (1911), 280–5, in a notice by V. B. Redstone entitled 'Cullum Letters'. When Mr Redstone wrote (1911), the manuscript was in the possession of Mr Gery Milner-Gibson-Cullum, owner of Hardwick House, which Thomas Cullum purchased in 1656. It is now in the West Suffolk Record Office, Bury St Edmund's (E 2/29/1.1), and is here used through the courtesy of M. Statham, archivist. The manuscript contains some 50 folios ($5\frac{1}{2} \times 7$ in.). References can easily be identified by the year of the account.

[3] Cullum, *op. cit.* p. 179.

[4] *Suff. Arch.*, *art. cit.* p. 281.

and we now know that one branch began to thrive in Elizabeth's reign until it was able to dispose of a manor or two and adopt the style of 'gentleman' in the 1630's.[1] But this was not John Cullum's branch. All we know about his position is to be found in his son's account-book. He must have been able to raise £50 or £60 to apprentice him to a good city company, and he left him £200 in his will to be paid when the apprenticeship was over. The eldest brother John, and a sister Susan, were each able to lend him £100 when he got a chance to buy a share in his master's business. There are glimpses of an 'uncle Bradshaw' in the cloth trade, with whom the young Thomas invested a few pounds; of a 'cousin John Johnson' of Limehouse and Blackwell Hall; and of 'cousin Field, glover'. What we seem to have here is a well-to-do yeoman family of a type that was common enough in Suffolk—the head of the family farming a patrimony and able perhaps to rent one of the many little manors, while the cadets and cousinhood included provincial mercers or clothiers, one or two of whom had made their way to London. It was a thriving class, from which gentry periodically sprang.

In February 1607 Thomas was apprenticed to John Rayney, draper, of Gracechurch Street, London. Eight years later, with his freedom in sight at Lady Day 1616, he opened his little account-book. Christmas was the time to take stock. 'In the name of God amen, amen. This Booke is for the proper[2] accompt of me Thomas Cullum Draper begineing the 30th of December anno domini 1615.' He found that the savings of his apprenticeship—'this little stock which by God his mercie I have saved'—amounted to £92. 2s. 6d. Of this, £17 was in ready money, £10 had been 'ventured with my uncle Bradshaw', and the rest was held by individuals who had either borrowed small sums at interest or owed Thomas for small services. After thanking God for

---

[1] This history can be traced among the deeds and wills in the Barnardiston MSS., West Suffolk Record Office, e.g. 613/95, 160, 126, 213. The successful branch called themselves Cullums 'on the Hill, Thorndon'. The last of them, Thomas Cullum the elder, called himself 'gentleman', instead of yeoman as previously, in a deed of 22 March 1636-7. His will, confirmed in 1641, left his property to a kinsman, Tobias Frere, of Harleston, Norfolk. The Thomas Cullum of this article acted as a trustee for these Cullums on two occasions, 613/366, 374.

[2] 'Proper' was used to denote the individual's own trading account, in distinction from partnership or factorage accounts.

the fact that he himself owed nothing, he then made a note of the £200 that would be paid to him by his brother John under their father's will in three months' time. He would have £292. 2s. 6d. to begin business.

For the next five years he lived with the Rayneys as a wage-earner. It was no doubt the prudent thing to do. Mr Rayney gave him £20 when he got his freedom in 1616 on condition that he would work another year for a wage of the same amount. In the second and third years he got £30, and £40 in the last two. These wages, together with his other earnings, gave him the chance to scrape together a little capital, and by staying in the Rayney shop—a thriving establishment—he assured himself of a junior partnership as soon as he could afford it.

TABLE 6. 'That first thousand!'

	1615			1616			1617			1618			1619			1620		
	£	s.	d.	£	s.	d.	£	s.	d.	£	s.	d.	£	s.	d.	£	s.	d.
Wages	—			20	0	0	30	0	0	30	0	0	30	0	0	40	0	0
Interest	—			19	10	0	23	8	0	40	14	0	54	10	0	66	5	0
Sales	—			14	2	0	31	13	0	26	3	6	33	14	5	5	18	0
Dyeing	—			37	16	9	47	14	1	45	14	8	36	18	9	51	16	0
Gifts	—			222	4	0	2	4	0	1	2	0	—			104	15	9
Expenses	—			20	12	7	22	11	0	18	4	0	25	18	1	36	12	7
Stock	92	2	6	385	2	8	497	10	9	623	0	11	752	6	0	987	9	8

Each Christmas he sat down to figure out his stock and enter the results in his book. He had other books, even at this early date, such as 'the little book of my expenses'—and how little those expenses were!—but the stock book showed him where he stood. He drew up a double statement. One was a little sum which started with the previous year's figure and then produced the new figure by adding the year's gains and deducting his living expenses. The other, which balanced, was an inventory of his stock as he found it at the end of the year, so much in 'debts' (that is, investments) and ready money, less anything he owed himself. It was in this form, with a few elaborations as his business developed, that he kept this book for the next forty-eight years.

During his five years as a wage-earner, Cullum raised his capital to just under £1000. Nothing would seem as slow again as that first thousand! Table 6 shows how it was done. Wages have already been explained. Gifts included the initial legacy of £200, Mr Rayney's £20, a pound or two from his mother, and a loan of £100 from his stepfather which he got for nothing in the fifth year and hoped to keep. The legacy was at once put out to earn money in two twelve-month loans. When these were repaid, he collected £462—almost all his capital—and loaned it to Mr Coulson, a dyer with whom he was doing business. This loan was renewed annually, and increased at one point to £563. The only other loan of any size was £50 to his brother, Daniel Cullum, for three years. The rate of interest is not very clear, but there are indications that it ranged between 8 and 10 per cent. The sales were either of dyestuffs or cloths. He made £29 by selling cochineal to Coulson in 1617, and was buying indigo to make a little profit in 1619. The cloths he dabbled in included a cloak made for himself which he sold for £3, a red cloth 'ventured with uncle Bradshaw' which cost £10 and made a profit of over £9 and some items called 'paragons'. Finally, he ran a small dyeing business which brought in rather more than his wages; some of the 'stuffs and remnants given by clothiers, dyers, and clothworkers' which he dyed and sold may have been perquisites.

His expenses, which in later years are itemised, only appear in gross. Mr Rayney provided board and lodging; 'apparrell' and 'sickness' are the only matters mentioned. The amount is fairly stable and very modest for a man of thirty, or thereabouts, living in London. One guesses now that Thomas Cullum had high ambitions and endless self-control. What mattered was what he saved.

When he made up his accounts at Christmas 1620, he must have looked forward to a brighter New Year, for he was at last in a position to enter a partnership with his master. Like all the associations of the period this was undertaken for a term of years. The initial stock was to be £10,000. Cullum was to put up one-eighth of the capital in cloth and cash and get a corresponding share of the first year's profits. In the second year he was to put in more money and own a seventh of the stock; in the third year, a sixth.

Between January and September 1621, Cullum put up his share, about half in cloth and the other half in cash, £1250 in all. The cloth had been bought, or ordered, before the New Year began, and the accounts of 1620 contain details of sums paid for rowing, shearing, dressing and finishing. We are told nothing about the market, but if this partnership conformed to the type which Cullum and *his* apprentice practised, many years later, the draperies were sold partly to dealers and partly to retail purchasers at the London shop. Having spent over £600 on cloth, Cullum could not raise another £600 without borrowing; so it was in these months that his brother John, his sister Susan, and one or two old East Anglian friends came forward with fifty or a hundred pounds apiece. Before the year ended, the partnership had brought him a profit of £205. 5s. on an investment of £1250. In 1622 he put in another £240 and made a profit of £245 on £1695. In the third year, 1623, he set his profit at £302.[1] The dyeing business was allowed to fall off—it has now become 'petty'—but it still brought in about £20.

This partnership was the beginning of high hopes, and Thomas acted accordingly. In the first year he took an apprentice; in the second, a shop; in the third, a wife. The apprentice was a Suffolk boy, Edward Goodwin, son of Thomas Goodwin, Esquire, of Little Stoneham. He brought £80 with him, which was added to stock. For a year the new master and his man boarded with old Mr Rayney; but then we hear of 'a lease of the howse and shop at the blew boars head which cost me £100' and of another £30 'laid out in charges about my shopp'. The wife soon followed.

Mrs Cullum was well chosen. In an epitaph, composed for her fifteen years after she had spent herself in childbirth, the poet wrote,

> If that all women were but near so good as shee,
> Then all men surely might in wives right happy bee.
> Would any know, how virtues rare in her did take,
> I say no more; she was a Crispe, born of a Pake.[2]

These names meant something in All Hallows, Lombard Street, where Mary Crisp was baptised, married, and buried. Her father,

---

[1] The precise amount of the third year's investment cannot be discovered from the accounts, as the partnership was being liquidated at the time they were made. The gain of the two previous years is about 16 per cent and 14 per cent, but it should be remembered that some fraction of the assets would turn out to be bad debts. Cullum made no attempt to estimate this fraction while the partnership was in being, but at the end of the next year's trading (i.e. at Christmas 1624) he put his desperate debts at £268. Those of the partnership must have been included in this figure.

[2] Cullum, *op. cit.* p. 180.

Nicholas, was a London merchant.[1] Her uncle Ellis would soon be sheriff. Her cousin Nicholas, Ellis Crisp's son, was embarking on the career in African trade that would make him one of the wealthiest men in London. One sister was married to Abraham Reynardson, a future Lord Mayor of London, another to George Strode, merchant, later Sir George; a third would marry a Mr Whitacre with an address in Amsterdam. The Pakes, her mother's family, are less familiar to us; but from a letter or two in the Cullum collection we can see that they had means, piety, and cultivation. They occupied the chief pew in the parish church of Bromefield and liked to give their girls a good education in a fashionable household.[2]

Of course there were many richer merchants than Nicholas Crisp, senior, but the connexion was promising enough. Thomas and Mary were married 18 February 1623. Six hundred pounds was bestowed immediately as part of Mary's portion, with £100 to follow on the birth of each child. They got £80 worth of plate at the wedding, and Thomas was soon able to include father Crisp, uncle Crisp, grandmother Pake, and brother Abraham among his creditors. Naturally his expenses went up. 'My wedding about £100. Childbed lynen about £15. My wife's lying in about £20...Household stuffe about £100, Apparell £20, dyate expenses £138.' From £40 in 1621 and £70 in 1622, the expenses jumped to £268 in 1623 and £354 the year after. But in spite of this, and the necessary borrowing, the growth of his own stock was reassuring: 1621—£1155; 1622—£1349; 1623—£2118. The second thousand had come a lot quicker than the first.

If there was any thought of continuing the partnership after the stipulated three years, nothing came of it. Perhaps Cullum had outgrown any arrangement which his old master was prepared to make; but what-

[1] The *D.N.B.* describes Nicholas Crisp as an alderman, in the article on Cullum, but this was an error. A. B. Beaven, *The Aldermen of the City of London* (1913), vol. II, p. 67, n. 92.

[2] Rebecca Pake, Mary's mother, seems to have received an excellent education in the household of some distinguished lady. Her father, John Pake, is described as 'the chiefest parishioner' of the parish of Bromefield, Essex. Her mother, Anne—the 'grandmother Pake' of the account-book—was able to lend Thomas Cullum £500 in 1625. See Cullum, *op. cit.* pp. 180–2 and *Suff. Arch., art. cit.* pp. 280–5. For the Pake pedigree, see G. G. Milner-Gibson-Cullum, *The Cullum Family* (1928), pp. 143–4.

ever the reason, he launched out on his own in the beginning of 1624. There is nothing in the account-book, between this date and the outbreak of the Civil War, to suggest that he ever looked back. The record is one of steady enrichment. But we often find ourselves sighing for more information. The purpose of the account-book was to keep a record of his own stock as it existed in cloth, 'Debts', cash, plate or real estate. This job was done when he had noted what was 'received into stock' by way of gifts or gains, deducted his expenses, cast out or scaled down the bad debts owing to him, and then balanced the resultant figure with what he found in his inventories after his own indebtedness had been taken out. We never see the inventories themselves, which would tell us what draperies he was handling, what middlemen he was financing, who were his retail customers, and what proportion of his capital was in foreign trade or money-lending. The 'buying-book' which kept a record of his purchases from Blackwell Hall factors and provincial clothiers, the 'cash-book', the 'book of expenses', the daily journal, and the classified ledger, which are not mentioned but must have existed in some form or other, and the masses of indentures, bonds, recognisances and acquittances have all disappeared. Moreover, some of the items that are recorded are somewhat ambiguous from a modern point of view. The term 'gained by trade' (from one Christmas to the next) appears in every account; but how was the figure reached? If the partnership records of a later date are any guide, it was done by taking the difference between the inventories at the two dates—a procedure which inflates the real profit, as some charges, such as wages and the allowance for bad debts, have still to be deducted.

Let us begin by summarising the obvious features of this phase—the first half of a career which we have chosen to divide at the end of 1641. He ceased to be a mere freeman of the company in 1626, when he held the office of warden of the yeomanry,[1] and he was admitted to the livery in 1627. Having graduated into a privileged circle of about eighty to a hundred members,[2] he remained there until his promotion

[1] *Court Minutes, 1640–67*, f. 204A, Drapers' Hall, London.
[2] A. H. Johnson, *The History of the Worshipful Company of the Drapers of London*, pp. 111, 87, 191–2. The court (Master, four wardens, and assistants) contained about thirty members; the freemen declined from over 2000 in James I's reign to about 1500. Many members were not

to the Court of Assistants in 1643. He kept a shop in Gracechurch Street, with a growing number of apprentices. According to the Company's register of admissions and his own account-books, eleven sons of provincial merchants and squires, from London, Suffolk, Yorkshire, Shropshire, Somerset and Worcester were admitted for periods of eight or nine years between 1624 and 1642.[1] Those who came in before 1634 paid, on the average, £80 apiece; the last two £100 and £120, respectively. A stepbrother, Robert Butts, was also taken into the shop from 1632 to 1634 on a somewhat different basis; in return for an investment of £500 he received about £80 a year in wages.

A shop of this size suggests a heavy investment in the domestic market, which is what we would expect of a successful 'draper shop-keeper' as distinct from the members of the Drapers' Company who had large interests in foreign trade. But here we are on doubtful ground. The account-book has several incidental references to his purchases of cloth from factors and his employment of dyers in the finishing process, but it is very unenlightening about his markets or about the proportion of his capital which went into loans. It is only when declaring a desperate debt that we learn that he had lost about £70 in a voyage to the Barbados, or that such and such an individual had defaulted on both the principal and interest of a loan. We may perhaps surmise that if money-lending had been a large operation in these years he would have employed a term which he had used before, 'gained by interest', but there is no certainty about such an inference where the record is so bald.

Clear enough is the steady enlargement of his capital. Table 7 will indicate the fluctuations, especially in the depression of 1634–7, but, on the average, he added about £1000 a year to his capital in these eighteen years, until he was worth about £20,000 in 1641. The sums which he had originally borrowed from friends and relations were paid

engaged in the drapery business. A hostile petition put the number of London families so engaged in 1634 at 140; in their reply the drapers said 250. *Calendar of State Papers, Domestic Series, 1634–35*, pp. 375, 487, 511.

[1] See also Johnson, *op. cit.* IV, 137, 'A List of those assessed for the Poll Tax, August 1641', where the number of his apprentices may be compared with that of other members of the Company. He is here described as 'woollen draper'.

off, and the only debt he carried in the last years seems to have arisen out of a suretyship. His procedure for dealing with the desperate debts among his own assets varied; for the first seven years he gave them a book-keeping value—20 per cent at first and then a token £5—but thereafter he simply recorded the mounting total as a footnote to the annual statement. They stood at £1794 in 1641.

TABLE 7. *Stock account, 1624–41* (£)

	Initial stock	Gains by trade	Other additions*	Total	Expenses	Desperate debts†	Total	Final stock	Net gain
1624	2,119	1,015	60	3,194	354	219	573	2,621	502
1625	2,621	1,000	180	3,801	467	41	508	3,293	672
1626	3,293	1,478	104	4,875	651	35	686	4,189	896
1627	4,189	2,015	80	6,284	569	31	600	5,684	1,495
1628	5,684	1,775	10	7,469	604	10	614	6,855	1,171
1629	6,855	1,771	80	8,706	574	44	618	8,088	1,233
1630	8,088	1,944	—	10,032	722	34	756	9,276	1,188
1631	9,276	1,903	80	11,259	720	247	967	10,292	1,016
1632	10,292	1,669	100	12,061	639	321	960	11,100	808
1633	11,100	1,605	40	12,745	662	—	662	12,083	983
1634	12,083	1,678	—	13,761	776	135	892‡	12,869	783
1635	12,869	1,594	80	14,543	854	59	913	13,630	761
1636	13,630	1,542	50	15,222	760	169	929	14,293	663
1637	14,293	1,770	26	16,089	856	179	1,035	15,054	761
1638	15,054	1,637	—	16,691	573	65	638	16,053	999
1639	16,053	2,093	207	18,353	560	385	945	17,408	1,355
1640	17,408	1,927	—	19,335	540	118	658	18,677	1,269
1641	18,677	2,145	230	21,052	629	321	950	20,102	1,425

  * Usually apprenticeship fees; occasionally a small legacy.
  † Also includes total losses, i.e. debts 'cast out', in the current year as well as those which have turned 'desperate'.
  ‡ *Sic.*

His expenses emerge clearly enough, though we could wish for more details within the categories. The decade 1632–41 may be used as a sample (see Table 9). In two years, 1635 and 1637, the total in each year is just over £850, but this was due to a heavy purchase of 'household stuff' in one year—£140, and his wife's funeral—£257—in the other. In the three years following his wife's death, they fell to about £550. 'Dyate' is the heaviest item, ranging between £238 and £377 with an average of £294. It is always accompanied by 'extraordinary expenses', which may have included the cost of company entertainments. These run as low as £30 and as high as £100 with an average of £67. Rent averages £73 for the period, but is rising somewhat. He had not yet entered the stage where he was buying real estate on any scale. He leased his own house and shop, a quay, a garden, and a

TABLE 8. *Inventory, 1624–41* (£)

	Cloth	Good debts	Plate	Cash	Total	Owing	Own stock	Desperate debts
1624	1,456	2,351*	80	30	3,917	1,296	2,621	269
1625	1,896	2,857*	90	227	5,070	1,777	3,293	310
1626	1,785	3,788*	90	159	5,822	1,634	4,188	356
1627	2,568	4,391†	90	127	7,176	1,492	5,684	331
1628	2,997	5,090†	100	113	8,300	1,444	6,856	333
1629	3,319	4,704†	100	398‡	8,521	432	8,089	306
1630	3,435	7,227†	100	156‡	10,918	1,642	9,276	325
1631	3,194	6,750	100	486‡	10,530	238	10,292	572
1632	3,811	7,391	100	298‡	11,600	500	11,100	873
1633	4,185	8,472	100	145‡	12,902	818	12,084	833
1634	3,743	9,027	100	499	13,369	500	12,869	1,022
1635	3,573	10,378	100	172	14,223	593	13,630	1,081
1636	3,328	11,242	150	102	14,822	530	14,292	1,113
1637	3,614	11,164	150	124	15,052	—	15,052	1,113
1638	3,276	12,302	150	323	16,051	—	16,051	1,153
1639	3,023	14,130	150	104	17,407	—	17,407	1,538
1640	2,803	15,776	150	106	18,835	158	18,677	1,646
1641	2,712	16,465	150	909	20,236	134	20,102	1,794

* Includes about £50 as a value assigned to desperate debts.
† Includes £5 for the same.
‡ Includes a garden lease valued at £25–£15.

smaller shop which he sublet. The amounts spent on repairs are small— an average of £8 a year—but he had paid £145 to put the quay in order when he first acquired it, and it still receives more attention than anything else. Some of the rent is apparently paid for property outside London, but this is impossible to identify. 'Apparel'—for his family and servants, costs more than rent;[1] an average of £77 per annum. A draper of the Livery was obviously expected to maintain a high

[1] See account-book, 4 January 1630, where £500 was borrowed from his brother-in-law George Strode, 'to pay interest or lend him as much'.

standard. 'Household stuff', by comparison, accounts for less than half this sum. The amounts are naturally irregular, but the average—after the £140 already mentioned has been included—is only £33. One notices elsewhere in the account that the value of his plate, which had been £80 at his marriage, is only £150 twenty years later. Ostentation in the home was obviously not Cullum's style.

'Fyring' and 'phizicke' are two items in the budget where the average for the decade is about the same—£20 and £17 respectively; but there is obviously more consistency about the first than the second.

TABLE 9. *Expenses, 1632–41* (£)

	Diet	Extra-ordinary	Rent	Repairs	Apparel	House-hold	Firing	Wages	Physic	Total
1632	238	102	55	7	89	10	20	93	25	639
1633	300	64	60	18	59	25	23	90	22	661
1634	300	86	55	4	113	30	20	98	49	755
1635	377	50	77	1	70	140	27	95	17	854
1636	343	68	76	4	94	33	27	102	12	759
1637	342	31	91	2	50	14	11	45	11	856*
1638	277	57	94	9	64	33	18	18	3	573
1639	272	88	76	3	57	16	19	23	5	559
1640	245	55	80	4	68	22	15	49	2	540
1641	248	74	66	27	112	12	20	42	28	629
Average	294	67	73	8	77	33	20	65	17	682

* Includes £257. 13s. 11d. 'per my wife's funerall shee dying in childbed and buryd privat'.

There was one year before this decade began in which 'phizicke' cost the staggering sum of £79, and it was £49 again in 1634. We can appreciate his feelings when he was able to say in 1638 'phizicke but £3. 7s. 0d.' and in 1640 'phizicke but £2. 9s. 0d.' Wages—'of men and maids'—are complicated in this decade by the ambiguous position of his stepbrother, Robert Butts, who received a sum called wages but who had also brought £500 of capital into the business for which no visible interest was paid. So long as he was there, the wage bill was just under a hundred pounds, but it had never been higher than £76 before he arrived and it fell below £50 after he had gone. Two items are conspicuous by their absence in the accounts of this decade. One is taxes, though they may be concealed either in extraordinary expenses or in his 'debts' as loans. The other is interest payments. After reaching a peak of £95 in 1626, these had dwindled to £7 in 1631 and then disappeared.

We began by sighing over the silences in these accounts. One paradox remains for which no adequate explanation can be offered. It will be seen from Table 7 that while the capital increases from about £2000 in 1624 to about £20,000 in 1641, the 'gains from trade', which were £1000 in the first year, are only double that in the last, with a range of £1500–2000 for the greater part of the period. Why was he not receiving a proportionate return? One hardly imagines that he was putting his gains in his sock. The Inventory (Table 8) shows that, apart from a fairly stable investment in unsold cloth, and trifling sums in plate and ready cash, his gains were in 'debts hoped good'. Some proportion of these must have been in his own cloth business, on the lines suggested by the records of his early partnership with John Rayney or his later partnership with William Nicholl. But where were the rest, and what was happening to them? He seems unlikely to have loaned money for nothing—a practice which only appealed to him where the recipient was going to lend him an equivalent sum for nothing.[1] If he was waiting for a deferred return, we can only say that it never arrived. And if the debts were not in fact good, but bad, why did he not say so? There must be some explanation, other than the improbable supposition that the return on capital was dwindling in the way these figures imply, but it eludes this writer. In default of an explanation, we can only offer the suggestion that he was prepared to treat debts as good which yielded no return for years on end, and that he had no alternative but to go on taking such chances.

As we enter the second half of Cullum's career we are faced by the question, how would he conduct himself in the Civil Wars? The evidence is slight enough, but we are not prohibited from eking it out with a little guess-work. When the revolution started, he was a self-

---

[1] See account-book, 4 January 1630 where £500 was borrowed from his brother-in-law George Strode, 'to pay interest or lend him as much'.

made man in his fifties who could look back on twenty years of steady enrichment. But his estate was still modest in comparison with the really big city fortunes, and he had not yet held the highest offices in his own Company—neither master, warden, nor assistant. In the absence of strong commitments, the impulse of such a man would be to play safe, following the lead of bigger men, attending to his business, and hoping for the kind of agreement between King and Parliament that would enable him to go on prospering. He was not, like his wife's cousin, Nicholas Crisp, a monopolist and farmer of the customs who would find it hard to detach himself from the court if he had wanted to.[1] Nor, on the other hand, can we feel sure that his piety, and the influence of some Puritan relatives, had brought him within the Puritan fold. It may have, but there is no conclusive proof.[2] These two factors—court affiliation and religion—were the sort of things that often turned an individual into a resolute partisan. But one guesses that Cullum had no good reasons for being a partisan; that his country had not treated him at all badly, whatever disgruntlements he may have felt; and that his heart was really in money-making. If such a man must be labelled, nothing more exclusive than 'moderate royalism' or 'moderate presbyterianism' will serve.

If space permitted, we could attempt to chart his course through the storms that followed. When Nicholas Crisp, already a marked man, moved over to Oxford in 1643,[3] Cullum stayed in London. If he was not to lose his livelihood, what else could he do? He was elected Master[4] of his Company while Pym was struggling to reverse the tide of royalist successes; headed the list of contributors to an emergency

---

[1] For Crisp, see *D.N.B.*; D. Brunton and D. H. Pennington, *Members of the Long Parliament* (1954), pp. 54–5; M. F. Keeler, *The Long Parliament, 1640–41* (1954), p. 147.

[2] Cullum's piety is stamped on every page of his account-book and reflected in the epitaphs on himself and his wife; W. A. Copinger, *The Manors of Suffolk* (1905–11), VII, 40; John Le Neve, *Monumenta Anglicana* (1717–19), V, 56. There are hints that grandmother Pake, who died in his home in 1639, was a good Puritan. *Suff. Arch.*, *art. cit.* pp. 280–5. Cullum also loaned £12 in 1620 to 'Mr Nathaniel Ward, preacher'—almost certainly the well-known divine of Ipswich, England, and New England, who at this time was just beginning his career. But we are still uncertain where Cullum stood. His master, John Rayney, in whose house he had lived eight years, endowed a preacher and a lecturer, but seems to have left instructions that they should comply with the rules laid down by Laud. Johnson, *op. cit.* pp. 111, 186.

[3] *D.N.B.*

[4] *Court Minutes, 1640–67*, 31 A (7 August, 1643), Drapers' Hall, London.

loan;[1] and played an essential part in the parliamentary victory as a Commissioner of Excise.[2] How enthusiastic or unenthusiastic he felt, it is impossible to say; but he was clearly among the 'presbyterian' combination at the end of the war which hoped to seal off the revolution. As sheriff in 1646–7, he had his moment of dangerous living in one of the crises which preceded the Army's seizure of power and spent some months in prison.[3] But he was released in March 1648 before any of his colleagues. Had he been able to clear himself, or was he prepared to carry compliance further than the rest? All we know is what he said in his petition, which was certainly humble enough.[4]

Thomas Hobbes once remarked that the City was 'not very good at venturing'. He was referring to political adventures, and Cullum's prudent career seems to illustrate his point. The old alderman must have shaken his head over the catastrophic turn which English politics took in January 1649. Republicanism! toleration! What sinful absurdities. But business must go on. Besides, he was getting no younger. So he gave up the Excise in 1650, resigned from the aldermanship in 1652, and moved out to the country in 1657. When the Restoration finally came, the man who had kept his sufferings for the royal cause within very tolerable limits was still able to claim his reward. He was among the dozen City men to get a baronetcy in 1660,[5] though it cost him £2000 in 1662 to insure himself against awkward questions.[6]

[1] *Court Minutes, 1640–67*, p. 33 A. The Drapers subscribed £3750. Nearly all the bonds were in the names of sons or relatives, presumably as a precaution against a royalist victory. Cullum was the largest contributor, his eldest son Thomas putting up £1035, the next son, John, £517. 10s. See also Johnson, *op. cit.* pp. 111, 161.

[2] At the same time he became alderman of Cordwainer Ward. Beaven, *op. cit.* II, 67.

[3] S. R. Gardiner, *Great Civil War* (1893), pp. 111, 335–7, 351–2; *Journals of the House of Commons*, V, 315–16; *Calendar of State Papers, Domestic Series, 1645–47*, p. 600.

[4] *Journals, op. cit.* V, 319, 495, 498. Two pamphlets in the Thomason Collection (British Museum) printed 28 and 30 September 1647, in protest against the imprisonment of the City officials, add nothing to our knowledge of the incident. For Cullum's petition to the House of Commons, see Thomason Collection, E 432 (2).   [5] Beaven, *op. cit.*

[6] The Act of General Pardon (12 Car. II, c. 11) had not included those responsible for arrears of excise, and an act (13 Car. II, c. 1) was passed to recover these sums for the King's use. Cullum was called to account for the period September 1647–September 1650 and required to pay £2000 as arrears and £200 as a fee to the auditor. The account-book contains a letter of 13 March 1660–1 from his son John, warning him that Colonel Birch wanted to inspect the accounts; it also has the note, under 1663, 'paid into the Exchequer to buy my peace and Birch 2200'. Whether this was a legitimate recovery of arrears, or not, it is impossible to say. See *Calendar of Treasury Books, 1660–67*, pp. 342, 529–30.

How had he fared in twenty years of civil war? When we turn once again to the economic biography,[1] we find additions being made to his capital in at least four different ways. Two of these—trade and overseas investment—we have seen before; the other two—profits of office and rents from real estate—are new. The office need not detain us, although it was obviously lucrative. At Christmas 1643 there is the entry, 'a quarter's salary in the Excise, £110'. The amount rose rapidly; for the years 1644–50, when the employment stops, the figures were £943, £1472, £1788, £1531, £1033, £1229, £1103. The author of the pamphlet who complained of 'Aldermen and Common Councilmen as have great profits by the continuance of the war' was conservative when he put the value of Cullum's job at £1200 per annum: the average was about £1300.[2]

Trade was the same business as before. He took in six more apprentices in the first decade, but then stopped, as he was reducing his commitments in the shop. One of these newcomers, William Nicholls, who was admitted in 1643 and presumably received his freedom in 1651, was paid the same compliment by the ageing Cullum as his old master, John Rayney, had once paid to him: he was taken into a partnership. The accounts of this association have survived and furnish our best indication of what was involved in the drapery business. They take the form of an annual statement in which an inventory is taken of the assets, in cloth, 'great debts unto chapmen', 'small debts', and cash, and the total is divided, for book-keeping purposes, in the proportion of 3:1 between the partners. This statement is accompanied by an itemisation of the great and small debts. From these accounts, together with the entries in the account-book, we can see that Cullum had put up £4500 and Nicholls £1500 in 1652, and that Cullum's proportion of the stock at the inventory a year later was £5190. He therefore recorded that he had 'gained in trade in partnership with William Nicholls—£690'. The chapmen remained much the same individuals throughout the seven years for which there are records. It is assumed

---

[1] For the remaining references to Cullum's accounts see Table 12, 'Stock Account, 1642–63', at the end of this chapter.
[2] Broadside entitled 'A Second Centurie'.

that these were wholesale distributors of cloth. The 'small debts', contracted by a variety of individuals with different occupations, many of them with London addresses, are presumably those of retail purchasers.[1]

This partnership lasted four years, with the gains of each year left in: thus for 1652 Cullum's investment was £4500, gains £690; for 1653, investment £5190, gains £720; for 1654, £5190, gains £690; for 1655, £6400 (a further £200 declared 'doubtful'), gains £732. These returns decline from about 15·3 per cent in the first year to 11·4 per cent in the last, and when the partnership is eventually liquidated, some of the debts will be cast out as desperate. In 1656 they formed a second partnership, with Cullum putting up two-thirds, or £4600, and Nicholls, one-third, £2300. Cullum's gains for the first year were £673, or about 15 per cent; for the second year, £613 on £5273, or 11·6 per cent. One is tempted to wonder if the declining return was not simply due to the slowness with which some of the debts were recovered. Cullum wound up this partnership at the end of the second year (January 1658), but two years later (December 1659) he still had about £300 of debts to collect under the first partnership and over £400 under the second.

These partnerships represented only a small investment of Cullum's capital in his later years.[2] If the category 'gains by trade' or 'gains by trade and stock' is examined for the whole period, 1642–63, it is seen to fall into three phases. In the first, from 1642 to 1651, he was on his own, putting the greater part of his effort, one imagines, into the drapery business, and crediting himself with gains which rose annually from about £2000 to £2900 (this, of course, is over and above the income from excise). In the second phase, of partnership with Nicholls, the gains were closer to £2000 per annum; he had no cloth business outside the partnership, and he was increasing his investment in overseas trade. He had been admitted to the freedom of the East India

---

[1] These accounts are in a separate MS. entitled 'Account of Sir Thomas Cullum, 1646–58', E 2/29/1.2, West Suffolk Record Office. This contains the partnership accounts, 1652–8, and a few accounts for 1646–7 when Cullum was sheriff. Up to forty-five chapmen with 'great debts' are listed; up to ninety individuals with 'small debts'.

[2] The partnership profits are separated from his other 'gains by trade' in Table 12.

Company in 1647,[1] and he invested in the second general voyage of 1648, realising £53 when the divisions were made in 1653.[2] In the same year he listed a gain of £60 by 'united stock',[3] and we find him referring once more to East India Company dividends in 1656. In the third period, from 1658 to his death, he had liquidated the partnership with Nicholls, retired to the country, and was living on an income derived from rents and stock. The latter was producing just under £1000 per annum in these last seven years, and from the frequent references to 'united stock' we may be justified in inferring a considerable investment in the Far East.[4]

Finally, there is the investment in real estate. He was in no hurry about this. He was fifty-seven years old before he made his first investment in rents and over sixty before he did so heavily. Perhaps the incentive was the insecurity of the times. The first purchase of six houses for £800 (four in the Minories, two on Tower Hill) came in 1644, after he had written off £623 as desperate debt in the previous year and was gloomily introducing a category of 'doubtful debts' between the 'good' and the 'desperate'. He seems to have got at least a 10 per cent return on this modest experiment, for the rent in the following year was £82. Of course we may be making too much of coincidences in the accounts, but the next one is too tempting to resist. After a taste of prison, and the shocking spectacle of the regicide, is it surprising to find that 1649 was the year in which real estate looked really tempting? He spent over £10,000 on London property, which he listed (see p. 132) together with previous purchases.

If we assume that the 'half-moon' and the 'key' were wholly in his own occupation, the rest was rental property. It had cost him about £10,450,

---

[1] E. B. Sainsbury, *A Calendar of the Court Minutes, etc. of the East India Company, 1644–49* (1912), p. 229.

[2] W. R. Scott, *The Constitution and Finance of English, Scottish and Irish Joint-Stock Companies to 1720* (1910–12), pp. 11, 119–23.

[3] United stock was a subscription for trade to the East, undertaken in 1650 and reorganised in 1652, which brought East India and Assada adventurers to terms and united them (*ibid.* p. 123).

[4] Some receipts have survived in which John Massingberd, Treasurer of the East India Company, acknowledged Cullum's investments, as follows: 4 October 1647, £250 in the second general voyage; 9 February 1649–50, £100 first payment for his adventure in the united joint stock; 17 April 1650, second payment ditto £100; 10 October 1650, third, £100; 3 January 1650/1, fourth, £100; March 1657, fifth, £100; 11 October 1651, sixth, £100.

Cullum's real estate acquisitions, 1649

	£
In leases, Tower Hill 400, Half-Moon 600, Key 100	1,100
12 houses, 1 stable in Limestreet with furnishings	4,600
8 houses, 1 warehouse, Bowlane	2,000
1 house in Bishopgate Street	450
9 houses in Warwicklane	2,500
4 houses in Minories on which bestowed 150	500
	£11,150

and, if he had received all the rents and fines that were due in the following year, he would have got about £925, or a little less than 9 per cent. However, there were both heavy losses in the expected rents (£166) and heavy expenses on repairs (£112). In the next seven years, he cut the losses down to a few pounds, spent over £1500 on the improvement and enlargement of the properties, and raised the rental to about £1140. It is hardly worth calculating what the average return was for these years, as we have his own conservative estimate of the long-term expectations from such property. In 1656 he settled the Limestreet and Warwicklane houses, then valued at £9300, on his eldest son, who was getting married, and calculated that with his wife's portion of £2000 this ought to give him an income of about £800 a year; i.e. about 7 per cent. No doubt he was doing rather better than this himself.

The loss of these rents was more than made up in the same year by the purchase of a country estate. He paid £18,000 for it, and had spent another £2500 in improvements before he died. From this source, and from the balance of his London properties, he enjoyed a rental income in his last years of about £1350 per annum.

So much for the different items—profits of office, gains by trade and investment, and rents—which were 'received into stock'. The reductions of the gross gains by bad debts and expenses remain to be considered before noting the net improvement of capital. The opening of the Civil War obviously aroused the worst apprehensions about the security of his estate. At Christmas 1642, his desperate debts had stood at £1888. After a year of war he added £623 to this figure and wrote on 26 December 1643, 'so there resteth betwine fear and hope these sad troublesome times belonging to my proper account £20,151'. In the next year, £644, he added the category 'doubtful debts' to those already employed; so he now has 'good debts' (£17,798), 'doubtful debts' (£4298), 'desperate debts uncast' (£2667) and those debts, admittedly few, which had become so desperate in the past as to be 'cast out' and not further recorded.

The 'doubtful debts' ran over £4000 a year for the next four years, but in 1650 they descended from about £3000 to under £400. This was not done by treating them as desperate, but it should probably be associated with the fact that in these years he admitted to having 'lost' about £1500 loaned to his royalist relations, Sir Nicholas Crisp and Sir George Strode. If this interpretation is correct, some of the doubtful debts had been cast out without passing through the desperate stage. In 1652 a low point of £150 was reached, then they climbed again until they stood at about £2000 in the last years. Meanwhile the desperate debts were increased by small transfers every year, with an occasional big one. In 1646 they jumped by nearly £500 to over £3000; in 1655 by £2842 to £6372. The occasions when he was able to report that a few pounds of desperate debt had become good again were rare, but it is equally rare to find them cast out. One exception was in 1656 when 'Hudens desperate debt now circa £3200' was compounded for £500 and the balance cast out. This brought the total down to about £4000 where it remained until 1660 when he increased it by £3017 'lost by weavers hall bills'. The new figure, £7317, was not much altered by the time of his death.

Finally, there were the expenses. These included certain heavy items which we shall reserve for separate treatment—the costs of the shrievality in 1646-7 and some abnormal family expenditures such as funerals and marriage settlements. The routine expenses had increased. The range in the decade before the war had been £550-£850 per annum. Between 1642 and 1658 the cheapest year, 1644, was £726 and the dearest, 1651, £1375, with an average of just under £1000 a year. 'Physicke' is one item which dwindled—no doubt because he was no longer supporting a wife who bore him a child almost every year. The average was about £5 a year, apart from one year when the death of an adult daughter brought the bill up to £25, and another, inexplicable year, when it soared to £61. Wages were another exception to the upward trend; after running between £40 and £50 for a decade, they dropped to £11 in 1651 and stayed there. This seems to be the amount that he was paying for household service, and one infers that he had either stopped paying a wage in the shop or found some other means of charging it. Rent remained fairly stable until the expiry of a lease and the addition of a coach-house and stable raised it by about £50 to £134. Diet, which had averaged just under £300 before the war, went up by about £70. Firing averaged £23 as against the earlier £19. Apparel, which had been £77, produced an average of about £100, but the amount varied sharply from year to year; between 1652 and 1655 it was about £150, of which £100 was spent each year on his eldest son, Thomas. The most irregular of all the expenses were those on 'household stuff'. In 1654, the year he bought a coach, they were £68; in other years they were as little as one, two, or four pounds. He spent no more in this area than before the war, and much less than might be expected of a man of his means.

The two items in the regular budget which rose most were 'repairs' and 'extraordinary expenses'. The former naturally increased with his purchase of real estate, but they exaggerated his expenses as they included the cost of new building and were certainly compensated for by improved rents. The dearest year which we referred to, in which his expenses were £1375, included £405 spent in this way. The extraordinary expenses, which had averaged £67 before the war, jumped to £158 in 1643 and continued to climb. If three years are ignored, in which the figure was obviously swollen by the shrievality and a funeral, the average for 1642–58 works out at about £250; they were over £350 in the early fifties and had tapered down to £220 by 1657. His promotion to the Court of Assistants in 1643 must have increased his responsibilities, and the amended description of this category—

'extraordinary expenses *and rates*'—indicates the incidence of war taxation.

These expenses are far from being a guide to what the Civil War cost Cullum. To know that, we would need to know the full history of his debts, including both the private investments which went bad and the loans to government which were never repaid. These figures merely tell us what happened to those routine living expenses which he was in the habit of paying out of the cash account of his business. As such, we may be surprised that they were not more, when we take into consideration both the demands of a steadily improving station and the impact of the war.

Such a man was well able to bear the burden of being sheriff, and one of the interesting features of his accounts is the record of what his year in office cost. The times were austere, but the scale of entertainment was still considerable. We learn, for instance, that he had to hire a cook, under-cook, and cook's labourers, a steward, a butler, a porter, two under-porters, a yeoman of the wine cellar, a running porter, a scouring woman and maid, a coachman, and a footman. The services of this staff for a year cost £134. There were also plate, linen, furniture, firing, apparel, and horses to be bought, not to mention the food, which still included about twenty kinds of poultry, austerity or no austerity, and the wine. By deducting his normal expenses from the swollen budget of the year 1646–7, we can arrive at some estimate of the total cost. The average of the years preceding and following the year of office has been used to calculate the 'normal' expenses.

TABLE 10. *Sheriff's expenses, September 1646–September 1647*

	£	s.	d.
Added to plate	130	0	0
Diet 1646: £1134 – £397	737	0	0
Extraordinary expenses 1646: £404 – £244	160	0	0
Apparel 1646: £172 – £89	83	0	0
Household stuff 1646: £336 – £10	326	0	0
Firing 1646: £79 – £25	54	0	0
Diet 1647: £1969 – £397	1572	0	0
Extraordinary expenses 1647: £487 – £244	243	0	0
Firing 1647: £68 – £25	43	0	0
TOTAL	£3348	0	0

To meet a part of this substantial sum, the sheriff received gratuities from the great city companies (his own being expected to make the biggest) and the profits of the sheriff's jurisdiction. Cullum recorded the following allowances:

TABLE 11. *Sheriff's allowances, 1646–7*

	£	s.	d.
Drapers	{ 33	6	8
	{ 163	0	0
Grocers	107	14	0
Mercers	67	0	0
Clothworkers	79	10	0
Haberdashers	27	8	0
Salters	40	10	0
Dyers	29	0	0
Goldsmiths	46	10	0
Brewers	50	0	0
Leathersellers	12	0	0
Fines and Tolls	191	0	0
Sessions	11	5	0
Gifts or perquisites	32	10	0
'More as sheriff from the Compter'	63	8	6
TOTAL	£954	2	2

So Thomas Cullum's year in office cost him £2394 over and above his normal expenditure. However, he was the better off by £130 worth of plate, which he kept, and he was able to sell off some of his surplus property. We know that a certain Sam Barnard, who had sold him the extra pewter he needed at 1s. 2d. a pound, had contracted to take it back again when the year was up at 1s. 10d. a pound. In this way, or by sale, he recovered £250 for 'household stuff, wine, pewter, horse, and other bargains'. We may therefore put the cost at about £2000. According to custom, any citizen worth £10,000 or above had to accept the office of alderman or sheriff, or pay a fine. Cullum thought he was worth about £28,000 at Christmas 1646, and his income that year, from office, trade, and rents, was over twice what it cost him to be sheriff.

We have still to review the provisions which such a man thought suitable for his family. Before his wife died at the age of thirty-six in

The Rising Merchant

July 1637, she had born him five sons and six daughters, seven of which children must have died in infancy. His wife's own death was an inexpensive event by the standards of the age; he buried her 'privately' for £257. Other scraps of evidence, between this date and the outbreak of war, suggest respectable dignity rather than great wealth. When his wife's father, Nicholas Crisp, died in 1641, the legacies to the grandchildren were only £80 for Thomas, the eldest, and £50 each for John, Rebecca, and Mary. When Rebecca was married to Job Throckmorton in 1642, the portion was £2000—a substantial sum, but not the figure which needy aristocrats had in mind when they bargained for aldermen's daughters. Job Throckmorton was, in fact, a merchant. Moreover, Cullum continued to live with restraint even though his fortune was climbing by over £2000 a year. He made no move to buy land, spent no more than was decent on his merchant's home, and buried his daughter Mary in 1649 with no more pomp than he had spent on his wife. There is a sobriety about this scale of living which consorts well enough with the conventional image of the Puritan business man, but Puritans had no monopoly of thrift, and we do not know whether his piety was tinged by Puritanism or not. All we do know is that after years of patient accumulation, and at a very advanced age, he finally allowed himself to be stirred into bolder social ambitions than those of a merchant. Perhaps the children were pressing; perhaps the dream of a landed estate had always warmed the Christmas bookkeeping. Had not John Rayney finished up as a landed gentleman in Kent? The son of his old master was now Sir John Rayney, baronet, of Wrotham Place. Why not become Thomas Cullum, Esquire, of Hawstead and Hardwick—with a suitable title, if the King ever came into his own again?

The purchase was made in 1656 at a time when he was negotiating, or had just negotiated, the marriage of his eldest son. Thomas, who was twenty-eight, may once have expected to follow his father's footsteps, but it was a squire's future which faced him now. The bride was Dudley (or Dudleia) North, daughter of Sir Henry North, of Mildenhall, Suffolk. The Norths were new nobility of the last century, descended from Edward, the first baron, who had climbed via the law and the

City into the Court of Augmentations, where more than one Tudor fortune had been made. The head of the family lived at Kirtling, near Newmarket. A cadet branch had been established at Mildenhall by the second baron and was now represented by Sir Henry, who can have been no stranger to the alderman, for he had married none other than Sarah Rayney, Sir John's daughter. The Norths had been refreshing their fortunes with City marriages since the days of the first baron, and Sir Henry, who seems to have done well enough out of a Rayney, was quite prepared to see his daughter marry a Cullum. We have already seen how the young couple started with £2000 from the Norths and over £9000 from the alderman, in real estate. Cullum gave them another £50 in pearls and over £300 to be spent on 'household stuff'; and they could look forward, at no very distant date, to inheriting the splendid property which he had bought for himself. Hawstead Place and Hardwick House had belonged to a premier Suffolk family, the Drurys, which had exhausted its male line on the death of Sir Robert in 1615. A house which had entertained Elizabeth, received Anne Bacon as the bride of Sir Robert, accommodated John Donne as a secretary, and nourished itself on an income of about £6000 a year in Sir Robert's day, was no mean establishment. The estate had passed to Sir Robert's three surviving sisters, and Cullum's purchase was negotiated with their heirs.

The alderman was sixty-nine at this date, and for the last eight years of his life he lived among these new-found mercies. The Restoration was received with a thankful heart. It enabled him to dignify his family with a baronetcy and to hope that some doubtful debts, such as the £2182 which his cousin, Nicholas Crisp, still owed him, would become good again. There were losses; but they were a small price for peace of mind. Each Christmas the quivering pen was made to do its duty and the record kept of 'God's great mercies to me and mine'. At the end of 1663 he balanced the books for the last time. So far as the family is concerned, they show that Thomas had been given another £1500, that John had been set up as a draper with £5000 and the prospect of inheriting London property, including his father's shop, to the value of another £5000, and that Rebecca had added £1000 to her original portion of £2000. Quite apart from anything they would inherit after his death, the children had been given £19,660 in his lifetime.

This last account—the forty-eighth in the series—shows an income from rents and stock of £2335 and a capital of £43,805. We have seen how his income had passed through several phases since 1641. Beginning with about £2000 a year by trade, it had reached its peak between 1645 and 1650, when trade, office, and eventually rents, were producing amounts which ran between £3800 and £4700 a year; then, though rents were increasing, the office disappeared and the trade contracted, bringing the range down to £3700–3200 a year for 1651–7; finally, after large settlements on the children, we reach the phase represented by this last account, where the level was £2300–2500. As his expenses (in the widest sense of the term, i.e., gifts, bad debts, new building, as well as ordinary living expenses) never exceeded his income in any year from 1643 to 1655, his capital naturally rose. From a base of £20,000 it reached a peak of nearly £48,000 in 1655; after which family settlements, a serious bad debt, or an expense like the purchase of his pardon, held the total down. Even so it had risen to almost £47,000 in the year before the last account.

Having followed Cullum from his apprenticeship to the grave, we are naturally curious as to how typical his history was. Economic biographies of this intimacy are exceedingly rare, so no precise answer is possible. However, there is a certain body of impressions about the wealth of London merchants at this time which has been culled from contemporary gossip, estate records, and the testimony of royalists. Using this material as a rough yardstick, certain observations may be ventured about Cullum's experience. It is clear that in the competition for wealth he started late and low. He was twenty-nine before he was out of his apprenticeship, thirty-three before he was worth £1000; and there was no one behind him to give him a vigorous lift. If the origins of the really rich men in his generation were known, it would probably be found that very few of them started with as little as he. It is equally clear that in the twenty years between his marriage and the civil wars, he never, as the saying goes, struck it rich. There were men around him who made his patient gains look like a snail's progress; adventurers in foreign trade, projectors, monopolists, farmers of customs; men on the inside waxing hugely fat. Sir Arthur Ingram, of an older generation, gave his daughter £10,000 to marry Lord Holland about the same time as Rebecca was getting £2000 to marry Job Throckmorton. John Harrison, who was about Cullum's age, had built himself a palace in Hertfordshire a whole generation before Cullum moved out of Gracechurch Street. John Jacob, a younger man by a decade, but a customs' farmer who was the son of a customs' farmer, was making £3000 a year in 1633 to Cullum's £1600. Closer home than all these was cousin Nicholas Crisp, twelve years younger, but swarming to the dizziest heights with the help of a good start (an alderman's son) and a fine entrepreneurial gait.

But there were compensations. When the monopolists came to grief in 1641, Cullum went on climbing. Two years later be became, in the eyes of some disgruntled observers, a kind of monopolist himself; a job-holder farming the excise, boosting himself as the others had done before. But there were limits to his powers. Among the slopes beneath the pinnacles, after a climb which neither economic nor political blizzards had much disturbed, he found his level. It was not the top; but it offered a comfortable shelter for the seven baronets who succeeded him.

TABLE 12. Stock account, 1642–63 (£)

	Initial stock	Gains				Total	Expenses	Desperate debts	Total deduction	Final stock	Net gain
		Trade	Office	Rent	Misc.						
1642	20,102	2,042	—	—	—	22,264	2,870[1]	94	2,964	19,300	−802
1643	19,300	2,051	111	—	120	21,582	808	623	1,431	20,151	851
1644	20,151	1,886	943	—	—	22,980	727	156	883	22,097	1,946
1645	22,097	2,280	1,472	82	126	26,057	871	30	901	25,156	3,059
1646	25,156	2,783	1,788	101	853[2]	30,681	2,250[3]	458	2,708	27,973	2,817
1647	27,973	2,595	1,531	101	837[4]	33,037	2,991[3]	40	3,031	30,006	2,033
1648	30,006	2,709	1,033	101	263	34,112	945	1,088[5]	2,033	32,079	2,073
1649	32,079	2,934	1,230	541	565[6]	37,349	1,392[7]	440	1,832	35,517	3,438
1650	35,517	2,556	1,104	924	—	40,101	1,323[8]	110	1,433	38,668	3,151
1651	38,668	2,766	—	934	600[9]	42,968	1,375[10]	503	1,878	41,090	2,422
1652	41,090	690 / 1,282	—	927	400	44,579	1,162	147	1,309	43,269	2,179
1653	43,269	720 / 1,503	—	943	110	46,546	1,129	—	1,129	45,417	2,148
1654	45,417	690 / 1,582	—	1,036	—	48,725	1,135	—	1,135	47,590	2,173
1655	47,590	732 / 1,752	—	1,140	750[11]	51,964	1,243	2,842	4,085	47,879	289
1656	47,879	673 / 1,766	—	1,133	1,150[12]	52,601	10,775[13]	8	10,783	41,818	−6,061
1657	41,818	614 / 1,255	—	1,357	550	45,594	4,928[14]	100	5,028	40,566	−1,252
1658	40,566	979	—	1,378	328	43,251	612	—	612	42,639	2,073
1659	42,639	930	—	1,348	50	44,967	990[15]	—	990	43,977	1,338
1660	43,977	1,129	—	1,348	650	47,104	1,549[16]	3,017	4,566	42,538	−1,439
1661	42,538	989	—	1,528	50	45,105	561	50	610	44,495	1,957
1662	44,495	944	—	1,348	500	47,287	510	—	510	46,777	2,282
1663	46,777	988	—	1,346	—	49,111	5,081[17]	225	5,306	43,805	−2,972

[1] Includes a marriage portion of £2000. [2] £130 added to plate; £200 by a lease; £120 by an apprentice; £403 gratuities for sheriff's expenses. [3] Includes sheriff's expenses. [4] £100 by an apprentice; £487 sheriff's fees; £250 by Ralph surplus goods. [5] Includes £1013 debt cast out. [6] 'Gained by Triplet's bill exchanged per myne upon goldsmith's hall per his Weavers hall, £315; gained by debentures bought per Warwicklane houses, £250.' [7] Includes funeral of daughter. [8] Includes £116 'lost rents', £112 repairs. [9] Includes £200 by a lease, £400 for new building. [10] Includes £31 'lost rents', £405 for new building. These elements also enter into the expenses for 1652–5. [11] £150 by an apprentice, £600 for building. [12] £750 added for new building: £400 for household stuff which he takes into account before giving it to his eldest son. [13] £9300 in real estate and c. £400 in goods before giving it to eldest son. [14] £4000 given to his second son, John. [15] £590 given to son-in-law, Job Throckmorton. [16] £630 given to his son John in household goods. [17] £2200 to buy his pardon; £341 expenses; and two debts given to his son John Cullum (Nicholas Crisp's, £2183, and Walker's, £358).

CHAPTER IV

THE COURTIER—IN AND OUT OF OFFICE

SIR THOMAS CORNWALLIS

THE Cornwallises were one of those families which rose from the squirearchy to the peerage, under the Tudors and Stuarts, by cultivating a connexion with the court over several generations. They acquired, so to speak, a hereditary interest in a household office, and they seem to have had the qualities of bravery, tact, and competence that were needed to catch the sovereign's eye. The founder of the family was a fourteenth-century merchant; a sheriff of London in 1378, whose heir was settled as a squire on the borders of Norfolk and Suffolk by the beginning of the fifteenth century. A century later they were still squires, but the lordships in Brome and Oakley had been enlarged by lands in the neighbouring towns, and William Cornwallis, a younger son who succeeded three childless brothers, was a substantial figure among the clients of the house of Howard when he died in 1519. The court connexion began with his heir, Sir John, who distinguished himself in the earl of Surrey's expedition of 1521 and became steward of the household of the young Prince Edward in 1538. It was continued by Sir Thomas, the treasurer of Calais and comptroller of Queen Mary's household. It was resumed again, after a long interval of recusancy, by Sir Thomas's younger son Sir Charles, the ambassador to Spain from 1605 to 1609 and the treasurer of Prince Henry's household. And it was completed by Sir Charles's nephew, Frederick, who was rewarded at the Restoration for a lifetime of service in court and camp by being made Baron Cornwallis of Eye, and—inevitably— treasurer of Charles II's household.[1]

[1] *D.N.B.* (Sir Thomas Cornwallis; Sir Charles Cornwallis); Copinger, *op. cit.* III, 239–43; A. R. Bateman-Hanbury, 'Brome Hall', *Suffolk Archaeology*, XIV, 227–32; Blomefield, *op. cit.* II, 171.

The Courtier

One of the most interesting chapters in this history of a rising family is the lifetime of Sir Thomas Cornwallis, who succeeded to his inheritance before the death of Henry VIII and outlived Elizabeth (1544–1604); for Sir Thomas shows us what it meant for an estate to experience both turns of the wheel. He belonged to the court gentry for five gratifying years and then to the country gentry for forty-five; a Marian courtier whose hopes were blasted by a Protestant succession. His accounts, which are among the manuscripts of the earl of Iveagh, at Elveden, Suffolk, are no more complete than such records ever are, and the lonely explorer has all the usual fears that he may lose his way among these fog-bound figures. But some contours emerge: the shape of the estate at his succession, a few of the windfalls of office, the effects of inflation on land values, the incidence of recusancy, and the levels of expenditure during the long years of retirement. Recent controversies about the fortunes of the gentry have emphasised the need for case studies. Sir Thomas's financial history is offered as another modest but concrete example.

INCOME (1540–95)

We shall begin by endeavouring to trace the course of his income, starting with the family estate at his succession in 1544, then moving forward to gauge its enlargement during his years of office, and ending with the evidence supplied by a good series of receivers' accounts in the reign of Elizabeth. We have no idea of the level at which his father was living during the last six years of his life when he was steward of Prince Edward's household, but if the worth of a man was partly measured by his 'port', which in this case is unknown, it was more solidly established by the amount he had put into land and the provision he was able to make for his younger children. We have Sir John's will, and a series of bailiff's accounts for his principal properties in Suffolk and Norfolk. The former upholds his reputation for successful management. He left alms in Brome, Oakley, Stuston, Thrandeston, Yaxley and several other towns; houses in Brome, Frense, and 'elsewhere'; a wardship, procured from the duke of Norfolk, for his younger son Richard; an archdeaconry, procured from the bishop of Norwich, for another younger son William; portions of 300 marks for his two unmarried daughters; an annuity for a brother; and various other legacies.[1] The bailiff's accounts[2] suggest that he had doubled his rent roll in five or six years. Table 13 shows that in 1540 various properties were bringing in a clear annual income of about £115 a year. But at least one of these, Monks Brome, had been very recently bought from the duke of Norfolk to enlarge the ancestral seat at Linghall, and a new purchase was made in each of the next four years. Though two of the original manors disappear for reasons unknown, and Palgrave drops out because it was assigned to a member of the family, the net income was over £200 a year by the time Sir John died. This improvement was almost wholly due to the purchases: rents and farms were more or less stable and profits of court, as we have learnt to expect of this period, were not yielding more than a few shillings;[3] except in the case of Tytteshall, where there was a large windfall. To this basic £214 a year, some increment would have to be added. The will refers to property in London and Middlesex, which is not shown here, nor do we know anything about the profits of farming at Brome, where northern cattle were fattened for the market and there was also a foldcourse for sheep. Though a firm estimate is out of the question, we may guess that the heir was worth not less than £300 a year—a very respectable patrimony for a squire in 1544.

The son of Prince Edward's steward might have expected some favour under Henry VIII and Edward VI, but it may be that his Catholic connexions interfered with his prospects when Protestantism got the upper hand. But if he gained no important office before Mary's accession, at least he was not prevented from making his mark. He was knighted in 1548; commended for his bravery in Kett's rebellion; and

---

[1] Copinger *op. cit.* III, 240.

[2] Iveagh MSS. (Cornwallis Box 7). I owe my access to the Iveagh MSS. to the courtesy of the earl of Iveagh, Elveden Hall, Suffolk, and of Mrs Alan Rowe, The Elms, Ixworth, Suffolk.

[3] The accounts record three categories of income: (1) 'rents and farms'—i.e. rents of assise and leases, combined in one figure; (2) profits of court; (3) occasional sales. Rents and farms remained unchanged, except in the case of Linghall, the seat, where they rose from £5 to £11—but we do not know whether this was due to alterations in the amount of land leased, or to improved rents. Profits of court in the first and last years were as follows: Linghall—1s. 6d., null; Brome Priory—12s. 3d., 11s. 6d.; Hoo Hall—1s. 6d., 1s. 6d.; Thrandeston—2s., 15s. 11d.; Tytteshall—null, £16. The windfall at Titteshall may have been due to the accession of a new lord.

made sheriff of Norfolk and Suffolk in 1553. It was this position, which he held during the critical days after Edward VI's death when Mary was appealing for support in his own territory, that gave him his chance. He began the new reign as one of the men who had saved the throne for the Queen; and ended it, as the inscription on his tomb reminds us, 'in especial grace and trust of his mistress at her untimely death'.

TABLE 13. *Deliveries from Cornwallis manors, 1540–45 (to nearest £)*

	1540	1541	1542	1543	1544	1545
Linghall in Brome	5	9	4	2	8	6
Brome Priory	15	16	16	16	15	15
Hoo Hall in Oakley	22	22	20	21	20	14
Titteshall	23	24	22	26	25	25
	—	—	45	57	44	48
	—	—	—	25	21	26
Thrandeston	21	21	20	21	22	23
Stuston	9	9	7	7	8	8
Facons in Stuston	—	—	—	—	2	4
Hyxley	12	10	—	—	—	—
Rowton	—	13	—	—	—	—
Mellis	8	8	8	8	8	8
Palgrave	—	6	6	—	—	—
Thorpe Abbotts	—	—	—	—	26	28
Purchased lands	—	—	9	9	9	9
TOTAL INCOME	115	138	157	192	208	214

Our impression of his income during these peak years falls into two parts. In the first place, we can see clearly enough what he was drawing from his lands in the three years between Michaelmas 1555 and Michaelmas 1558, though this was before he had fully sampled the royal bounty. Secondly, we can see how much spending money passed through the hands of his household officers in 1559 and 1560. This is certainly not the whole picture, but it is instructive enough.

The basic revenue from land can be seen in a receiver's account of 1555-6,[1] which shows the gross receipts for that year, and in two nearly identical bailiffs' accounts for 1556-8.[2] The income has more than

[1] Iveagh MSS. (Cornwallis, Box 3). [2] *Ibid.* (Cornwallis, Box 8).

doubled since 1544, being £448 in the first of these three years and £443 in the last. It is of interest to see how this has been done. Three factors were responsible, in unequal proportions.

(1) New acquisitions, both of whole manors and of additions to old manors;
(2) moderate improvements in leasehold income;
(3) a bigger income from copyhold fines.

No doubt there was also a fourth—the additions which must have come through the marriage of Sir Thomas with Anne Jernegan—but as these have not been isolated, they are included among (1).

The new acquisitions were undoubtedly responsible for the greater part of the increased income. In each of the parishes of Brome, Oakley, Thrandeston, and Palgrave, where the family was already established, a new manor had been added: Davillers in Brome (£7 p.a.), Beauchamps in Oakley (£6 p.a.), Ampners in Thrandeston (£2 p.a.), and the manor of Palgrave (£22 p.a.—without including profits of court). This last was clearly a gift from the Queen. The patent of 27 March 1555 shows that it was given to Sir Thomas, and his wife Anne, one of the gentlewomen of the Privy Chamber, without fine or fee.[1] Another grant of the same date was the reversion of the manor of Westhorpe, with its two parks, 'in consideration of his services to the queen, especially in the rebellion against her at Framlingham, Suffolk, and for the labour and costs he has been at in the town of Calais, of which he is now Treasurer'.[2] Westhorpe brought in £33 in 1558, but £8 had to be paid as an annuity to the individual whose present interest had been bought out. Over and above these acquisitions, we also find Kilverstone (£21 p.a.), Barnes (£31 p.a.), a tenement in Needham Market (£3 p.a.), and a mass of lands and tenements in Basildon, Essex (£64 p.a.).

About £180 p.a. of new income can be attributed to these additions, but if we knew the whole history of the older properties, which were producing a bigger leasehold income, we might find that new purchases had also played their part there. A prosperous landowner was constantly

[1] *Patent Rolls* (Philip and Mary), 1554–5, p. 67.   [2] *Ibid.*

adding to his properties as opportunity offered, and each new 'quillet' or farm would swell the leasehold income. It is probable, however, that some moderate improvement of rents had occurred, as leases fell in. There is enough detail in the accounts to show that Tivetshall manor and Thorpe Cornwallis were still under their old leases in 1558: but Monk's Brome had gone up from about £15 to £18, Hoo Hall had doubled its value from £20 to £40, Facons (Stuston) produced £10 a year compared with the previous £4, and there are suggestions that the rents in Thrandeston, and the rents of the purchased lands in Tivetshall, had improved by a few pounds. Precision is impossible, but we may guess that £30–£50 a year of new income was coming from this source.

The balance of the new income came from two quarters. Linghall, which Sir Thomas was not occupying while he divided his time between houses in Calais and London, was rented to his receiver, Edward Golding, who paid £33 p.a. for the rent of the site, park, demesnes, and foldcourse. Secondly, the fines paid by copyhold tenants for the transfer of lands in the manorial court had shot up. This 'casualty' was not expected to yield more than a few shillings in Sir John's lifetime, but in 1558 Palgrave produced £21 in fines and Thorpe Cornwallis £14.

We must remember that this £450 p.a. (if we may use round figures) was no more than the minimum income from land, for it included only rents, in the broadest sense of the word, and the proceeds of a few wood sales. Profits were being made out of the sale of stock, even though Linghall was let, and there were doubtless other opportunities of making money out of the estates. But there is only one piece of evidence which takes us outside the realm of guesswork, and that is the receiver's account for 1555–6, which gives us not only the rents from lands but also 'all other sums received from 6 March 1555 to 22 May 1557'. This account merits a little study for it seems clear that the accountant, Edward Golding (the farmer of Linghall), was looking after Sir Thomas's English revenues while his lord was absent abroad. There is enough detail to show receipts from the sale of stock, modest payments under bonds, sums due in London and Lynn, and small annuities; but the Calais establishment, and almost everything which would be regarded as the profits and expenses of office, was someone else's responsibility. The main heads of the 'charge' are as follows:

	£
Arrears in ready money	about 400
Arrears in debts	about 235
Rents for one whole year ending Michaelmas, 1556	448
Annuities for the same period	16
Other receipts for two years March 1555–May 1557	592

Possibly the arrears of £635 were nothing more than the unpaid net income of the previous year; but at all events we can make a good guess at the income of the current year. The sum of £448, £16, and £296 (one half of the 'other receipts') is £760, and certain deductions would have to be made for allowances, and for the fact that thirteen months, not twelve, were involved in the 'other receipts'. So it looks as though Edward Golding was raising a net income of about £650–£700 out of the estate business and a few other miscellaneous sources. The distinction which this implies between a minimum and a maximum income from land is in line with what we shall find later among the fuller records of the Elizabethan period.

When we leave the relatively safe ground of bailiffs' and receivers' accounts and try to form some estimate of the income from office, we are almost completely at sea. All we can say of the Calais appointment is that very large sums of money passed through his hands. He returned to England two months before the town was lost to the French, and while still comptroller of Queen Mary's household, was required to account for the last five quarters of his treasurership (namely, from 6 October 1556 to 7 January 1558).[1] From the charge side of this account, we see that arrears and income (including several thousand pounds worth of grain and provisions) came to £45,000. From the discharge side, we learn that while Thomas, lord Wentworth, the deputy, claimed £880 for his establishment, and Sir Anthony Aucher, the chief marshall, was allowed £300 for his, Sir Thomas, as treasurer,

---

[1] Iveagh MSS. (Cornwallis, Box 1).

claimed £1793. The bulk of this sum was for an establishment of personnel, and £350 was demanded in miscellaneous fees. After all allowances and payments had been claimed, £7160 remained in debts, of which £3776 was owed by the purchasers of grain and victuals, and £3485 by the Treasurer. He was given a complete exoneration for this official debt, under a royal warrant of 4 April 1558, on the grounds that this amount was in the hands of his deputies when the French captured the town. Later gossip had it that Sir Thomas built his house at Brome out of the profits of Calais (with a malicious innuendo that he sold it to the enemy), but we have no means of knowing either his gross receipts, his expenses, or his net gains.

We are not, however, without some knowledge of his total income in his last years of office. The series of household accounts, which records the annual expenditure of his officers during the reign of Elizabeth, begins on 1 December 1557.[1] It therefore includes one whole year while he was still comptroller of the household (he vacated the office, after the funeral of Queen Mary, on 14 December 1558) and another year in which payments were still flowing in. By examining the amounts which the spending officers were given, and the sources from which they came, we can try to discover the *least* that Sir Thomas was worth at this peak period. The first account period was not a year, but ten months; that is from 1 December 1557 to Michaelmas 1558. Three officers were involved, Lady Cornwallis, Simon Goldingham the steward, and Edward Golding the receiver. Lady Cornwallis, who was responsible among other things for the household in London, started the period with £689, of which £329 came from her husband's foreign receipts, £34 from a John Tyndale of Calais, and £326 from Simon Goldingham. Goldingham started with £1703, which he had received partly from his master, and partly from sources which were not specified but no doubt included the receiver, Edward Golding; and we learn that it was from this sum that he paid his mistress her £326. Golding's charge is not shown, but we can see that before handing over his revenues he had spent £237. From all this we may infer that at the very least the receipts for this ten-month period were £689 plus £1377

---

[1] Iveagh MSS. (Cornwallis, Box 1).

plus £237; that is, £2303. The income was certainly bigger than this, for apart from the possibility that Golding was left with money on his hands, there is the probability that Sir Thomas himself had more money than is shown.

In the second account period—a full year running from Michaelmas 1558 to Michaelmas 1559—Lady Cornwallis got £540, of which £427 came direct from her husband and Goldingham contributed less than £100; Goldingham started with £1985; Golding spent £122; and an overseer of works, Richard Barwick, was given £60 from the foreign account over and above sums paid to him out of the budgets of Lady Cornwallis and Simon Goldingham. A little simple arithmetic suggests that the income for this year—which is subject to the same reserves about assets of the lord withheld from this system—was at least £2494.

From this level of affluence, which reflected the profits of office, the descent was rapid. With Sir Thomas retired to the country, and his expenditure funnelled through one officer, the cash defrayed was £1061 in 1560, £1533 in 1561, £1138 in 1562, and £1212 in 1563.

We can throw little light on where the peak earnings of 1558-9 came from. He must have had several stewardships,[1] but the indirect income from such sources, as distinct from the few pounds in fixed fees, is unknown. He must have had wardships, like the grant of the three daughters and co-heirs of William Halse, which was made out in his own name on 12 July 1557,[2] but we do not know how many or what they were worth. In the last month of the Queen's life he secured some more favours. On 14 October 1558 he got a licence to buy and export 600 sacks of wool a year for the next six years;[3] a privilege which he could sell to some merchant. Two weeks later he was given 'in consideration of his service', the manor of Wilton in Cleveland, Yorkshire, for a yearly rent of £50.[4] Here we are on firm ground, for we know that this was equivalent to a clear grant of about £180 a year, independent of large windfalls which would accrue from fines and other sources; so the minimum revenue from land has been raised to at

---

[1] One was the stewardship of Colnes Hundred, Suffolk, at £4 a year. *Patent Rolls* (Philip and Mary), 1557–8, p. 256.

[2] *Ibid.* p. 209.   [3] *Ibid.* p. 455.   [4] *Ibid.* p. 418.

least £630. Finally, five days before he surrendered his office, he got another reward—a thirty-year lease of the manor of Walsham, Suffolk, for a fee-farm of £47. 15*s*., which he promptly sold to Sir Nicholas Bacon, the new Lord Keeper.[1] How the rest of his income was made up, in fees, gratuities and profits, is one of those mysteries of office-holding which no estate-study of the sixteenth century has so far solved.

We now enter the best documented phase of Sir Thomas's career—the thirty years from 1565 to 1595, for which twenty receiver's accounts have survived.[2] With these we return once again to the minimum income from land. The deliveries from each manor have been abstracted (to the nearest pound) in Table 14. The total for each year may vary by a pound or two from the addition of these approximations, as it is the accountant's figure (the sum of the charge, to the nearest pound) which has been adopted. The allowances, deducted to produce the net income, are those which may be regarded as a legitimate cost, as distinct from payments such as fees and gratuities, or amounts spent on the purchase of land, which were also included in the receiver's allowances. They come to just under £60, and are made up of a fee farm for the manor of Wilton (about £50), certain tenths to the crown (about £5), and a fee for respect of homage (about £3). The accounts are uncomplicated by any arrearages, as the accountant paid up in full each year; or by any other item of income, except an annuity of £10 a year from the bishopric of Ely, which has been omitted from this table.

If we turn first to the total net income, we find that in 1565 it is at least £200 a year larger than it had been in 1558—about £650 a year compared with about £450—but this was almost entirely due to the addition of Wilton, which produced its first revenues in 1559. From £650 it climbs to £1000 a year in 1573, and then fluctuates between £1000 and £1200 for the next twenty years, with the exception of three windfall years (1579, £1264; 1593, £2297; 1594, £1518). In reality, the course of improvement was probably smoother than this, for 1573 (£1005) and 1574 (£1100) were also windfall years and the

[1] *Ibid.* p. 400.
[2] Nineteen of these accounts are in Iveagh MSS. (Cornwallis, Box 8); the account for 1575 is in the Folger Library, MS. 1553.1.

TABLE 14. Income from Cornwallis manors, 1558–95 (£)

	1558	1565	1567	1570	1573	1574	1575	1577	1579	1582	1583	1584	1586	1587	1590	1591	1592	1593	1594	1595
SUFFOLK																				
Ling Hall (Brome)	43	15	20	21	80	69	69	99	55	84	83	83	85	38	38	52	53	54	52	61
Brome Priory	18	8	7	17	25	23	23	24	25	23	23	23	8	7	8	16	22	16	16	18
Davillers (Brome)	7	5	5	8	7	12	23	12	12	12	13	13	6	6	8	6	7	7	7	7
Hoo Hall (Oakley)	23	34	38	80	71	68	94	109	115	102	99	120	112	123	137	137	137	143	153	155
Beauchamps (Oakley)	6	5	2	2	2	2	1	1	1	2	1	1	1	3	2	3	3	3	2	3
Purchased lands (Brome and Oakley)	—	27	53	—	—	—	—	—	—	—	—	—	—	—	—	—	—	—	—	—
Woodhall (Thrandeston)	24	19	20	21	31	26	49	26	26	31	27	29	34	30	32	33	30	30	31	31
Ampners (Thrandeston)	2	2	2	2	2	2	3	2	2	2	2	3	3	2	2	3	2	2	2	2
Facons (Stuston)	10	10	5	4	5	6	3	9	11	9	11	4	8	9	8	10	11	11	12	10
Boylands (Stuston)	3	12	7	7	7	6	5	7	10	8	7	6	7	7	18	9	8	10	8	10
Palgrave	44	69	47	23	34	50	34	28	27	29	40	27	27	37	32	40	49	31	40	31
Fenhouse (Palgrave)	—	—	—	—	—	—	—	—	10s.	10s.	10s.	10s.	10s.	10s.	10s.	10s.	10s.	10s.	10s.	10s.
Westhorpe	19	52	47	52	49	39	109	70	132	117	119	138	220	185	192	192	198	191	193	185
NORFOLK																				
Tivetshall	34	34	99	91	118	94	103	112	104	137	133	144	138	140	230	148	141	154	149	135
Purchased lands in Tivetshall	53	70	76	80	108	90	93	90	98	88	91	87	90	90	93	103	105	96	109	106
Thorpe Cornwallis	38	43	44	41	47	61	51	44	148	70	51	57	57	110	48	46	48	47	55	44
Kilverstone	21	27	22	29	30	28	24	—	—	—	—	—	—	—	—	—	—	—	—	—
Boylands (Scole)	—	7	15	8	8	8	11	8	8	11	9	9	16	13	10	13	13	8	21	15
A manor (Scole)	—	—	—	—	—	—	—	—	—	—	—	6	7	7	28	—	8	10	23	7
Chapel in the Fields (Norwich)	—	—	—	—	6s.	6s.	7s.	6s.	6s.	6s.	6s.	6s.	6s.	6s.	6s.	6s.	6s.	6s.	6s.	6s.
ESSEX																				
Basildon	64	41	67	67	69	66	68	77	102	137	70	71	75	76	121	121	116	116	121	121
YORKSHIRE																				
Wilton	—	177	185	228	364	500	479	284	438	242	246	244	238	234	235	237	243	1418	579	301
TOTAL	443	658	763	780	1062	1158	1233	1004	1322	1105	1027	1067	1134	1117	1346	1174	1191	2355	1576	1241
Allowances	—	—	—	50	57	58	60	59	58	58	58	58	58	58	58	58	58	58	58	58
NET INCOME	443	658	763	730	1005	1100	1173	945	1264	1047	969	1009	1076	1059	1188	1116	1133	2297	1518	1183

basic values may not have reached £1000 a year until about 1580. But to bring out the factors behind these figures we must go into a little more detail.

First, we notice that the enlargement of the estate almost ceased after Sir Thomas retired from office. It did not quite do so. A little manor in Scole seems to have been bought between his retirement and the beginning of these accounts. About £1000 was put out between 1565 and 1570 to buy lands in Brome and Oakley. £400 was spent in 1571 to buy Chapel in the Fields, a town house in Norwich. And another £500–£700 was spent in small sums, annually, over the next twenty years. But all this cannot have added as much as £100 p.a. to the annual income. Territorial expansion by leaps and bounds had stopped.

Second, though these are inflationary times, some rents do not expand. On inspection, these turn out to be manors with very little or no leasehold income, so the most obvious means of raising the income was missing. Davillers (Brome) had only a £2 lease in 1558; Beauchamps (Oakley) a 12s. lease; Ampners (Thrandeston) and Boylands (Stuston) no leases at all. Facons (Stuston) had about £7 in leases in 1558, but there seems to have been very little improvement in the next forty years. Occasional fluctuations were produced by copyhold fines, as in the case of Boylands (Stuston) in 1590, when £18 was taken instead of the usual £9 or £10; but none of this was of much account. They were all small manors (tiny Fenhouse in Palgrave with its 9s. rent being the smallest) and they were doubtless bought for their position.

It was a very different story with the bigger manors. If we look at Wilton, the last minute pay-off for Sir Thomas's services, we see at once how entry fines and wood sales could swell the rental under inflationary conditions. Wilton was rented under beneficial leases where the normal rents changed very little in these thirty years. The apparent jump in income between 1567 and 1570 (£185–£228) is an illusion: the difference is due to the fact that before 1570 the fee-farm of £50 was deducted at source while afterwards the deduction was made among the receiver's allowances. During the whole period, Wilton produced about £230–£240 a year; but there were half a dozen exceptional years when the yield was vastly greater. In five cases (1573–5 and 1593–4) the bulge was due to entry fines, and if we had more accounts for these two periods when twenty-one-year leases were being renewed, we would probably see the impact of fines on them. The account of 1575 informs us that some £850 was charged for the renewals of that time and collected over a period of five years (1573, £131; 1574, £248; 1575, £245; 1576, £176; 1577, £44). When the same leases came up for renewal twenty years later, over £1500 was collected in the two years, 1593–4, with more instalments to follow, no doubt, in the accounts which are missing after 1594. Another windfall was due to the demolition of Wilton Castle, which only a decade before had been described as a serviceable fortress. Today it is a grassy mound, Sir Thomas having made £189 in 1579 from the sale of lead, iron, timber, and stone. By the time we get to the end of the period, wood sales in themselves could produce an exceptional year: £23 in 1574 and £19 in 1579, they made £245 in 1595.

The beneficial lease, with its low and relatively stable rent combined with as high an entry fine as the demand would bear, seems not to have been common in East Anglia. Fines were a regular feature of copyhold tenure, but so far as leasehold land was concerned, the normal practice in the sixteenth century was not to take fines but to raise rents. This process can be seen at work in several of the manors. When the manor of Tivetshall was obtained from the crown in 1542, the demesnes were being farmed by John Oldham for £15 a year. They were still under the same lease in 1565, with a total net income ranging between £35 and £50, as profits of court and wood sales rose and fell. But a glance at the table shows an income of about £100 a year between 1567 and 1579, and £130–£150 from 1579 to 1595. Similarly, the 'purchased lands' in Tivetshall brought in about £50 a year in the 1540's, about £70 in the 1560's, and just under £100 in the last twenty years. Hoo Hall in Oakley, one of the oldest of the Cornwallis manors, was another property where the income steadily increased. New purchases may have played their part in raising the income from about £20 in the 1540's to £70–£80 in the early 1570's; but no purchase of any consequence occurred after that date, when the income doubled once again. The leasehold land at Hoo Hall greatly exceeded the copyhold land; much of it was let on a year-to-year basis, and there was also a warren and a mill. This was a well balanced, flexible property where there were no impediments to a rising income.

At Woodhall, in Thrandeston, there is only a 50 per cent increase in the *total* net income between 1545 and 1595—from about £20 a year to £30. But here the opposite conditions prevailed. The total charge, in 1558, had been made up of about £20 in rents of assise and £4 in leases. Only the latter was flexible.

A final illustration of rising rents may be taken from Basildon, Essex. This substantial property, with its demesnes, marshlands, urban tenements and woods had been bringing in over £60 a year in 1558. The receipts of 1565 were abnormally low and those of 1579 and 1582 abnormally high. Perhaps as late as 1588 there had only been a £10 increase in the total income, but then something substantial must have fallen in, for in the 1590's the receipts are about £120 a year, which is double what they had been.

In still other cases the income increases (independently of 'windfalls', of which we shall speak shortly), but we cannot be so positive about the cause. The financial history of the estate on which the lord has his seat is often excessively complicated, because of his absences, his building or parking activities, and the allowances which he makes to his eldest son. The effect of all this is to produce wide fluctuations in the leasehold income, which are only completely intelligible where there are detailed bailiffs' accounts. The income which reached the receiver, which is what we principally rely on here, is not the best index. With this caveat, we may note that Linghall, the Cornwallis seat, produced on the average about £5 a year when it was occupied by the lord in the 1540's. This no doubt represented little more than the rents of assise of copyholders and freeholders, which were just under £5. When it was rented in 1558, the net income was £43, made up as follows: rents of assise £5, farm of house, park, etc. £20, farm of foldcourse £14, other farms £8, less £4 in allowances. Between 1573 and 1586 it was again in effect rented as Sir Thomas was charging his eldest son, William, £43 a year for the lease of the house, park, cattle and foldcourse, and collecting from all sources about £80 a year. The increase seems to have been chiefly due not to the family lease, which the son enjoyed on much the same terms as the receiver had done when Sir Thomas was treasurer of Calais, but to an improvement in 'other farms'. When Sir Thomas resumed control of the house and foldcourse in 1587, the other sources, which had produced about £10 a year in 1558, brought in £38 in 1587 and £61 in 1595. It must be repeated, however, that without more knowledge about the administration of the seat, the whole of this improvement cannot be safely attributed to inflated rents.

Westhorpe is another case of an expanding income at the cause of which we can only guess. When the reversion was given to Sir Thomas in 1555, the patent referred to a manor with two parks (a Great Park and a Little Park). We know that in 1558 rents of assise were £16, the farm of the demesnes £11, wood sales £4, and profits of court £2 = £33. Between 1565 and 1574 rents and farms had risen to about £40 a year and the 'casualties' might bring in another £10 = about £50. In 1574 the receipts were £70, the regular income having jumped to about £54. Then, in the following year, a Westhorpe 'New Park' takes its place beside the old Westhorpe, with an income of £62 p.a., making a total for the next four years of £120–£140. In 1587 the two Westhorpes were combined and the receipts for the rest of the period average about £190. Just how these results were achieved is a mystery. We can only say that there is nothing here, or in the records of expenditures, to suggest that new purchases, or any large outlay of money, was involved.

A final word may be said about the role of 'casualties'. Only two instances have been found of fines being charged on leases in the East Anglian manors; in 1582, a fine of £66 was paid by the lessee of a tenement in Basildon, Essex, to obtain the renewal of the lease for twenty-one years, and in 1584 £9 was paid in Bacton for another twenty-one-year lease. Otherwise, the only fines recorded here are those imposed on the transfer of copyhold tenements. This was the commonest source of variation in the manorial income and the amounts could represent substantial additions to the rental. The case of Palgrave has already been mentioned. As exhibited in the bailiff's account of

1558, the manor consisted only of rents of assise, valued at £22, and the fines for that year were £21. In 1565 the receipts of £69 included £49 in profits of court, and the comparable figures for 1574, 1583 and 1587 were £50 (£28 profits), £40 (£19 profits), £37 (£28 profits). Amercements for small offences as well as fines on land were included among profits of court, but we can safely assume that fines were responsible for all but a tiny fraction of these sums. The other recurrent casualty was the income from woods, nowhere large on these manors, if we except £89 raised at Tivetshall in 1590 and £245 at Wilton in 1595, but often producing additions of £20–£30.

Such was Sir Thomas's basic income from land in the thirty-five years of country life which followed his retirement from court. From a level of £600–£700 a year his income rose to a level of £1100–£1200 a year, without the injection of more than about £1500 into the purchase of income-producing property. Like many other large land-lords, he owned several small properties which failed to keep pace with the rise in values, and at least one big one (Wilton) which did so by a gigantic harvest of fines every twenty years. But there were others, like Hoo Hall, Westhorpe, Basildon, and Tivetshall, where a relatively smooth improvement was possible. On the whole, he cannot be said to have been unlucky in the structure of his empire, whether we look at properties like Linghall and Hoo Hall which had been in the family since the early fifteenth century, or at his father's purchases, during the dissolution of the monasteries, or at the rewards which he got for his own services. They all bore up well. Indeed a survey such as this may suggest that the difficulties of 'mere' landlords in a period of inflation have been exaggerated, but of that we can better judge when we turn to the other side of the story—the cost of living.

Meanwhile, we must remember our earlier distinction: that even in these years this was not the whole income. The accounts of expenditures kept by his household officials show that during the 1560's the sums entrusted to them each year exceeded the minimum revenue from lands by anything from £100 to £400. Thus in 1564–6, when the landed income was about £650, the steward accounted for £985, £994 and £972; and in 1567–9, when the landed income was about

£750, the amounts were £858, £1162 and £887. At this point these records of gross receipts stop, but there is an isolated account for 1582 which shows us where the increment, or at least some large part of it, came from. In that year, the receiver, William Crowe, added to his own duties those which had previously been discharged by Lady Cornwallis, who had just died. In other words, he became responsible for all receipts and disbursements, and his ordinary receiver's account was followed by another in which he accounted for ready money received and spent in 1582. Here he not only credited himself with the cash produced by his own receiver's account, but also with the arrearages and income of the 'foreign account'. The arrearages were £184 and the income, described as 'Forreyne Receptes...as corne, cattle, slaughte skynnes and suche other thinges as appearethe particulerlye by the booke thereof' came to £234. No detailed foreign receipts seem to have survived among the Cornwallis records, but they obviously included the profits of husbandry as well as windfalls like marriage portions and legacies. If our figures are typical, the additional income which a landed gentleman derived from these sources was not trifling.

EXPENDITURE (1557–97)

We have already commented[1] on the curious chance that has let us know so much about the income of the gentry and so little about their expenditure. This poverty of information gives a distinct interest to the unbroken series of Cornwallis accounts which cover the forty years from 1557 to 1597. These are annual summaries, varying a little in their title and organisation, but sufficiently described by the form of words which becomes standard—'A Briefe Collection of all the Accompts for the Charges and Expenses of Sir Thomas Cornwaleys, knight, for one whole year'.[2] During the first two years while Sir Thomas, the office-holder, was maintaining several establishments, the centralisation of expenditure under the supervision of one official was out of the question, so there are several separate accounts, followed by a summary statement. Thus in 1557–8 there are four accounts as follows: (1) Lady

---

[1] See chapter I, pp. 10–12.   [2] Iveagh MSS. (Cornwallis, Box 1).

Cornwallis's expenditures; (2) the expenditures of Simon Goldingham, steward of household; (3) the expenditures of Edward Golding, receiver—that is, the allowances claimed in his account. These three accounts were all organised on charge-discharge principles, but (4) was simply a summary of the expenses in the previous three. This consolidated statement comes as close as we can get to a complete record of annual expenditure—the unknown element being such receipts and disbursements as the lord chose to withdraw from this system.

In the second year, 1558-9, the same principles held, but six accounts were shown. In addition to the accounts of Lady Cornwallis, Simon Goldingham, and Edward Golding, there were separate accounts for Richard Carman, bailiff of husbandry, and Richard Barwyke, a surveyor of works; all of which were summarised in the final statement.

The loss of Sir Thomas's office in November 1559 obviously simplified the problems of management. We hear no more of his house near the Charterhouse in London, or of Copthall, Essex, where he had also resided. He retired to East Anglia and divided his time between his seat at Brome and a town house in Norwich. The expenses were consolidated in a single annual statement except on rare occasions when a prolonged absence from home made a separate account necessary. For about a decade (1560-70) the annual statement was drawn up by the steward, Simon Goldingham, or his successor, Edmund Oldham: but then Lady Cornwallis carried the responsibility until her death in 1581. During this period, they seem to have dispensed with the services of an officer who was solely the 'steward of household'; we find one man combining the jobs of steward and receiver, and after Lady Cornwallis's death, it was this officer who took over.

An interesting feature of the accounts is the amount of descriptive detail which appears in the explanatory note at the head of each annual statement. These always cover the movements of the lord, which included his annual migrations from Brome to Norwich, his examinations by the council and imprisonments for recusancy, his visits to London 'to shewe himselfe to the Quenes Majesty' or to attend to litigation. Each year of 'the building of Brome' is formally recorded and there are many details about the building activities there and at

Norwich. We hear of the 5000 deaths in that city which forced the family to spend the whole of 1579 at Brome; about the accident which killed John Cornwallis, Sir Thomas's grandson, in 1594, when a block and tackle which was being used to build a new gallery fell on his head; and about the matrimonial difficulties of Sir Thomas's daughter Mary, whose husband, the young earl of Bath, refused to cohabit with her.

The system of book-keeping was superficially simple. Quarterly journal books were kept in which expenditures were noted as they occurred. At the end of each quarter the items contained in these were then sorted and classified under different heads in a book known as 'the book of titles'. The four books of titles furnished the material for the greater part of the annual summary and had to be produced at the audit. Occasionally some matters might be withdrawn from the journals and books of titles and made the subject of separate accounts: it was common for 'foreign' accounts, building accounts, and husbandry records to be kept separately. Finally, the expenditures of the receiver were embodied in the annual summary and the 'allowance' section of his account was also produced at the audit.

Table 15 has been compiled out of these records,[1] and at the risk of exhausting the reader we must examine the categories used by the accountants. The 'foreign expenses' were the most diverse of all. They included taxes (subsidies), the ransom of a captain captured at Calais (£316), marriage portions and trousseaux, executors' expenses, the redemption of an annuity, an unsuccessful experiment in coal mining,[2] travel expenses, building expenses, and money laid out in the purchase of land. Presumably there was some correspondence between the

[1] The following adjustments have been made in compiling this table: (1) the nearest pound has been adopted for each item and the totals embody these approximations. (2) The annuity of the heir, William Cornwallis, which was shown among these expenses, in the original manuscripts, from 1572–5, was then deducted at source in the bailiffs' accounts for 1575–97. Here we have followed the earlier procedure and carried it in this table throughout. (3) The receiver's payment of £58 a year in out-rents, which is shown in these manuscripts, does not appear in this table, as it was treated as a manorial expense in Table 14, and deducted there (see Table 14, Allowances). (4) Where the receiver's expenses, in these manuscripts, are not broken down, it has been necessary to make arbitrary assignments, on the analogy of other years, between expenditure on fees and expenditure on the purchase of land. It is thought that none of these approximations involves serious distortions.

[2] '£39. 11s. 11d. expended in digginge to fynde a cole myne at the said Sir Thomas his mannor of Wilton in Yorkshiere, but not yet brought to effect (1592).'

expenses charged on this account and its income, but the latter must have bulged with the arrival of 'casualties' like marriage portions, and the former rose above the £100–£250 level to peaks like £640, £730 and £1203. Nor were all the items peculiar to this category. A journey or a marriage might be charged on the foreign account, but it might also be made the subject of a separate account. Land, which was sometimes paid for out of the foreign account, was also bought by the receiver and charged among his allowances. Annuities were even more the receiver's responsibility, but that does not stop a mother from giving her son an instalment out of the foreign account. Convenience was as persuasive then as now.

This ambiguity extends to building. If Sir Thomas kept a 'Building Book' for his houses at Brome and Norwich, similar to those in which neighbouring lords had recorded the cost of building Hengrave or Redgrave, it has not survived. Building expenses were charged in the foreign account and we have only been able to make it a separate category in Table 15 because the accountant frequently describes a particular work, and its cost, in his headnote. Even so, we have often had to bracket foreign expenses and building expenses, because works are mentioned without any note of their cost, and it is probable that in years where no reference was made to building, small expenses were being carried in the foreign account. This makes it impossible to determine the exact amount spent on this typical activity, but the main outlines are clear enough.

Sir Thomas had no sooner retired from court than he started to build. In his first year at Brome he spent about £30 rebuilding the aisle of the parish church where his ancestors were buried and where, in due time, he would give thought and money to his own tomb. But meanwhile it was an earthly habitation that interested him. A man no sooner succeeded in the sixteenth century than he built himself a new home—and more than one if he could afford it. Sir Thomas had just seen his income halved, but he could still look forward to the margin which enabled the gentry to build their houses out of income over a period of eight, ten, or a dozen years. In 1562 the author of the headnote reported that Sir Thomas, his lady and the children were living at

TABLE 15. *Cornwallis expenditures, 1558–97* (£)

First decade

	1558	1559	1560	1561	1562	1563	1564	1565	1566	1567	1568	1569*
Minimum income†	—	c. 2300	—	—	—	—	—	658	—	763	—	—
Spending money‡	c. 2300	c. 2500	1061	1553	1138	1212	985	1054	972	1055	1162	887
Foreign expense	119	640	138	730	171	82	80	67	44	45	70	67
Building	48	—	28	—	133	244	126	135	155	58	36	94
Fresh achates	231	160	59	44	38	36	8	11	13	16	22	23
Gross provisions	101	257	352	291	331	395	426	304	244	211	387	204
Household necessaries	313	122	42	47	55	24	17	21	22	35	93	26
Husbandry necessaries	—	36	47	53	60	37	42	43	47	63	49	19
Apparel	381	160	106	141	41	30	24	21	24	20	39	42
Gifts and rewards	174	125	92	47	52	69	56	111	153	116	117	116
Wages	82	86	{100	127	152	180	171	204	207	234	223	227}
Fees and annuities	63	60		—	—	—	—	—	—	—	—	
Heir's annuity	—	—	—	—	—	—	—	60	—	197	—	—
Land purchase	42	—	—	—	—	—	—	—	—	—	—	—
Miscellaneous	116	—	—	—	—	—	—	—	—	—	—	—
Stable	122	78	61	54	22	20	4	19	16	1	22	2
TOTAL EXPENSES	1792	1724	1025	1534	1055	1117	954	996	925	996	1058	820

* Sir Thomas was away from home 10 October 1569–10 August 1570.

† Minimum income: this is the income shown in Table 14 (with the addition of a £10 annuity from the bishopric of Ely which started in 1573). In other words, it is the income from manors, after the deduction of bailiffs' costs and out-rents paid by receivers. For the use of the terms minimum income from land, see pp. 147, 148, 157–8 above.

‡ Spending money: this is the ready cash entrusted to the spending officers. The figures are taken from the expense accounts, where they are given there. In two cases, 1565 and 1567, the amounts known to have been spent on the purchase of land by the receiver, before he handed his revenues over (£60 and £197, respectively), have been added. The spending money in 1566 and 1569 is low, because prior payments for the purchase of land were also being made by the receiver in these years, but in the absence of his accounts we do not know the size of the instalments; about £300, not recorded in our table, may have been spent in this way between 1565 and 1570. The spending money for 1582 has been obtained from an account which shows that in that year the receiver's revenues yielded £910 and the foreign account £234, i.e. £1144. Where the figures allow us to compare the spending money with the actual expenses, we find that there was a small surplus at the end of the year, which was returned to the lord.

Second decade

	1570	1571*	1572	1573	1574	1575	1576	1577	1578	1579§
Minimum income	730	—	—	1015	1110	—	—	955	—	1274
Spending money	—	—	—	—	—	188	—	—	—	—
Foreign expenses	641	280	245	438	470	266	232	280	274	198
Building	—	—	—	—	—	—	120	—	—	—
Fresh achates	7	63	73	67	73	43	66	60	73	86
Gross provisions	122	242	251	238	258	248	218	251	367	222
Household necessaries	3	89	24	58	45	56	40	38	42	33
Husbandry necessaries	29	44	—	1	—	—	—	5	3	10
Apparel	83	85	103	92	94	48	55	76	84	78
Gifts and rewards	108	95	51	44	69	50	68	43	77	95
Wages	123	110	59	82	79	81	76	88	122	92
Fees and annuities	—	180	56	55	69	146	76	146	146	67
Heir's annuity	—	—	136	136	128	160	160	160	160	230
Land purchase	360	473	45	20	40	24	20	11	—	—
Miscellaneous	{305† 183‡}	—	—	—	—	—	—	—	54	—
Stable	11	8	14	26	16	14	28	30	37	63
TOTAL EXPENSES	1975	1669	1057	1257	1341	1324	1159	1188	1439	1174

* This account is for 1¼ years, that is, October 1570–31 December 1571. Previously, they have run from Michaelmas to Michaelmas; hereafter from 31 December.

† Expenses of Sir Thomas's journey.

‡ Marriage expenses of William Cornwallis, the heir.

§ Sir Thomas away from home 25 April–4 June and 17 October–31 December.

Cornwallis expenditures, 1558–97 (£) (cont.)

Third decade

	1580*	1581†	1582‡	1583	1584	1585	1586	1587§	1588‖	1589¶
Minimum income	—	—	1057	979	1119	—	1086	1069	—	—
Spending money	—	—	1144	—	—	—	—	—	—	—
Foreign expense	271	1203	⎱283	243	⎱223	—	243	200	⎱220	⎱219
Building	—	—	⎰	—	⎰	—	—	65	⎰	⎰
Fresh achates	24	97	115	170	152	—	186	157	113	164
Gross provisions	190	234	205	187	194	—	282	113	110	149
Household necessaries	35	48	26	35	27	—	56	66	64	11
Husbandry necessaries	12	5	—	—	—	—	—	—	—	—
Apparel	14	84	31	17	49	—	38	56	45	25
Gifts and rewards	43	147	39	84	39	—	31	69	244	56
Wages	98	145	77	77	75	—	84	69	61	47
Fees and annuities	128	146	58	58	58	—	50	50	50	50
Heir's annuity	220	220	205	210	231	—	227	192	190	190
Land purchase	—	8	60	11	—	—	5	3	15	17
Miscellaneous	—	—	—	—	—	—	—	—	—	—
Stable	14	16	19	16	15	—	41	56	12	39
TOTAL EXPENSES	1049	2353	1118	1108	1063	—	1243	1096	1124	967

* Sir Thomas stays in London till May. Accountant notes that his expenses are not included as not yet made up. He returned again in October.
† In London till Lady Day. Another short visit in November.
‡ Journey to the west country, April–July.
§ In London, July–September and again in October, where he was detained for the rest of the year.
‖ Confined in London all year.
¶ Allowed to return to Brome in May.

164

Fourth decade

	1590	1591	1592	1593	1594	1595	1596	1597
Minimum income	1198	—	1143	2307	1528	1193	—	—
Foreign expense	⎰ 279	276	⎰ 248	179	165	214	238	207
Building	⎱	150	⎱	42	120	244	91	121
Fresh achates	109	202	137	114	119	112	111	—
Gross provisions	150	25	235	334	232	379	628	482
Household necessaries	41	—	138	50	40	21	49	171
Husbandry necessaries	—	—	—	—	—	—	10	9
Apparel	26	36	32	37	38	20	37	28
Gifts and rewards	173	56	59	58	61	73	66	103
Wages	76	49	80	76	53	106	68	124
Fees and annuities	45	46	45	40	35	35	35	35
Heir's annuity	220	192	206	201	216	195	190	190
Land purchase	132	—	—	100	77	13	—	24
Miscellaneous	—	—	—	—	—	1000*	200†	—
Stable	9	16	22	11	22	16	10	10
TOTAL EXPENSES	1260	1048	1202	1242	1178	2428	1733	1504

* Marriage portion for Francis Cornwallis, the eldest daughter of the heir.   † Marriage portion for another relative, Elizabeth Cornwallis.

Thrandeston as this was 'the fyrst yeare of the buylding at Brome'. Seven more accounts were dated in the same way before the reconstruction was finished and in these eight years about £1000 had been spent. But Sir Thomas no sooner had a country house to his liking than he began to plan a town house in Norwich. A certain Miles Spencer, dean of the college called Chapel in the Fields, had arranged its dissolution with considerable adroitness and kept the mansion house for himself.[1] In time his nephew, William Yaxley,[2] inherited it, and it was this young man, a fellow Catholic, who sold the house to Sir Thomas for £400 in 1571. In 1573, after a lull in building which had lasted no more than three years, extensive work began at Norwich—a new gallery, a porter's lodge, a new hall, a better kitchen, a court paved with Purbeck stone. This lasted six years, and though the costs are not so easily separated from the foreign account, some £700 or £800 must have been involved. After another brief lull (1579–82), building began again in 1583 and continued in some form or another until 1596—a new wing at Norwich; towers, courtyards, a park, a mill, a granary, a dairy and a costly gallery at Brome; a tomb inside the church and alms houses outside. The costs are again a matter for guesswork, but the gallery alone (where the accident occurred which killed the little grandson) consumed all the sums recorded for 1593–6 (£497) and these did not include wages of masons and carpenters that were paid by the eldest son, Sir William Cornwallis. All in all, the building activities of this retired courtier must have consumed close to £3000.

It has sometimes been thought that the expense of these mansions which sprang up all over Tudor England lay less in their fabrics than in the costly furnishings that went into them; a great deal of brickwork, carpentry, or masonry could be commissioned, when labour was cheap and much of the materials came off the estate, for the price of a service of plate or a set of hangings. But this is hardly borne out by these accounts. 'Nesessaries of household', which must have included expendable objects as well as permanent furnishings, seem to have con-

---

[1] B. Cozens-Hardy, 'The Norwich Chapelfield House Estate', *Norfolk Archaeology*, XXVII, 352.
[2] This is the same William Yaxley who was the ward of Sir Nicholas Bacon; see chapter II, pp. 84–8.

tained few extravagant items. We know that the £171 spent in this category in 1597 included over £100 on the furnishings of one room, the Chapel Chamber—£61 for a bed and other pieces and £44 for hangings. But a glance at the series shows that the annual expense was usually somewhere between £20 and £50 and that it had soared above this on only three occasions since Sir Thomas left office—£93 in 1568, £89 in 1571 and £138 in 1592. Of course the possibilities that Sir Thomas had equipped himself before he left office, or that he was using the foreign account for this purpose, cannot be excluded; but so far as these forty years are concerned, it seems unlikely that heavy expenses would have been left unnoticed.

'Fresh achates' was the title given to fresh meat, game and dairy produce. The expense varied with the scale of hospitality and the resources of the estate. In the two years of court life, with which the accounts begin, it was £231 and £160. In the first year of country life it fell to £59, and dwindled away to £20 or less throughout the 1560's. In the 1570's it was usually about £60 or £70, and in the next two decades above £100. Doubtless the improvement of Sir Thomas's income which began in the 1570's, and the rising agricultural prices, lay behind the average annual expenditure for each decade—£27, £61, £131, £122.

The other category concerned with food was 'Gross provisions'— but it also involved much more. It was the most expensive of all the 'titles', if we except the foreign account: £314 p.a. in the 1560's, £241 p.a. in the 1570's; £185 p.a. in the 1580's; £330 p.a. in the 1590's. It included not only food for men and beasts, such as wine, sugar, spices, herrings and oats; and household provisions like salt, soap and coal, but also livestock and seed-corn. Substantial sums could be paid for a hundred wethers at 7s. each or a score of Cheshire steers at 30s. This is the only category which became more expensive when Sir Thomas left office; and it is easy to imagine that his country house and farms (which had been largely let) needed restocking. But as we are unable to get behind the gross figures, we can throw very little light on either the heavy expenditures of the 1560's or the steady decline which was only reversed in the 1590's.

'Necessaries of husbandry' is one of the less satisfactory 'titles' because of the doubt of what it involved and the suspicion that there must have been a change of procedure. As expenses on buildings and stock were carried elsewhere, the title must have been designed for implements and equipment, but some labour charges have also been included in our table. Thus, the £63 spent in 1567 was made up of £17 described as 'charges in husbandry' and £46 of wages to hedgers, ditchers, mowers, threshers and shearers. Similarly, the bulk of the expense in 1560, 1561, 1568 and 1569 was made up of costs which had been recorded in the quarterly books of workmen's wages. But it will be seen from the dwindling amounts after 1571 that this item must have been removed; and from 1581 virtually nothing was recorded. There is no such mystery about 'Stable charges', which included the purchase of stock as well as saddlery. These stood at peaks of £122 and £78 in the last two years of office, and then fell away until trifles like £4, £1 and £2 were recorded between 1564 and 1569. Judging by annual averages within the four decades of country life, this proved a modest and fairly stable item; £22 a year in the 1560's, £25 in the 1570's and 1580's, £14 in the 1590's. A recusant who found it prudent to stay at home could no doubt economise on his stable.

The title 'Wages' covered the fixed sums paid quarterly to household servants and retainers, as distinct from the 'workmen's wages', already mentioned, which applied to husbandry and odd jobs on the estate. A book of titles for the summer quarter of 1562 shows sums running from 20s. for the steward down to 4s. for the underlings; with most of the servants getting between 6s. and 10s. These quarterly wages may have risen a little in the next thirty years, but probably not very much: there were other ways of tempering the winds of inflation to a household servant. The annual payroll was just over £80 in the last two years of office, but the form of the account in the 1560's prevents us from separating wages from fees and annuities. It averaged £91 p.a. in the 1570's, £81 p.a. in the 1580's, £79 p.a. in the 1590's. The decrease may not have involved any reduction in staffs—sons with housekeeping budgets at Brome and Norwich could have been carrying some of the expenses. Some fifty servants may have been involved. At least Sir Thomas's son-in-law, Sir Thomas Kytson, with a similar payroll at nearby Hengrave, was carrying fifty individuals in the 1570's for about £90 a year.[1]

Though the opportunities of servants varied, it would be safe to assume that their wages were the smallest part of their earnings. Quite apart from bed, board and livery, they lived in a society where high and low expected to be tipped. Ninety per cent of the 'gifts and rewards' were tips—a steady stream of small sums, seldom exceeding a pound, bestowed on cooks, musicians, tradesmen, household officers, wayside poor, and all the innumerable people 'bringing presents and taking pains'. The other 10 per cent might have to be dignified with another name, if only because they were given to equals or superiors. They also cost more. The wedding gift, the New Year's gift, the gift to kinsmen and allies, the ring of gold set with a very fair turquoise (£13. 6s. 8d.) and twelve yards of satin (£7. 4s. 0d.) which were given to my lord bishop after being billeted on him, and the three and a half yards of taffeta (£2) which his chaplain expected.

Where details have survived, these gifts and rewards are often disappointing to the student in search of the gratuity which oiled the wheels of influence. They are so unpolitical. The Kytson accounts, which are detailed, contain almost nothing of unusual interest until the record of small tips, during a visit to London in 1575, is interrupted by the item—'Payed by th'andes of my master as so moch by him gyven in reward to the Ladye Suzan Bourchier for her travell [? travail] in suinge out my master his license to travell LXVI^{li} XII^s iii^d. In reward to Doctor Julio for the lyke matter X^{li}.'[2] Sir Thomas Cornwallis also visited London, in search of favours, and the two peaks reached by 'Gifts and rewards' in 1581 (£147) and 1588 (£244—during a period of preventive arrest) no doubt reflected his needs. But if the analogy with the Kytson accounts holds, it is unlikely that these records contained much beyond the ebb and flow of routine gratuities. On the average, this item was just a little heavier than the wage bill—£93 p.a. in the 1560's, £70 in the 1570's, £84 in the 1580's, £81 in the 1590's.

'Fees and annuities' present certain problems. We see them in 1558–9,

---

[1] Hengrave Hall MSS. 82 (3); Cambridge University Library.   [2] *Ibid.*

when they were running at about £60 a year, then for over a decade they were merged with wages. If we assume a fairly stable wage bill, fees and annuities must have risen in these years, and when they were separated again in 1571, the figure was £180. From this date on, the information has to be derived from the receiver's allowances and though these are quite precise in most years, in others the proportion spent on fees and annuities has to be conjectured, on more or less plausible principles, from the gross sum. The series printed in Table 15, is probably a reliable approximation. As an illustration of their scope, the £146 of 1577 was made up as follows: William Deal, for lands sold by him, £10 p.a.; Henry Cornwallis, brother of the lord, £10 p.a.; William Cornwallis, brother of the lord, £10 p.a.; Margaret, relict of Richard Cornwallis, brother of the lord, £20 p.a.; Charles, younger son and Anne his wife, parcel of jointure, £70 p.a.; Mary, younger daughter, for her exhibition, £20 p.a.; John Thurston, lawyer, £1 p.a.; Thomas Whipple, subseneschal of Suffolk, £1 p.a.; John Godfrey, subseneschal of Norfolk, £1 p.a.; James Hunter, £2 p.a.

As the circumstances of the family altered, the amounts fluctuated. The total dropped sharply in 1572 to below £60 because the eldest son was provided for elsewhere. It rose again to £146 in 1575 because the younger son, Charles, was put on this payroll at £70 a year. It stayed at that level (except for a year or two when Charles was paid out of the foreign account) until 1581, when his annuity was redeemed by a capital sum which helped to swell the foreign account of that year. Thereafter, as the last daughter married and older relatives died off, it fell away from £58 to £35.

The decline in this account was, of course, offset by the cost of providing portions for girls and land (or a capital sum) for boys. When Elizabeth Cornwallis married Thomas Kytson, of Hengrave, in 1561, the portion was £600, the trousseau £160, and £11 was distributed in gifts to the household officers at Kenninghall, where the duchess of Norfolk, in whose household Elizabeth had served, presided over the marriage. When Alice Cornwallis married Richard Southwell, of Horsham St Faiths, in 1570, the portion was 1000 marks and the trousseau £83. The marriage of the youngest daughter, Mary, to the earl of Bath in 1578, seems to have been made, and repudiated, so hastily that nothing was properly settled; but there was another generation to come after these girls. In 1595 Francis Cornwallis, eldest daughter of Sir William, the son and heir, was married to Edmund Withipole with a portion of £1000, and in the second last year of the accounts we find another girl, Elizabeth Cornwallis, being helped in her marriage with a gift of £200.

William, the eldest son, married Lucy Nevil, daughter and co-heir of Lord Latimer in 1570 at a cost of £183. The portion paid by the bride's family to Sir Thomas is not known, but the young couple received immediately an allowance of about £130 p.a. which rose to about £160 after five years and to over £200 in less than ten years; at which level it remained. Charles, the younger son, married Anne Nichols, widow, in 1574, and we have seen how they got an annuity of £70, which was charged on 'Fees and annuities'. But the manor of Kylverston, Norfolk, disappeared from the land revenues in the year of the marriage, and we know from Sir Thomas's will that it was assigned for jointure to Charles and Anne. We may assume, therefore, that they also had the benefit of this property, worth about £30 a year in 1574. If Sir William's allowance, and the value of Kylverston, be added to the amounts in 'Fees and annuities', it will be seen that the cost of maintaining dependents might approach £400 in the peak years, independently of any benefits in board and lodging. On the other hand, the portions brought into the family by the brides of William and Charles were a contribution to maintenance. In William's case, the lands assigned for jointure were worth at least £200 a year at the time of the marriage, so it is likely that the portion was somewhere between 1000 marks and £1000.[1]

Of the remaining items in the budget, we have already discussed the comparatively modest expenditure on land. The figures printed under this head in Table 15 are not quite accurate. We can see that of £1000 known to have been spent on land in Brome and Oakley between 1565 and 1570, about £300 is not shown here: and some of the small sums of later years are guesses within the framework of the receiver's

---

[1] It is possible that Lucy's portion took the form of a settlement in land.

allowances. None the less, the general impression of two substantial purchases (the town house, in 1571, being the other) followed by a small annual outlay is probably reliable. 'Apparel', the only other item in Table 15, is unambiguous. It covered the needs of Sir Thomas, his family, and those of his servants who were entitled to livery; and it was one of those expenses which was always inflated by the claims of public life. It was £381 and £160 in the last two years of office. In 1560, when it might have fallen, the new Queen made a progress to Ipswich and it cost Sir Thomas £50, of the £160 spent in that year, to make a suitable appearance. In 1561 it was again high (£141), but for the rest of that decade it averaged only £30 a year. In the 1570's it was £80 a year; in the 1580's £40; in the 1590's £32.

Behind this pattern there no doubt lay the changing circumstances of the family. Children who were grown up, but not yet independent, would increase these charges, and reductions could be expected in later years. However, there were special circumstances like marriages or visits to court which would swell the expense, whatever the time of life. These are not usually shown in this column but elsewhere. Thus the foreign column of 1561 contains £160 spent on Elizabeth's marriage apparel; Alice's trousseau cost £83 in 1570, of which only £33 was carried under 'apparel'; the expenses of William's marriage in the same year, which included £100 for the bride's clothes and £30 for the groom's, formed a separate account; and visits to London, like the one in 1570 when Sir Thomas spent nearly £40 on clothes, were either accounted for separately or charged on the foreign account. As we have no accounts for Sir Thomas's enforced stay in London from 1587 to 1589, the total expense must have been greater than appears here.

Thanks to the explicitness with which the movements of the lord are recorded in the headnotes, we know all the important journeys made by Sir Thomas in these forty years; and a word must be said about each because of the possibility that not all the expenses are shown in these accounts. The first was in the account year, 1569–70, when the arrest of the duke of Norfolk led to a round-up of his clients and associates. An account has survived entitled the whole expenses of Sir Thomas Cornwallis 'in his trouble' as engrossed by Thomas Laughter, the accountant who attended him. Sir Thomas left Brome on 10 October 1569, with a party of six men, and reached the court at Windsor, via Newmarket and St Alban's, on the 12th. There he was first examined 'upon some articles touching the Duke of Norfolk' and being found 'not to be any weye touched with any disloyalty towards his Prince' was then questioned 'upon matier of religion and being found to embrace the Catholique faith nowe termed papistical and refusing to come to the church to communicate in prayer according to the religion and lawes sett fourth and established', he was committed to the custody of Bishop Jewel, at Salisbury, while his lady was ordered to remain at Brome. He was in Salisbury from 29 November to 6 June, when he was transferred to the custody of the dean of Westminster in London. Pardoned in August, he was escorted back to Brome by a party of twenty, which included his wife, his eldest son, his daughter Elizabeth, and her husband Thomas Kytson.

This absence of ten months cost £305. Riding charges and diet were £128, foreign charges £7, necessaries £15, apparel £38, stable £26, alms £3, physic £3, gifts and rewards £84. Riding charges, apparel and gifts were the things which made such journeys expensive. In 1558, a year of office in which movement was inescapable, riding charges had been £116. Then, as now, people saved a great deal of money by staying at home. The gifts and rewards—£9 at Windsor, £56 at Salisbury, £12 at London, and a few pounds *en route*—have been preserved in detail. They contain nothing above £2, apart from the ring and satin for the bishop. Of course Sir Thomas may have had a private slush fund, but if so, we know nothing of it.

Unfortunately, we have no itemised expenses for the later journeys. Some of them can be roughly appraised, others are immeasurable. The brief trip of 1574—'made one voyage to the court aboute June to shewe himselfe to the Quenes Majestie'—was probably carried in the heavy foreign expenses of that year. Another, of the same type, in May 1578, may also have been taken up in these accounts. But we cannot feel so sure about the visits of 1579–81, occasioned by the deplorable mess which followed Mary Cornwallis' precipitate marriage at Hengrave with the young earl of Bath, a student at Cambridge. The way in which the marriage was engineered by Sir Thomas Kytson and then frustrated by the intervention of the boy's mother can be read elsewhere.[1] From the point of view of Sir Thomas Cornwallis, it meant that his daughter had been deserted within two weeks of the wedding, with very painful consequences for both his pride and his pocket. This took him to London in the spring of 1579 and again in October, where he stayed until the following May. The headnote informs us that Sir Thomas carried his grievance to the council, and that a committee under Burleigh's chairmanship urged the earl to accept his wife, only to hear him refuse. It seems likely that the earl, under his mother's Protestant thumb, was pleading disparagement through marriage with a Catholic; but whatever the rivers of feeling, personal and religious, may have been, Sir Thomas found himself with no alternatives but to swallow his pride or institute suit. He sued—and when the case came before the Court of Arches in the autumn of 1580, that meant another six months in London.

In all, this had involved some fourteen months' absence. When the foreign account was made up at the end of 1581, it reached the gigantic peak of £1203, but we are told that this included the redemption of a £70 annuity (on terms unknown) as well as recent visits to London. If it were not for the complication of the annuity, one might be tempted to think this the whole bill, but it might be safer to assume that it only covered the visit of October 1580–March 1581, and another short visit of November 1581 which had been undertaken on Sir Thomas Kytson's behalf. On this hypothesis, we have no record in these accounts of the visits of 1579–80, with their expensive application to personages like the Lord Treasurer, the Lord Chamberlain, the earl of Leicester, and the bishop of London. One mitigating factor would be the keen sense of responsibility felt by Sir Thomas Kytson, a very wealthy man, for the situation he had helped to create. His town house in the Augustine Friary was put at the disposal of his father-in-law and sister-in-law for the greater part of their stay and there were doubtless other offers. But this may still have left Cornwallis a few hundreds out of pocket.

A journey of 1582 (Easter to July), undertaken at the desire of Sir Thomas Kytson, need not detain us. It involved a brief visit to London

---

[1] John Gage, *History and Antiquities of Hengrave* (London, 1822), p. 187.

to complete the marriage settlement of Kytson's daughter, who had married Lord Cavendish; a leisurely inspection of Kytson's lands in Devonshire; and a visit to the redoubtable countess of Shrewsbury, the bride's mother-in-law, in Derbyshire, which had to be abandoned when the news reached them that Lady Cavendish had died in childbirth. In so far as the expenses of this rural tour were not taken up in these accounts, or met by Kytson, they would not be excessive. But the final absences of 1587–9 were another matter.

The story of what happened to one prominent but pacific recusant in the great crisis of Elizabeth's reign may be told by the accountant.

1587...about the beginninge of July he made a voiage to London to obteyne favor in payment of the mulct A penall statute imposeth upon Recusantes. But the same Sir Thomas his case beyinge commytted to the order of the Lord Treasurer and Mr Secretarie, and not sortynge to such spedie ende as was hoped of, the said Sir Thomas retourned to his house in Brome VII September, and havyinge disposed of his household affayres, made another jorney to London in the ende of October for fynishinge his said suyte, but the same still procedyinge A very slowe corse, and the said Sir Thomas makeyng his abode at Mr Taylor's house in Wodestreet he was with other Catholikes by Direction from the Lords of Her Majesties privie Counsell convented before the Archbishop of Canterbury and other Comyssioners for matters Ecclesiasticall and on St Andrewes even commytted to the custodie of the Bishopp of London, where remayninge onlie one day and two nightes he was by favor of my Lord Treasurer upon suyte to hym made, removed to the house of Mr Blague at Lambith.

1588...Sir Thomas remayninge at commandement...at Mr Blagues house...and fallynge ther verie sicke, was (in Februarie) by favor obtayned of the said Lords licensed to remove to Sir Thomas Kytsons house in London, wher he remayned till the beginninge of September; when he had licens to be at the house of Mr Taylor...with libertie to be about the citie as farr as Higate.

1589...Sir Thomas remayned at commandement...untill the beginninge of May when he obteyned favor of the Lords of Counsell to go downe to his house in Brome for three monethes before the expiracion wherof he had Further favor to make his abode wher he should best like, untill he should agayne be called for.

This was no martyrdom, and there is no evidence in these records that Sir Thomas's recusancy cost him anything by way of 'mulct'. But we can hardly believe that the expense of a twenty-month absence is included here, even if several of them were spent in bed at his son-in-law's. The only item which seems to reflect a stay in London, with suitable attention by Sir Thomas's servants to all the begging faces at court, is the size of 'Gifts and rewards' in 1588—£244.

This uncertainty about the inclusion of all the travel expenses is the only serious doubt we need feel about the comprehensiveness of these accounts—and it may well mean a difference of £1000. Litigation is never singled out for special mention, except in the case of Mary Cornwallis and the earl of Bath, but the folds of the foreign account were ample enough to look after ordinary legal expenses. The same may be felt about other omissions, like additions to plate and jewellery. In so far as a set of official accounts ever told the whole truth about the expenses of a magnate, these bear the stamp of reliability.

What are we to think of these expenditures when we view them as a whole? Three simple observations seem in place. First, in view of the difficulties some ex-courtiers are thought to have experienced in ad-justing their scale of living to a reduced income, Sir Thomas seems to have managed well enough. The spending money available in the first year of retirement was less than half what it had been in the two years before, and every category save one was drastically reduced. Eco-nomies in entertainment, furnishings, dress, transport, travel and wages seem to have cut the bill from about £1800 a year to £1000.

Secondly, it seems as if the emergencies which had to be faced were all manageable. Abnormally expensive years were bound to be experienced by people in Sir Thomas's position. Daughters needed portions; friends got into trouble; some offices and some law suits were costly; strategically placed lands came on the market which had to be bought. As the surpluses of the gentry were usually locked away in land, and no provision had yet been made for long-term borrowing, these corners could only be turned by a limited number of expedients. A windfall might be wrung out of the estates: a good marriage con-tracted; a creditor might be persuaded to accept an annuity instead of a capital sum; and short-term loans could be raised from business men or friends. In the last resort—which was the routine expedient—it would soon be necessary to meet the debts by selling land, unless friends were unusually good-natured, or something else turned up. The best proof of the solidity of Sir Thomas's position is that he sold no land. This fact justifies us in assuming that his borrowings, of which we have almost no record, were never damaging. Moreover, a glance at the tables shows us how some of the corners were turned. The first abnormal year was 1570, when the expenses soared to double the usual level under the pressure of two marriages and an expensive journey But there must have been method in the double marriage, for one could be made to pay for the other. If over £500 had to be paid out this year, as part of Alice's portion of 1000 marks, William's bride could bring in that and more. On top of everything else, £360 was found in this year to wipe out the payments still due on a land purchase of 1565. It *might* have been borrowed to meet an inflexible deadline, but as the creditors were his own servants, that seems unlikely. We would guess that it came out of Lucy's portion. Similarly, 1595 and 1596 were expensive years, chiefly because £1200 had to be spent in marriage portions; but the huge fines from Wilton in 1593-4 had more than made this possible. We are not so well informed about the only other year when the expenses were twice as high as usual (1581—£2353) or about one or two years, like 1571, when he may not have had in cash the £400 that he needed to buy Chapel in the Fields. But if he had to borrow, his son-in-law, Sir Thomas Kytson, could have tided him over.

Finally, we return to a question already raised when we looked at his income—whether the difficulties of landlords in a period of inflation have not been exaggerated. Though the irregular incidence of 'casualties' makes the calculation hard it would seem that during the years when Sir Thomas was a 'mere' landlord (1560-95) his income from rents had improved by not less than 80 per cent—a figure which is in line with what we know to have happened to other estates in the same locality during the same years. The money income from the sales of meat and grain, which formed a substantial part of the 'foreign receipts' must have followed a similar, or sharper curve, though we know nothing about its details. Meanwhile, what about costs of living? Here again there are difficulties of presentation, but if we look first at the average annual expense within each of the four decades, the recorded figures are £1048, £1358, £1236 and £1449. The first would be £30–£40 higher if we added the extra amount known to have been spent on land; and it is also pertinent to notice that no emergency year occurred in this decade, whereas there is one peak, of roughly the same size, in each of the other three. The third figure might be a £100 higher, if we decided to add £1000 for unrecorded travel. But without making any of these corrections, which tend to flatten the curve, it is still flatter than the graph of income. A study of the individual items within the annual budget reinforces this impression. The cost of finding a portion for a daughter rose from £600 to £1000, and there are two categories, 'Fresh achates' and 'Gross provisions' in which the effects of the inflation in agricultural prices can be either seen or surmised.[1] But no such trend appears in 'Wages' or its companion 'Gifts and rewards': in 'Apparel', 'Household necessaries', or 'Stable charges'. Fees and annuities, being fixed charges, are not affected, though it may be that the allowances granted to the two sons are higher than would have been thought necessary in an earlier generation. On the whole, the predominant impression left by these expenses, treacherous as some of their features are, is surprise that they should show so much stability. Nor was this a man who was compromising his standards to preserve his solvency. He built himself two houses, did all that was expected for his children, preserved his credit among the first families of the county, and had himself interred in a suitably impressive tomb. As a 'mere' landlord, the retired courtier seems to have managed well enough.

[1] It is possible that a close scrutiny of the Brome Household Accounts would reveal more stability than might be expected. A superficial comparison of the sums spent weekly on fresh food and ~ross provisions between 1571–5 (Cornwallis, Box 3) and 1594–1605 (Cornwallis, Box 4) suggests that the heavier expenses of the later period were due less to inflation than to fluctuations between a household of about twenty individuals and one of forty to fifty.

CHAPTER V

THE MERE LANDLORD

IT has been usual to suppose that the inflation of our century presented serious problems for rural landlords, and some of the most striking theories of the controversialists have been based on this supposition. On the face of it, the reverse might have been expected. Why should landlords suffer when agricultural prices were rising? The explanation relied, in varying degrees, on three arguments; one was the supposed inelasticity of tenures—such as the long lease or the inflexible copyhold—which prevented the landlord from getting his fair share of rising values; another was the unbusinesslike psychology which was thought to have deterred some of them from making the necessary adjustments; the third was the belief that the rise in the cost of living may have exceeded the scope of improvement on all but the best managed estates. Under the influence of these conceptions, two notions were widely propagated. One was the image of the 'improving landlord', the standard-bearer of the modern capitalist spirit, who was able to prosper, while so many others declined, through his adoption of rational techniques. On this view, the inflation was a profoundly disturbing challenge which could only be overcome by novel remedies.[1] The other was the image of the impoverished 'mere landlord' whose only sure escape from his problems was an injection of income from the money made out of office, or business. On this view, the inflation was equally disturbing, but the remedies often lay outside the scope of land management.[2]

More recently, there has been a certain tendency to undermine the basic premise of landlord embarrassments without going the length of overthrowing it. A study of certain Northamptonshire families led

---

[1] This view is everywhere discernible in the writings of Professor R. H. Tawney. It was also an integral feature of the Marxist and quasi-Marxist theories of the 'bourgeois revolution'.

[2] H. R. Trevor-Roper, 'The Gentry 1540–1640', *op. cit.*

one cautious authority to insist that it was at least necessary to suspend judgement about the scope of agricultural profits; these families seemed to have enjoyed substantial increases in their agricultural income; some others could be shown to have founded a fortune out of land, and many more might be shown to have improved fortunes which had been founded by other means. Nevertheless, there was too little evidence to allow us to rule out the possibility that others suffered from a lag between rising income and rising expenses, or from holdings which did not permit particular kinds of farming.[1] Another reviewer, generalising from the gleanings of scattered estate-studies, was somewhat bolder. What impressed him was the way in which attention had been distracted by fat 'court gentry' and famished 'country gentry' from a solid mass of prosperous landlords who seemed to have thrived on rising values from at least the 1580's, and who formed the backbone of the parliamentary leadership in the civil wars. But this was more an impression of wealth than a demonstration, and it was still supposed that the secret of prosperity might have something to do with special resources and skills—though perhaps the skills were not novel at all, but strictly traditional.[2]

Here again, as we rub our eyes in the midst of this conflict of theories, the problem is to find the kind of evidence that may help to resolve it. The commentator on the Northamptonshire studies, already quoted, pointed out that 'without information about annual income for a long succession of years' it was difficult to be positive about the history of a single family; and that the work under review, in spite of its merits, did not contain such information. We have been luckier. We have already seen something of the rise in values on Bacon and Cornwallis manors, and we now return to the subject for a more thorough inspection. We shall begin with a glance at sheep-farming. This is the animal which is supposed to have turned sand into gold—but how much gold?

---

[1] H. J. Habakkuk in M. E. Finch, *Five Northamptonshire Families, 1540–1640* (1956), pp. xiv–xv.

[2] J. H. Hexter, 'Storm over the Gentry', *Encounter* (May 1958), p. 28.

The Mere Landlord

THE PROFITS OF SHEEP-FARMING[1]

The qualities of the old Norfolk sheep were preserved from oblivion by observant admirers just as the age of Bakewell was setting a term to its immeasurable days. Its face and feet were black, its chine thin, its legs equal to the distance it had to travel for its food, its constitution to the strains of being densely penned at night. Its flesh, though meagre to the point of comedy by modern standards, was greatly admired for its flavour. Its fleece, though a bare pound and a half in weight and not the best of its kind in its day, never lacked buyers either at home or abroad. And its dung turned a waste into an arable field. The observers who recalled its centuries of useful existence, though no sentimentalists, were sufficiently moved to plead for a suspended sentence when the judgement of a scientific age was first poised above it. They wondered if a breed adapted by the ages to its environment was not too good a treasure to be lightly cast aside.[2]

Hundreds, and sometimes thousands, of these sheep were kept in every village of the champion country. A few of them might belong to little men—the husbandman with a dozen, the shepherd with a few score which he was allowed to feed for nothing as part of his perquisites. But generally speaking, sheep-farming was the business of big men. It was the thriving yeoman who could afford to farm a manor, and still more the lords who were exploiting the privileges of the foldcourse[3] on their own account, that dominated the scene. Sometimes

[1] This section was written before the appearance of Dr K. J. Allison's instructive article, 'Flock Management in the Sixteenth and Seventeenth Centuries', *Econ. Hist. Rev.* 2nd series, XI, no. 1 (1958). Dr Allison studied the accounts of some ten flockmasters, including most of mine, with the important exception of the long, continuous series for Culford (1590–1618). His observations about flock management usually coincide with my own and he has furnished additional details on some aspects. I have somewhat more to say about prices and profits, thanks largely to the Culford accounts.

[2] William Marshall, *The Rural Economy of Norfolk* (1787), I, 362–7; Nathaniel Kent, *General View of the Agriculture of the County of Norfolk* (1796), pp. 102–5; J. Dugdale, *The New British Traveller* (1819), III, 592; IV, 268. Marshall commented on two varieties, the larger and commoner, weighing 15–25 lb. a quarter, and the smaller heath-sheep around Brandon and Methwold, of 10–15 lb. Dugdale said the fleece was 'nearly two pounds'. Nathaniel Bacon informed his father in 1572 that 120 sheep (that is, the long hundred) were expected to yield 12 stones.

[3] For the pastoral customs of the region, see K. J. Allison, 'The Sheep and Corn Husbandry of Norfolk', *British Agricultural History Rev.* vol. v, and my comment, 'The East Anglian Foldcourse: Some Queries', in vol. VI (1958) of the same journal.

these monopolistic patterns were resented. A lurid glare lights up the anger stirred by the big flocks in the days of Kett's rebellion. But in ordinary times they seem to have been accepted philosophically enough. The sheep accounts tell us how big the flocks were. These records are organised on the usual medieval principle of 'charge and discharge'. The account begins with a 'remainder figure', comparable to the arrearages in a financial account which shows the stock as the shepherd's charge at the end of the previous account year. It then records the additions by natural increase, purchases, or transfers, and the losses by disease, sales and other transfers, until the new remainder is reached. Doubtless the sheep encounter the vicissitudes of their lot in suspiciously round numbers, but this is the best evidence we have. A few examples may be given to show the scale on which the leading families of Norfolk were keeping sheep in the first half of the sixteenth century. In each case the figure is the 'remainder figure'; it would presumably be much bigger before the midsummer sales and smaller (though not as small as tradition says) after the reduction of stock for winter.[1]

The first accounts are those of the Fermours, of whose wealth in their day there is still a very beautiful reminder in the house at East Barsham. The record[2] is for a single year, 1520–1, and it deals—as often happens—with stock only. The records of purchases, sales, costs and profits, which some head reeve must have kept, are lost. Sir William Fermour was keeping sheep on twenty-five different grounds, each of which is accounted for. Some of the flocks were on his own foldcourses in the Barsham area, or on those rented from Hempton priory or from Ponte-fract College, Yorkshire (which owned manors in Taterford, Taterset

---

[1] It is usually impossible to find out from a sheep account how many were slaughtered at Martinmas, as the accounts were made up after Michaelmas and the slaughters, or sales, are not usually distinguished by date. Some particulars in the records of the Stiffkey flocks, which are too detailed to be mentioned here, have suggested to the author that the difficulties of keeping stock through the winter have been exaggerated.

[2] Norwich City Library MSS., 1583, xiii. The sites, and approximate remainder figures, are as follows: East Barsham, 1000; ? (torn MS.), 1120; Bayfield, 1517; Houghton, 368; Hocham, 13; Fakenham, 826; Irmingland, 626; Titleshall Burland, 230; Titleshall Warte, 944; Newton, 898; Taterford, 1118; Waterden, 1042; Billingford, 131; Saham, 677; Titleshall Newhall, 683; Barwick, 741; West Barsham, 34; Toftrees, 719; Hempton, 100; Thorpland, 480; Skulthorpe, 560; Sherneborne, 1026; Taterset, 1351; Causton, 31; Cromer, 860. Dr Allison gives a total of 15,568, which was apparently derived from twenty of these twenty-five flocks.

and Skulthorpe). One flock was at Houghton, where Edward Walpole accounted for it. Others were as far away as Causton and Cromer. The inter-manorial transfers were obviously complex, but there is too little evidence to disentangle them. Altogether, the Fermour shepherds were charged with over 17,000 sheep at Michaelmas. When Sir William died childless in 1557 he left 'to the pore men's boxe, of every town, where I have a flock of shepe going, 10 shillings'. It is interesting to recall that his brother Thomas, whose son was the heir, had been killed at Rising Chace in 1549 by the embattled peasants.[1]

The Townshends had a place in farming annals before they were linked with turnips. They stood for inter-manorial sheep-farming around East Rainham. The accounts at hand are for four years only, and they deal with only a portion of the flocks; but they include marketing details and a calculation of profits as well as the movements of stock.[2] They are the records of Thomas Townshend, who had been entrusted by his father, Sir Roger, with four flocks at the end of 1544; a wether flock at East Rainham, two breeding-flocks at Kipton and Barn (?), and a hogg flock at South Creake; amounting in all to 3000 sheep. But he altered the whole layout in the first year and increased its total by a third. One of the ewe flocks was sold off to a Norfolk breeder, while the other, at Kipton, was doubled. The flock at East Rainham was doubled and another flock of the same composition (480 wethers, 120 wether hoggs, 120 rams and riggs) was started at Shereford. Only at South Creake was the Michaelmas figure of the previous year un-altered—1200 hoggs and young wethers. The new total of 3960 was maintained through 1546 and 1547 and then pushed up again in 1548—to 4200—by more expansion at Kipton.

This was on the eve of Kett's rebellion. Just after it, we have a record of the flocks of Sir Richard Southwell, no mere landlord but the heir to a great fortune made at court and himself a prosperous courtier. He was an officer in the Court of Augmentations about the same time that Nicholas Bacon got his job there, but he had already been sheriff of

---

[1] Blomefield, *op. cit.* VII, 56.
[2] I owe my introduction to these manuscript accounts, which are in the Library of the London School of Economics, to Mr R. J. Hammond's M.A. (London) thesis. My figures for the Townshend flocks agree with Dr Allison's.

The Wealth of the Gentry, 1540–1660

Norfolk at the age of thirty in 1534–5. An account of 1550–1 shows that he was keeping over 13,000 sheep on fourteen different foldcourses.[1] A statute of 1533[2] had referred to 'covetous sheep-farmers' in the kingdom with as many as 24,000 sheep. How covetous they were is an open question, but there were obviously several Norfolk families with flocks between 10,000 and 20,000. If there is any truth in Walter Rye's story[3] that Sir Christopher Heydon used to give a Christmas dinner to thirty master shepherds at Baconsthorpe, he was certainly among them.

The same statute attempted to make 2000 (i.e. 2400, if we convert the long hundred) sheep a legal maximum,[4] and something like this was a common size for the home farms of leading gentry, who owned two or three courses in the neighbourhood of their seats. Culford, in West Suffolk, had been a sheep farm of this size for many generations under the abbots of Bury St Edmund's. A fragmentary account of 7 William Cratfield, abbot, suggests that it was as big then as it ever became; there were over 2000 sheep in the care of three shepherds.[5] At the dissolution, a branch of the Bacon family took a fifty-year lease of the property, and in 1586 it was bought by Sir Nicholas Bacon, of Redgrave, the eldest son of the Lord Keeper, who built himself a second seat there. This was the only one of his sheep-manors which he farmed himself, and the records have been luckily preserved among his bailiffs' accounts. Another, somewhat smaller, example of the same type was managed by Nathaniel Bacon, the second son, at Stiffkey, and eventually inherited by the Townshends. We shall return to both these cases shortly.

The economics of the business were relatively simple. Income was made out of the sale of wool, stock, skins, pasturage and the fold. Of

---

[1] Norwich City Library MSS., NRS 12396, 27 D 1. The sites, and remainder figures, are as follows: Tostes, 1292; Burcham, 724; Rudham, 946; Wesenham, 1549; Walsingham, 1053; Morton, 538; Ringland, 680; Totington Calcroft, 896; Totington Lodge Ground, 1138; Totington South, 812; Burneham ewe flock, 1292; Burneham hogg flock, 612; Horsham St Faiths', 711; Spixwith, 912. Dr Allison's total of 9880 for fourteen flocks in 1550 is far below mine. But his totals of 15,480 for 1544, and 1771 for 1561 (in Southwell accounts I have not seen) are higher.
[2] 25 Henry VIII, c. 13.   [3] Walter Rye, *History of Norfolk*, p. 131.
[4] For exceptions permitted by this statute, and certain informations based upon it, see Allison, *op. cit.* pp. 100–1.
[5] Bacon MSS. (Chicago).

The Mere Landlord

these, wool and stock were of course the biggest earners. When Nathaniel Bacon was asked by his father to find out the weight of a ewe's fleece, around Stiffkey, he replied that twelve stone might be expected from six score ewes[1] (the long hundred was invariably used in sheep arithmetic, and we shall find it convenient to use it here). Such evidence as we have suggests that a fleece of $1\frac{1}{2}$—2 lb. was common. The stock—which was kept much longer than would be thought efficient in the eighteenth century—was culled for sales at various seasons, with lambs, hoggs, young wethers, fat wethers and crones (the old animals) being the usual categories, and the price further depending on whether the sale came before or after the clippings. The other three sources would not bring in more than a few pounds. Tanners would buy the skeepskins and lambs' pelts. Agistment—or 'joysement' as it was locally rendered—brought in about £1 per hundred sheep in the middle of the century, but many flockmasters may have said then what Thomas Townshend reported to his father in the first year of his expansion—'Joysement—null, for the sheep be now all your own'. The hiring of the fold, or 'tath' as it was called, seems to have had a customary price of 1s. 4d. an acre until at least the 1570's.[2]

The initial outlay involved pasturage and stock. The manors, with their foldcourse privileges, provided the feed, but it might be necessary to rent extra closes, or foldcourses. The latter were rented in terms of their capacity, at so much per hundred sheep—thus a course for 1000 wethers at Stody, Norfolk, was rated at 50s. a hundred in 1570. The flocks were either wether flocks or ewe flocks. A breeding-flock, once started, could maintain itself with very little further resort to the market; we shall see how the Bacon flock at Culford was more or less self-sufficient. But the Townshends, who kept both kinds of flock, seem to have depended as much on the market as on their own ewes, and those who had only wether flocks were of course buying hoggs every year. Some idea of the lamb production may be gained from Nathaniel's report that six-score ewes at Stiffkey would rear four score, and with care five score.[3] Away from the sea, they might do a little better.

[1] Bacon MSS. (Garsett House, Norwich).
[2] Ibid.
[3] Ibid.

The Wealth of the Gentry, 1540–1660

The labour costs were light. The shepherd was a member of a hereditary vocation which enjoyed several little perquisites as well as wages.
A good description of his emoluments in 1580 has come down to us
from Saxlingham, a manor belonging to the Cleres. The shepherd
there had £3 a year in wages; a tenement containing one acre in two
pieces; his 'covenanted sheep'—a right to keep 80 in the lord's flock; his
livery; the bell wether's fleece; a marking lamb; furze and brakes for
his fuel; the right to keep three neats and one nag on the heath; and
the 'tath' of two acres per year. For this he paid a rent of 6½d., one hen,
suit of court—and all his lonely labours.[1] A pound or two spent on
extra labour and another pound or two on stores would complete the
bill. Sheep had to be driven from place to place, and teams were hired
annually for the washing and clipping. Hurdles had to be made in the
lord's woods, and carted to the sites, or bought. Tar and pitch—the
sovereign salve for scab—were imported from the Baltic and sold in
barrels to the big flockmasters. There were no other expenses except
hay and straw. A certain toll was taken of wool and stock before it
reached the market. Tithe had its regular claims on lambs and wool.
Some wool was reserved for liveries and other household uses. The
kitchen had its demands, though the stock surrendered there was often
charged to the household account. Gifts of sheep would be made to
friends and relations, and the Townshends, out of their thousands,
annually recorded the bestowal of two sheep on the poor.

How close can we come to discovering the profits which could be
made at different times in our century? Bearing in mind that we start
with almost no information at all, we may be grateful for the scraps
that can be collected. The best documented history is that of the lord
who has his own acres and a flock already started. We can offer three
examples of this: the Townshend flocks around East Rainham during
the four years 1545–8; a Bacon flock at Culford between 1590 and 1618;
and some flocks around Stiffkey in 1625–6 which had once belonged to
the Bacons and then passed to the Townshends. This is meagre enough,
but it is not without its interest.

[1] I owe this reference, which was taken from a Saxlingham Lease Book in his custody, to the
courtesy of Basil Cozens-Hardy, Esq., of Letheringsett, Norfolk.

The Mere Landlord

The earliest of these records is taken from a period which is usually thought to have been at the peak of a long boom. About a decade earlier a statute of 1533 had complained that agricultural prices were almost double what had once been customary. The figures quoted by the legislators were rough generalisations. They said that good fat sheep, that used to be sold for 2s. 4d. or 3s. were fetching anything from 4s. to 6s., and that a stone of wool had gone up, in some counties from 1s. 6d. or 1s. 8d. to 3s. 4d. or 4s., in others from 2s. 4d. or 3s. to 4s. 8d. or 5s. Prices in Norfolk and West Suffolk were probably at the low end of the national scale, but the only information we are able to use as a base is a valuation of a Bury St Edmund's flock which was being leased in 1525.[1] At that date, lambs were being rated at 8d., ewes and rams at 1s. 2d. If we ignore the lambs, and take 1s. 2d. to be the average price of mature sheep, this works out at £7 for the long hundred. A decade later (1536) another Bury lease shows ewes valued at 1s. 6d., or £9 for the long hundred.[2] For the local price of wool, we can go back to 1477–90, when the Townshends were getting 2s. 2d. a stone at the beginning and 2s. 8d. at the end.[3]

In 1545 Thomas Townshend was selling lambs at 1s. 1d., young sheep at 2s. 2d., ewes and fat wethers at 3s. 4d., crones at 1s. 6d., and a stone of wool at 3s. 4d. During the next three years some prices, such as those for lambs and young sheep, changed very little, while fat wethers rose from 3s. 4d. to 4s. 4d., crones from 1s. 6d. to 2s. 6d., and wool, after staying at 3s. 4d. for three years, jumped to 6s. 8d. The last year was the eve of Kett's rebellion, when peasants were complaining bitterly about the price of wool and the Somerset government was trying once again to limit the scale of sheep-farming. Meanwhile, Townshend's expenses hardly altered, with the exception of tar, which cost him 4s. a barrel in 1545 and 8s. in 1548.

Table 16 tabulates his profits. It will be noticed, on the income side, that he credits himself with sales to the kitchen. This item, which does

---

[1] Lease to John Crofts, of West Stow, Suffolk, 21 November, 17 Henry VIII, Add. MSS. 14849, 35*b* (B.M.).
[2] A sixty-year lease of the manor and stock of Ingham Hall, Suffolk Charters, no. 150, Bodleian Library.
[3] Allison, *op. cit.* p. 107.

not change, is made up, annually, of ninety-two wethers at 2s., forty-two lambs at 1s., and the sum of £12. 11s. 8d. 'paid to my lady in recompense of more to be killed this year'. He does not, however, place any money value on gifts of sheep or on the 20 stones of wool kept annually for shepherds' and servants' liveries. On the expense side, he spends about £30 a year in renting extra pasture, and pays his shepherds about £2. 13s. 4d. in addition to the usual perquisites. For the purposes of comparison with the later records, we have worked out the profit on each long hundred sheep. If we ignore the first year, which was one of reorganisation (a flock of 840 ewes was sold off at 3s. 4d. each and almost as many more young ewes bought at 2s.), the range is between £3. 12s. and £5 per long hundred. If we should decide to ignore the rent paid for extra pasture, on the grounds that feeding facilities are being taken for granted, and that no such element appears in the other two accounts that we are going to examine, then the profit per long hundred is improved by a little less than a pound.[1]

Next we can turn to the flocks which the Bacons were keeping at Culford in the generation after 1588, as illustrated by Table 17. This series—of about thirty years—has enough length to give a fair idea of the fluctuations which could be produced by variations in disease, lamb production, and prices. The prices ranged between twice and thrice what the Townshends were getting for their products in 1545–7, but they do so through a series of peaks and troughs, in which the peak of the second decade of the seventeenth century is no higher than the peak of the last decade of the previous century.

Thus, if we look first at wool prices, we find them rising steeply from about 5s. 6d. a stone in 1588–9 to 10s. in 1593, at which level they stayed until 1597, with a peak of 12s. 8d. in 1594. Then came a break. Because of low prices, no wool was sold in 1598 and a two-years' clip had to be unloaded in 1599 at 7s. a stone. None was sold again in 1600, and the sales of 1601 may have sunk to as low a rate as 5s. Then there

---

[1] Dr Allison presents the profits for the flocks of the Southwells, the Bedingfields, and the Townshends at certain points in the period 1544–62, and reduces them to an average profit per sheep. His figures for the Townshend flocks (1545–8) are in line with my own and produce an average of about £4 per long hundred. He offers no guesses for the period after 1562 (*op. cit.* pp. 111–12).

TABLE 16. *Townshend flocks, 1545–8*

	1545	1546	1547	1548
FLOCKS				
Ewes	—	1319	1319	1319
Rams and riggs	—	240	240	240
Wethers	—	1201	1201	1201
Hoggs	—	1200	1200	1200
TOTAL	3000	3960	3960	3960
Lambs	1050	960	970	960

	£ s. d.	£ s. d.	£ s. d.	£ s. d.
SALES				
Ewes	142 0 0	5 0 0	6 13 4	48 0 0
Rams	1 10 0	1 10 0	2 0 0	4 12 0
Wethers	100 0 0	53 0 0	50 13 4	49 9 4
Hoggs	16 0 0	106 13 4	106 13 4	41 18 0
Lambs	5 8 4	6 0 0	6 0 0	10 12 4
TOTAL	264 18 4	172 3 4	172 0 0	154 11 8
Wool	36 13 4	47 0 0	57 0 0	113 13 4
Skins	1 16 9	4 8 9	4 1 3	3 15 3
Kitchen	23 17 8	23 17 8	23 17 8	23 17 8
Miscellaneous	3 4 5	8	1 6	1 2
TOTAL	330 10 6	247 10 5	257 0 5	295 19 1
EXPENSES				
Ewes	79 3 4	10 0 0	10 0 0	16 0 0
Wethers	86 12 0	40 4 8	37 18 0	44 8 8
Hoggs	28 0 0	35 8 0	36 0 0	54 3 4
TOTAL	193 15 4	85 12 8	83 18 0	114 12 0
Pasture	25 5 2	31 5 2	31 5 2	31 5 2
Wages	8 10 0	10 10 0	10 10 0	10 10 0
Miscellaneous	3 19 4	3 18 4	5 11 0	5 14 6
TOTAL	231 9 10	131 6 2	131 4 2	162 1 8
PROFIT	99 0 8	116 4 3	125 16 3	133 17 5
Adjusted profit*	—	119 17 7	129 9 7	165 4 1
Profit per long hundred sheep	—	3 12 0	3 18 0	5 0 0

* Includes credit for 20 stones of wool (at current prices), kept each year for household use; and for 240 extra sheep, part of the profits of the last year. The latter have been valued only at 2s. each—they were probably worth more.

Table 17. *Culford flocks, 1588–1618*

	1588	1589	1590	1592	1593	1594	1595	1596	1597	1598	1599	1600	1601	1602	1603
FLOCKS															
Ewes	—	1633	1520	1538	1520	1398	1405	1390	1413	1437	1422	1436	1432	1311	1300
Rams	—	60	63	61	57	57	50	43	54	56	53	55	54	53	55
Hoggs	—	822	800	800	720	602	620	634	640	663	680	680	680	588	600
TOTAL	—	2515	2383	2399	2297	2057	2075	2067	2107	2156	2155	2171	2166	1952	1955
Lambs	1345	1588	1334	1297	1072	1103	1032	1306	1354	1348	1290	1297	979	997	1176
SALES															
Ewes	11	—	—	47	51	31	14	33	29	41	29	27	31	32	39
Rams	—	—	—	—	1	—	—	1	—	1	—	1	—	2	2
Hoggs	71	—	126	89	70	59	91	137	144	143	123	116	55	86	85
Lambs	36	—	51	48	44	49	44	68	91	77	52	50	27	24	53
TOTAL	118	—	177	184	166	139	149	239	264	262	204	194	113	144	179
Wool	40	39	65	65	62	71	72	71	86	—	104	—	49	61	71
Skins	3	6	3	6	8	6	12	2	3	3	4	3	11	2	4
Pasture	—	—	—	—	—	5	5	5	5	5	5	5	5	5	5
TOTAL	161	—	245	255	241	221	238	317	358	270	317	202	178	212	259
EXPENSES															
Stock	—	—	—	—	2	—	40	16	14	2	14	6	—	8	4
Wages	—	6	6	6	6	6	6	6	6	6	6	6	6	6	6
Stores	—	4	2	4	2	6	3	3	6	4	3	5	3	4	3
TOTAL	—	10	8	10	10	12	49	25	26	12	23	17	9	18	13
PROFIT	—	—	237	243	233	209	189	292	332	258	294	185	169	194	246
Profit per long hundred	—	—	11·8	12·1	12·2	12·3	11*	17·1	19	18†	13·4†	11·6†	8†	12	15·1

* Note the heavy purchase of stock in this year.

† The proceeds of wool sales in 1599 have been divided between 1598 and 1599. Those of 1601 have been divided between 1600 and 1601.

FLOCKS																
Ewes	1320	1340	1343	1360	1441	1448	1447	1460	1464	1475	1475	1475	1565	1339	1462	1475
Rams	56	56	55	57	56	58	56	45	56	56	56	56	58	50	52	53
Hoggs	606	610	616	660	700	709	700	708	703	700	700	700	702	603	680	703
TOTAL	1982	2006	2014	2077	2197	2215	2203	2213	2223	2231	2231	2231	2325	1992	2194	2231
Lambs	1213	1256	1202	1223	1308	1277	1352	1344	1203	1227	1179	908	1135	1460	—	
SALES																
Ewes	31	34	34	32	32	39	38	38	35	39	41	28	35	45	47	
Rams	2	2	1	2	1	2	2	1	1	—	—	2	3	3	—	
Hoggs	88	86	91	95	108	96	115	115	104	86	73	87	78	132	145	
Lambs	63	65	46	45	70	82	66	61	51	45	48	25	50	73	78	
TOTAL	184	187	172	174	211	219	221	215	191	170	162	142	166	253	270	
Wool	82	84	—	—	126	—	—	64	55	60	—	61	79	88	78	
Skins	4	4	2	—	3	4	3	2	4	6	11	17	4	3	4	
Pasture	5	5	5	5	—	—	—	—	—	—	—	—	—	—	—	
TOTAL	275	280	179	181	340	223	224	281	250	236	173	220	249	344	352	
EXPENSES																
Stock	6	—	—	5	—	—	—	1	1	2	—	14	—	—	—	
Wages	6	6	6	6	6	6	6	6	6	6	6	6	6	6	6	
Stores	3	3	3	3	3	3	3	3	3	3	3	3	3	3	3	
	15	9	9	14	9	9	9	10	10	11	9	23	9	9	9	
PROFIT	260	271	170	167	331	214	215	271	240	225	164	197	240	335	353	
Profit per long hundred	15·8	16·2	14·0‡	13·3‡	13§	14§	14§	15·2	13	12	12‖	10·6	14·6	18·3	19·0	

‡ The wool sold in 1608 was the clip of 1606 and 1607. In calculating the profit per long hundred, the proceeds have been divided between these two years, and deducted from 1608.

§ Wool was held over in 1608, 1609 and 1610, because of low prices. But when sales were resumed, over 300 stones produced in these years are unaccounted for. In calculating the profit per long hundred, we have added a minimum sum of £35 to the income of each of these three years (i.e. 100 stones at 7s. a stone).

‖ £60 has been added to the income of this year, for wool presumed sold but not recorded (an estimated 120 stones at 10s. a stone).

were four years at about 10*s.*, followed by another fall—no sales in 1606 or 1607, then 8*s.* a stone in 1608, none again in 1609 or 1610, then 7*s.*, 7*s.*, and 8*s.* for 1611–13. By 1615, the price was back again at 10*s.*, to stay there, or improve a little, for another three or four years.

Stock prices seem to have had similar ups and downs at this new level. Lambs began at 2*s.* 4*d.* and rose to as high as 3*s.* 6*d.* in the next decade. In the trough of 1599–1602, they were a little below where they had started, and by the good years of 1615–18 they were once again at 3*s.* or 3*s.* 6*d.* Of course these were average prices for the whole parcel, the best lambs fetching 4*s.* or 5*s.* in good years. Hoggs followed the same pattern, with a range between 4*s.* 6*d.* and 7*s.* Rams and ewes, culled out of the flocks, were sold more steadily at 4*s.* or 5*s.* As the best ewes were rarely bought, the flocks usually maintaining themselves, we do not often see their price; 7*s.* each was paid for some replenishments in 1597–8. And, of course, all the wethers were sold off as hoggs, as these were only breeding-grounds. Meanwhile, expenses were small and relatively stable. The senior of the two shepherds was receiving a slightly smaller money wage than the Townshend shepherds of the mid-sixteenth century—£2. 8*s.* a year, half that for his assistant. A barrel of tar was 17*s.* and more, but of course it was a trifling item. Hurdles were made in the lord's woods at Hinderclay for a few shillings. No extra pasture was needed.

One interesting feature of this record is the fact that the income from the sale of stock was more than double that from wool—a reminder that estimates which have been made of the profitability of sheep-farming on the basis of comparisons between corn prices and wool prices are taking no account of the more important element, if this situation is typical. When we examine the profit per long hundred, we naturally find considerable variation, with an exceptionally bad year of £8 and two or three very good ones of £18 or £19. But as the average for the first decade is 13·8, for the second 13·7, and for the last seven years 14·2, we may perhaps accept £14 as a rough estimate.

Six or seven years after the Culford accounts end, we catch our last good glimpse of a sheep farm around Stiffkey, where Nathaniel Bacon's old servants, who had outlived their master, were managing the flocks for the Townshend heir.[1] John Walker, sheep-reeve, was responsible for three flocks in 1625–6; 500 ewes on the Lizard fold-course in Stiffkey, about 450 hoggs on the Netherhall course in the same town, and 500 wethers on the neighbouring course at Merston, which Nathaniel Bacon had obtained from Sir Thomas Gresham, when he married his daughter Anne. So there were about fourteen and a half long hundreds altogether, or, to be precise, 1740 sheep. The ewes produced 500 lambs this year, which is better than the average Nathaniel had been taught to expect in the previous generation. The best lambs were sold at 4s. 4d., the worst at 2s. 6d., and 3s. 4d. was paid for fifty tithe lambs which were bought back from the parson. Crones were fetching 4s., wethers, 12s. 6d.; so the prices were comparable with the peak years of the previous decades at Culford. The wool sold, after tithe had been deducted, came to 166½ stones, with an extra 10 stones of locks. This was the clip of 1625 which was being sold in 1626; the clip for 1626 being about the same—162½ stones of wool and 13 of locks. This may have been a better production than at Culford, where a somewhat large flock seldom yielded heavier sales, or the difference may have been due to larger reservations at Culford for the household. Compared with Nathaniel Bacon's formula of 12 stones per long hundred, the production of the combined flocks, before deductions for tithe, was rather higher; but the ewe production, which may have been what he had in mind, was slightly lower. The price was equal to the highest ever obtained at Culford, and the accounts allow us to see the precise details. Of the 1625 clip, about 76 stones came from the wethers and was sold at 13s., 12s., and 11s. 6d. a stone; 47 stones from the ewes and 43 stones from the hoggs were sold at 12s. and 11s. 6d. The locks fetched 4s.

This little history has more than one interesting feature. When we examine the detailed record of the sale of the wool, which gives the name of every purchaser and the quantity he bought, we are confronted by the absorbing spectacle of the whole clip being sold off to the villagers and their wives in small quantities. One man took 10 stones; a few more 2 or 3 stones; while the rest was sold off in packages

[1] The account of John Walker, sheep-reeve; Norwich City Library MSS. 1572, 1 C 5.

of 1 stone or ½ stone. However active the big buyer may have been elsewhere in Norfolk—and he is prominent enough in both the corn trade and the meat trade—he was obviously doing nothing about Stiffkey's wool.

But we must return to our main interest—the evidence of the profits as shown in Table 18. About £200 was made this year out of flocks totalling 1450, besides the value obtained from the fold, and some small profit to the household. If we disregard the incidental benefits, this works out at a profit of just under £14 for every long hundred, which is comparable with the average returns at Culford in the previous period, though an account for one year can obviously be misleading. The only other evidence we possess for these flocks is an inventory taken at the death of Sir Roger Townshend in 1636–7.[1] From this it seems likely that their composition was as stable as at Culford; the ewe and hogg flocks were virtually the same size as they had been ten years before, and the wether flock a few score bigger. Nor were prices much different—the older wethers were valued at 10s. each, the younger ones at 8s., ewes at 7s., and ewe hoggs at 6s.

On the basis of these fragments, and with a full knowledge of their limitations, we may offer a rough guess at what the big flockmasters were making at various times in our century, on the assumption, which was obviously valid in many cases, that they had inherited their lands and their stocks. In the late 1540's, by which time profits must have been 50–100 per cent higher than in the 1520's, the owner of a thousand sheep (in long hundreds) might clear about £40 a year; at the time of the Spanish Armada, about £120; and thereafter, up to the 1630's, an average of about £140. The comparable figures for an owner of 10,000 would be £400, £1200 and £1400 a year.

It is difficult to see how landlords who were sheep-farmers had anything to fear from inflation. There was nothing to stop them from taking advantage of rising prices and the improvement in their incomes would enable them to absorb a higher cost of living. The plateau which

---

[1] H. L. Bradfer-Lawrence, 'Stiffkey alias Stewkey', *Norfolk Archaeology*, XXIII, 334. The author of this article, in querying the addition (p. 335, n. 34), has been confused by the long hundred.

The Mere Landlord

TABLE 18. *Stiffkey flocks, 1625–6*

RECEIPTS

	£	s.	d.
58 'morte' skins	1	11	2
208 'slaughte' skins	11	10	2
141 wethers sold	88	2	6
30 crone ewes sold	6	0	0
44 lambs sold at Rudham	7	6	0
100 lambs sold at Rainham	16	13	4
76½ stones of wether wool	47	17	6
90½ stones of ewes wool	51	14	3
10½ stones of locks	2	4	0
TOTAL	£232	18	11

EXPENSES

	£	s.	d.
50 lambs bought		8	6	8
Three shepherds' wages at £4. 0s. 0d. each plus liveries	13	8	0
Hired help at lambing time		10	0
10 dozen hurdles and carriage	2	0	0
2 stones of pitch for clipping		4	0
1 barrel of tar		18	0
24 pints of oil		6	0
For greasing 528 hoggs at 1s. 6d. a score	1	19	6
For washing 1748 sheep at 1s. a long hundred		14	6
For throwing sheep into the pit		1	0
For clipping 1147 ewes and hoggs at 3s. a long hundred, and 601 wethers at 3s. 4d. a long hundred	2	5	2
For five draggers for two days		10	0
For six winders for two days		8	0
For gathering up the locks for two days			8
For carrying the wool for two days		1	0
4 stones of cheese for the clippers		9	4
For driving lambs to market		3	0
17 lb. of redding		2	10
TOTAL	£32	7	8
PROFIT	£200	11	3

prices reached by the end of the sixteenth century may have deprived the industry of some of its earlier appeal, but there was no reason for concern. The rentier, who chose to rent his courses with a stock, seems to have got a reasonable return on his investment. The only person who was likely to get into difficulties was the yeoman farmer, who often rented his farm on narrow margins, and had to find his rent at fixed seasons, regardless of fluctuations in prices. At the same time, we can admit that sheep-farming was no short-cut to great wealth. Some yeomen may have advanced their prospects of becoming gentlemen by their good management of rented facilities; some gentry may have reaped windfalls from jumps in prices; but by and large it was simply a dependable livelihood for people in their various stations. We recall the remark of one celebrated smallowner who sometimes regretted the fortune which had turned a simple squire into the uncrowned king of England. He said he wished 'he had stayed by his woodpile and kept a flock of sheep'. The prospects of doing this comfortably seem to have been no less in Norfolk and Suffolk than in Cromwell's Huntingdon.

THE MOVEMENT OF RENTS ON THE BURES ESTATE, 1530–1654

From sheep-farming—the only form of demesne farming which was practised on a large scale—we may now turn to the landlords whose manors were always let. We have referred in an earlier chapter to the Bures Estate, on the borders of Suffolk and Essex, which drifted from its ancient moorings on the death of Henry Bures, in 1529, into the hands of Sir William Buttes, the court physician, and was eventually divided, after preserving its historic unity until 1599, between the Bacons and the Barrows.[1] A medley of evidence preserved among the Bacon muniments tempted us to see whether the movement of rents could be traced on the five 'manors' which made up the inheritance. After fitting the bits and pieces of the puzzle together, it became clear that the desired information was available for the whole estate up to 1589, for two manors up to 1624, and for one of them up to 1654. The year 1530 was used as the base date, but in the case of the manor with the longest records—Foxearth—it was possible to start as early as 1494, and thus produce a more or less continuous picture of income for 150 years.

---

[1] See chapter II, above, pp. 91–2.

The Mere Landlord

The five properties which the ancestors of Henry Bures had acquired in the thirteenth and fourteenth centuries were all within close touch of thriving towns. Three of them, Foxearth, Acton and Morevies (a manor in Great Waldingfield), lay a mile or two to the north of Sudbury; a fourth, Reydon, was just south of Hadleigh; and the fifth, Wherstead, about the same distance from Ipswich. No surveys have survived for any of them, but we have some idea of their structure. Foxearth—or Foxearth and Brookhall, to give it a fuller designation—consisted of two demesne farms, Foxearth Hall and Brookhall, which rented at about £10 apiece; Weston Mill, which may have brought in £3; some twenty or thirty copyholders and freeholders who paid about £17 a year in rents of assise; and a few acres of woods. As the out-rents were exceptionally heavy—nearly £9 a year—the net income was about £30 a year. Reydon had the same sort of structure, but was worth more. We know that one farm, Sulleys, brought in £8 a year, and the other, Reydon Hall, was worth at least twice that. Reydon Mill was a better mill than Weston Mill, and there were more woods here than at Foxearth. The rents of assise were about the same—£18— but the outrents were only 33s. So the net income must have been between £40 and £50 a year. Acton, the seat of the family, may have been worth between £60 and £70, but we know very little about it, except that there was the usual moated house, a demesne farm, a little wood, £35 in rents of assise, and only a few shillings in out-rents. Of Morevies and Wherstead, we know even less. They cannot have produced more than £15 and £10 a year, respectively, so they were the smallest of the properties, but how far the income was produced by a farm, and how far by rents of assise, it is not easy to say. The infrequency of a reference to an income from fines in the later accounts would suggest that the tenants were few, but we cannot be sure. Morevies seems to have included a quarter interest in a mill. Neither manor had any woods.[1]

---

[1] The descriptions of the manors in fines and inquisitions have not been thought sufficiently reliable to be quoted. Foxearth Hall, at the time of its sale in 1654 (which did not include the farm of Brookhall) was said to contain 240 acres, of which 64 were meadow and pasture, and there were 30 acres of wood; Bacon MSS.—Particulars (Chicago).

The figures used so far are rough estimates of the income at the death of Henry Bures. The chief evidence for the value of the estate at this date is a manuscript extent which was prepared at the time of the Inquisition Post Mortem, and which seems to have been a fairly accurate appraisal; at least its figures are consistently higher than those of the official I.P.M.'s,[1] as we can see from the following comparison:

	Acton			Reydon			Foxearth			Morevies			Wherstead			Total		
	£	s.	d.	£	s.	d.	£	s.	d	£	s.	d.	£	s.	d.	£	s.	d.
MS. extent	69	6	8	40	0	0	26	13	4	13	6	8	9	0	0	158	6	8
I.P.M.'s	40	0	0	36	0	0	18	0	0	12	0	0	6	0	0	112	0	0

The reliability of the extent can be checked by comparison with one or two leases. Thus Foxearth seems to have been leased at the figure which appears in the extent, though its real value was probably a little higher, as a relation had been given a long lease on favourable terms. Acton had been leased at £54 since 1525, but the higher figure in the extent—£69—may have included an estimate of the Hall in which Henry Bures had been living, which, together with some other appurtenances, had not been included in the farmer's lease. Reydon was worth about £56 in 1538, as compared with the estimate of £40 in 1530, but a raise may have occurred in the interval. In spite of these ambiguities, it seems likely that the whole value lay between £160 and £180, and perhaps nearer the higher figure, inasmuch as small irregular profits were often ignored in such extents. It is also probable that the values had been fairly stable since at least the beginning of the century. We know, for instance, that Foxearth, here valued at about £27, had been leased for £28 in 1494, and that the farm of Sulleys, in Reydon, had been leased at £8 since 1503.

From this base we can begin our inspection of a century of inflation. Within about a decade of Henry Bures's death, there are scattered glimpses of the values under Sir William Buttes, who bought the wardship of the four Bures girls and in due course arranged their marriages—Jane, to his eldest son William, Bridget to Thomas, Anne to Edmund,

---

[1] Henry Bures, Suffolk, Chancery series, vol. 48, no. 81; Essex, Chancery series, vol. 50, no. 86, vol. 80, no. 88.

and Mary to Thomas Barrow. By 1545 one of Sir William's sons becomes extremely useful to us. This was Thomas Buttes, who seems to have settled down to a long life as a 'mere' landlord, at the age of twenty-three, when his father made him lord of Riborough, in Norfolk. Two years later—in 1541—he received the livery of his wife's property and began to interest himself in her quarter-interest of the Bures Estate. The most useful feature of his records is a series of semi-annual receipts, at Lady Day and Michaelmas, which begin in 1547 and run from 1555 to 1589 with scarcely a break. These brief, methodical entries of his share of the sums which the Suffolk and Essex farmers brought twice a year to his brother, William's, home at Thornage, or his own house at Riborough, tell us quite precisely what each of the four co-heirs received *after deductions*; but as these deductions usually included the payment of dower to Henry Bures's widow, and annuities to one or two other relations, an accurate knowledge of these changing charges, as well as simple arithmetic, is needed to reconstruct the income of the whole estate from Thomas Buttes's accounts.

When these sixty years (*c.* 1530–90) are reviewed, with the help of all the available evidence, they are seen to fall into two equal halves. So far as the first half is concerned (*c.* 1530–60), we do not yet seem to have entered a period when improvements were expected at almost every expiry of a lease; but we do assume that a modest improvement took place between 1530 and 1547, though the ambiguous elements in the estimate of 1530 prevent us from being as precise as we would wish. Foxearth, which was leased at about £27 in 1530 is bringing in about £33 in 1547; Morevies has risen from £13. 6s. 8d. to £17; Wherstead from £9 to £10. 6s. 8d.; Reydon from £40 to £55. 5s. 5d. In the case of Reydon, we happen to know that this had been the income since at least 1538. Though the possibility that the estimate of 1530 was an understatement must be borne in mind, it seems likely that Sir William Buttes had taken his opportunity to improve some of the leases. However, it is clear that one of them was still unimproved. The farmer of Acton was paying no more in 1547 than he had paid in 1525 (i.e. £54), and no revenue is shown for the Hall which Henry Bures had then occupied. In all, the rents of 1547 came to about £176, and irregular profits such as fines and wood sales may have been producing another £20–£25 a year, so that a round figure for the net income at this date would be £200 a year. By 1559 there had been no further change in the leases, but wood sales were averaging about £40 a year in the late 1550's, so that the first half of our period ends with the estate producing about £225 a year.

In the second thirty years, this income is more than doubled: the average of the last four years (1586–9) is over £480. In the main, this is simply the result of increasing the rents whenever the leases fell in. Thomas Buttes began this era in 1559–61, when a *novum incrementum* was formally recorded on each lease. There was a second round of raises in 1572–4, and a third in 1585–6. If the leases of this last date are compared with those of 1530, it will be seen that farms have gone up about fourfold and mills about twofold. Wood sales are still making a useful contribution to the income, but they show no upward curve—it an average annual income is taken for each decade, it ranges between £30 and £35. Profits of court are of least importance, but there has been some pressure on them; from £2 or £3 a year in the 1550's they jump to about £10 in the 1560's and 1570's. On the one manor, Foxearth, where we can study the process, we can see the Buttes management doing what the Lord Keeper was doing on some of his manors in the same period; a standard fine of 2s. an acre was doubled. The inflexible rents of assise remain unchanged. Before the inflation began, they might have accounted for as much as half the value of a manor, and those that we know of on this estate (i.e. at Foxearth, Acton and Reydon) were producing £70 a year in 1530; but the steady decline in their relative importance is now well advanced.

Our view of the whole estate ends in 1598, with the last of Thomas Buttes's accounts. Thomas himself died in 1593, to be buried in an altar tomb at Riborough—a mere landlord who achieved the immortality in his parish church which is sometimes said to have been the privilege of 'court gentry'. The Bures estate was partitioned in 1599. Morevies was sold; Reydon and Wherstead became the property of the Barrows, Acton and Foxearth, of the Bacons. It is when the last two manors appear in the Bacon accounts of 1600 that we can resume our study of the inflation.

Recent investigation has taught us to expect a jump in values in the 1590's, and we certainly find it here; but the explanation which is sometimes offered, in terms of a long lag at last caught up, does not apply in any simple sense to these manors. It was merely a case of the fourth round of raises being bigger than the previous three—anything from 67 per cent to 93 per cent on the rent of a farm. Foxearth Hall was producing £42 in 1586, £81 in 1600; Brookhall, £40 in 1586, £66. 13s. 4d. in 1600; Acton £82 in 1586, £143 in 1600. Only on Weston Mill was there a small raise—from £8 to £9.

The remainder of the story is soon told. The farm of Acton was raised to £172 in 1616 and then removed from the accounts in 1624 while this lease was still running, and before the peak of the inflation had been reached. The uncertainty as to what the house and reserved land was worth in 1530, when the farmer was paying about £20 for the farm, makes it impossible to be precise about the increase, but it cannot have been less than fivefold, and may well have been more. If profits of court and wood sales are averaged for the period after 1600, they work out at about £5 a year, and £24 a year, respectively, though both are very irregular. Rents of assise continued to produce their original £35. On this basis, the annual value was £236 in 1624. If the estimate in the extent of 1530 was reliable—and it seems to have been high rather than low—this is an increase of 350 per cent.

Foxearth Hall was raised to £92. 10s. in 1623, £105 in 1633, and stood at £108 in 1654. Brookhall went to £76 in 1608 and £92 in 1633. Its value when it was separately sold to a Bacon steward in 1651 is not known, but it is unlikely to have been much more. Weston Mill was raised to £16. 10s. in 1623 and £25. 10s. in 1626, but was renewed at £24 in 1634. These three leases are respectively ten times, nine times, and six times more valuable than they had been in 1545. Meanwhile, we know from a particular which was prepared for the sale of the manor in 1654 that the woods were valued at £10 a year, the profits of court at £12, and the rents of assise at £18. On this basis, a property whose net income was about £30 a year in 1530 was £255 a year in 1654—an increase of over 800 per cent.

Here again, it is difficult to see how the mere landlord had suffered from the inflation. Nor was there anything remarkable about the way in which his rising income was achieved. He had simply raised the rents, and found tenants—often the same tenants—who were able and willing enough to meet each rise. The stability of the rents of assise, and the relative insignificance of the increased income from fines, is sufficient evidence that the copyholders were not suffering. Indeed, their lot might well be envied when we consider the unearned increment which had fallen their way. It is also interesting to discover that a prospective purchaser of Foxearth in 1654, though willing to pay about £3000 for it (this was minus Brookhall) had some reserves to express. He pointed out that it was surrounded by many poor towns—a sidelight on the condition of Sudbury, Clare, Long Melford and Lavenham at that date—and was inclined to fear that the tenants had been allowed too much liberty.[1]

THE MOVEMENT OF RENTS ON SOME BACON MANORS, 1540–1656

From the Bures Estate we can return once again to the Bacon Estate. Some indication of the rise in values during the Lord Keeper's lifetime was given in an earlier chapter, but here we can attempt to take a larger view.

First, we can look at the Mettingham College estate which Sir Nicholas bought in 1562, as the records for these properties run, with only a few interruptions, for a century and a quarter (1530–1656). The lands in question may have amounted, in value, to about one third of the total estate of the College at the dissolution; they were known as *Mettingham cum membris*, the manors of Ilketshall and Sheepmeadow, and several other farms in East Suffolk, being associated with the manor of Mettingham, where the College was located. The

---

[1] The materials in the above section have been based on K. J. Appel, 'The Bures Estate in the Sixteenth Century' (M.A. thesis, University of Chicago) as supplemented and corrected.

demesnes—the soil of which was described as 'verie good and holsome'—consisted of 1370 acres, of which 911 were pasture, 328 arable, 107 meadow, and 24 marsh. There were remnants of open fields in Mettingham, Bungay, Ilketshall St Johns, and elsewhere, but the bulk of the property was enclosed. The woods—about 180 acres—commanded good prices, thanks to easy access to the sea, and to the demand for ash with which the coopers made barrels in herring time (Yarmouth was twelve miles from Mettingham).[1]

A series of bailiffs' accounts, kept by the College between 1530 and the surrender in 1542, enable us both to make a rough guess at the annual value of this estate and to see precisely what were the rents of individual farms. The accounts show a fairly stable income of about £66 a year after deductions (rents of assise £40, farms £29, profits of court £3, expenses £6).[2] However, three assets were not mentioned here: the site of the manor of Mettingham, which was occupied by the College, the home farms and the woods. These assets produced an income of about £50 a year when they were leased at current values in 1542, so the annual value of the estate in the decade before the dissolution must be plus or minus £100. We may notice, in passing, that the tenth which Sir Anthony Denny paid to the crown, under the terms of the grant which gave him all the College estates, presumed an income of £73 from these particular lands, and that the *Valor Ecclesiasticus* of 1535 put their value as low as £42 (a result reached by reporting the rents of assise accurately, by undervaluing the leases, and by ignoring the assets in the hands of the College).

There was the usual flurry of activity on the eve of the dissolution. We know that the chaplains tried to hide the silver, until a simple brother betrayed them! A few pieces of demesne disappear inexplicably from the accounts and more wood was sold than usual. One or two leases were renewed at their old values for forty years and many more for twenty-one years. We assume that fines were charged for these

---

[1] Add. MSS. 14850, fols. 153–62 (B.M.). The other evidence in this section has been drawn from the bailiff's accounts, and other sources, among the Bacon MSS. (Chicago).

[2] The accounts show an income of about £70 a year, but they included the tenement of Shurlocks, and a few other pieces (about £4 in all) which disappeared at the dissolution. For the purposes of comparison with later history, these items have been removed.

renewals and it is interesting to find a trace of one of them in the later Denny records—a second instalment of £10 which was paid for the lease of Ilketshall, with the information that the other £10 had been previously paid when the master of the College renewed the lease. As the rent of Ilketshall was £10 a year, it may be that twice the annual rent was considered an appropriate fine for a new twenty-one year term.

Sir Anthony Denny, a favourite of Henry VIII, had no reason to complain of his grant. He was given all the lands of the College, in return for £1000 and his services, and the total value received, if reckoned on the basis of the 'tenths', must have exceeded £4000. The Denny accounts for our portion of the estate, which run from 1542 to 1550, are complicated both by windfalls from the sale of church property and by the new expenses, which included not only the tenths paid to the crown (about £7 a year), but also £40 a year in pensions to six chaplains (three survivors were still receiving £15 in 1550). For these reasons, we have not bothered to include a record of 'the charge' or of 'the deliveries' of these years in Table 19. But the information about rental income is there. The rents of assise are more or less unchanged. The leases of 1530, as renewed in 1541, are about the same, and to these have been added the newly leased home farms of the College—the Dairy House farm at £9 a year, Walshams at £10 a year, Morgans and the Conyger at £10 a year, and several more at £2 a year or less (£47 in all). With wood sales of £3–£4 a year, the whole income of the estate was about £120 a year, from which fixed expenses of £13 a year (the old out-rents and the new tenths) would have to be deducted.

A decade later, when Henry Denny, Sir Anthony's son, sold out to Bacon in 1562, the rents were very little bigger. Here and there we can see that a rent had been raised on the expiry of a lease (just as we can see that a bigger fine than the customary shilling an acre had been taken on the transfer of a copyhold); but in the main the old rents had simply been renewed. This was also the case on the very eve of the sale, when the Dennys followed the earlier example of the College by extending many of the leases for twenty-one years. Again we presume that fines were taken, but no evidence has survived. What we do know is the guarantee of the value of the estate which Bacon received. The Dennys promised a net income of £108 a year (roughly what they had received themselves) but went on to explain (1) that the Dairy House farm would be out of lease the following year, (2) that profits of court were being counted at no more than £2 a year, and (3) that neither the site of the College, nor the woods, were included in their estimate.

On this basis, and fortified by his own local knowledge of the lands, Bacon paid £3540 for the estate. This implies a much higher rate than the usual twenty years' purchase, but the explanation is clear enough when we turn to a survey which Bacon ordered within a month of his purchase. The authors of this meticulous document rated meadow at anything between 4s. and 8s. an acre, pasture between 2s. and 3s., enclosed arable at 2s., and open-field arable at 1s. 4d. They then compared the value of each parcel, as measured by these current rates of 1562, with the old rents, and found that the latter were only about a half of what the lands were worth. The Lord Keeper could do nothing about the leases which the Dennys had just renewed for twenty-one years, but he could make something of the lands which were in the hands of the lord, and of the woods, and he, or his heir, could look forward to a rich harvest later. The returns from the estate up to the Lord Keeper's death in 1579 (summarised in chapter II, Table 5A, above) suggest an average income of about £150 a year from all sources. In 1581, when his son was able to renew the Denny leases, the upward spiral which we have seen on the Bures Estate began in earnest.

The possibilities of these farms may be illustrated by a few examples. The manor of Ilketshall Hall was a farm in Ilketshall St John's of 268 acres (216 pasture, 37 arable, 15 meadow). All of it was enclosed, with two pastures bearing names—the Northfield and the Southfield—which suggest the existence of open fields at an earlier date. In 1530–40 it was leased by John Kegell for £10 a year. On 31 March 1561, Henry Denny let it to Robert Stroger for twenty-one years at £13. 6s. 8d.—about 1s. an acre. The next year, Bacon's survey found that it was worth more than double that, namely, £31. When the lease expired in 1581, the value had doubled again; Andrew Hawes, yeoman, of Barningham,

Suffolk, paid £60 a year for the next twenty-one years. It was £66 a year after the turn of the century, £152 in 1625, and £160 in 1646. This was sixteen times the rent of 1530 (or about fourteen times, if we adjust the rent of 1530 to include a fine of £20 for the negotiation of a twenty-one-year lease).

Pentocks was a farm of 130 acres, almost all enclosed, of which 85 were pasture, 33 arable, and 12 meadow. In 1530–40 it rented for £3. 3s. 4d. a year. On 22 June 1540, about two years before the dissolution, it was let by the Master of the College to Richard Vardon for forty years at the same rates. In 1562 the survey said it was worth £17. 3s. a year, but the old rent, passing from father to son, lasted until 1580. It was then let to Thomas Rouse, gentleman and servant of Nicholas Bacon the younger, for £25. 13s. 4d. a year for twenty-one years. At the next renewal, about 1600, it went to £44. 8s., and stood at £46. 4s. in 1646. This was about fourteen times the rent of 1540 (unadjusted for fines).

Sheepmeadow Hall was a farm of 96 acres (18 pasture, 18 meadow, 23 marsh, and 37 arable). In 1530–40, Thomas Bridges, bailiff, was paying £3. 5s. 5d. a year. It was leased to Thomas Petytt in 1561 for £3. 15s. 5d. a year, within a few months of the survey which put its annual value at £13. 13s. 10d. In 1579, when the lease expired, a yeoman of Sheepmeadow, Robert Allarde, took it on for nineteen years at £28. It must have been renewed at the same price, for it was still £28 in 1625, but by 1646 it had risen to £36. This was eleven times the rent of 1530 (unadjusted for fines).

Finally, we can look at the process on a smaller scale. Melmont Close, containing 20 acres of pasture, was let by Henry Denny in 1545 for twenty-one years at £1. 3s. 4d. a year, that is 1s. 2d. an acre. Wells Close, 10 acres of pasture, was let by the same Henry Denny for twenty-one years in 1561 at 13s. 4d., that is 1s. 4d. an acre. In 1562, this same land was being valued at 2s. 8d. an acre. The two closes were combined in one lease in the Lord Keeper's lifetime, and by 1546 they were rented at £15, which is 10s. an acre.

We have attempted to show the rising income on the whole estate after the Lord Keeper's death by a table of average annual returns for

The Mere Landlord

each decade. The rents of assise are stable. The profits of court, though doubtless bigger than the Master had collected in the days when copyhold fines were 1s. an acre, were still a trifling source. The woods might have been expected to produce more, and there is always a doubt as to whether bailiff's accounts are a complete record of these sales—a wood-reeve might be accounting separately. Still, the windfall of £451 a year for three years in the 1550's will be noticed. The possibility that the estate changed its size by purchase or sale, should not, of course, be ignored; but it seems to have been tolerably stable. On this showing, leasehold income multiplied over ninefold between 1530 and 1656. The increase in the value of the whole estate is harder to determine, owing to the absence of a precise value for 1530 and the problems created by wood sales; but an eightfold increase would be a reasonable guess.

TABLE 19. *The average* annual income from the Mettingham College Estates, 1578–1656 (£)*

	Total charge	Livery money	Leases	Rents of assise	Profits of court	Woods
1530–40	—	—	29†	40	3	3
1542–50	—	—	76	40	3	4
1578–9 (2)	249	127	112	40	11	3
1580–9	499	390	327	40	6	40
1590–9 (9)	477	404	351	39	8	22
1600–9	543	507	416	38	20	42
1610–19	578	570	485	38	14	32
1620–9 (8)	721	676	570	38	24	87
1630–9	712	662	610	38	13	29
1640–6 (5)	923	789	702	38	26	22
1653–6 (3)	1293	1031	706	38	9	451

* The averages are for each decade; where the available accounts are less than ten, the number has been inserted in parentheses.

† These are the farms which were leased in 1530: others were in the hands of the College. For comparative purposes, the figure for 1542–50 (namely, £76) should be used as a base.

From East Suffolk we may now turn to West Suffolk, where Nicholas Bacon had built up his first seat around Redgrave. Here, the manor of Rickinghall Inferior, *alias* West Hall, at the southern end of the little market town of Botesdale, affords a good view of the inflation. After the Court of Augmentations received it from the monastery of Bury St Edmund's, the rents of assise were rated at £14, the demesnes at £15, the profits of court at under £3, and there were 130 acres of woods for which Bacon paid a lump sum of £103. This was one of those purchases from the crown which were undervalued at the time of the sale: Bacon's survey of 1545, based on rates which ranged from 8*d.* to 1*s.* 8*d.* for arable, 1*s.* to 1*s.* 8*d.* for pasture, and 2*s.* to 3*s.* 4*d.* for meadow, showed that the demesnes were worth more than twice what the farmer was paying for them under an Augmentations lease of 1542. He obtained his first improvement in 1546 by displacing the farmer and raising the rent of the demesnes from £15 to £29. Another followed in 1570, when he added 60 combs of wheat to the money rent, thus almost doubling it again for his own lifetime and creating a permanent hedge against inflation. Further improvements followed in 1578, 1591, 1612, 1613 and 1637. By the last date, the demesnes were producing £143 in cash and 63 combs of wheat, which at 15*s.* a comb would be £47; courts were averaging £20; those woods which were not included in the farm of the manor were bringing in another £20; and rents of assise were £16. In other words, an income of about £37 in 1540 had been raised to £246 in 1640—an increase of between six- and sevenfold.

Here again one lease provides a good illustration of the possibilities of improvement. In 1545 two closes, Westhall Green and Trindelmere Green, which formed a continuous pasture of 120 acres and was considered the best in the farm, was let for £9. Bacon's surveyors, reckoning 1*s.* 8*d.* an acre, thought it was worth £10. In 1637 it was let for £75, twelve gallons of Spanish wine and twelve gallons of muscatel. This was an eightfold increase, with the pasture worth about 13*s.* an acre. However, the peak had been reached. By 1643 it was down to £67.

A few miles to the south of Rickinghall was the manor and park of Wyverston. If we take 1568 as our starting-point, the park of 254 acres was rented for £40 a year, a little Hall for £3, a close called Parker's Close for £1. 13*s.* 4*d.*, and a croft for 5*s.* In addition to these leases, rents of assise were worth £27, and the profits of court for that year were about £10. By 1624, the rents of assise, the profits, and the rent

of the Hall were no bigger, but the little croft had gone up from 5s. to
£2. 3s. 3d., Parker's Close from £1. 13s. 4d. to £18, and the Park was
repeating the now familiar history. On Bacon's death in 1578, it had
stood at £72. In 1587, a corn rent was introduced, by an arrangement
whereby the farmer was allowed to break up 95 acres, for which he
would pay a comb of wheat per acre, while continuing to pay 5s. 8d.
an acre, the previous rent, for the balance of the pasture, that is, £45 in
cash. Assuming that wheat was 10s. a comb, this would be about £92
in all. By 1639 the rent was £69 in cash and 100 combs, which would
make £144, if the wheat is converted at 15s. a comb. By 1652 it was
£90 and 80 combs, which is £150 if we convert at the same rate. If
we suppose that the Park had rented for as much as 1s. 8d. an acre in
1540, which would be £21 in all, the main lease had gone up sevenfold.
The difficulties of the conversion introduce obvious errors into this
sort of calculation, but we have tried to safeguard ourselves by being as
conservative as possible.

If the labour were considered worth while, we could pursue this
history on other manors. It would be complicated by various problems,
one of which has just been mentioned—all the manors around Redgrave
paid part of their rent in corn. Other problems would be the possibility
of additional purchases in the formative period of a large estate, the
changes in accounting procedure which sometimes transferred the
assets of one manor to another, and the extreme difficulty in pursuing
the history of the principal seat, such as Redgrave, where involved
arrangements were often made between the father and the eldest son.
Nor would we expect every manor to exhibit as big a rise as those we
have considered. Redgrave itself was a manor which consisted (apart
from its park) largely of rents of assise when Bacon bought it, because
the abbot had been turning demesne into copyholds on the eve of the
dissolution, in return for fines. Bacon was only able to rebuild the
demesne by buying out the copyholders, and though he did so at a
price which was modest in comparison with the later cost of land, the
improvements here, if they could be calculated, would no doubt be
less than on an estate like Mettingham.

He also bought one or two other properties which consisted wholly, or largely, of rents of assise, but here the significant thing is their relative unimportance compared with his other holdings. Some, like Wenhaston, a dilapidated little manor near Bramfield, in East Suffolk, were picked up as incidents of a larger purchase, and he quickly got rid of them by selling the copyholds to their tenants—often at a profit to himself. This was obviously a sensible thing to do with an inelastic property. Others he bought, and kept, for their position. The little manor of Mellis St John, which had belonged to the Knights of St John of Jerusalem, as part of their preceptory at Battisford, was one example; but its income, which barely altered, was under £10 a year. Ashfield was bigger; the rents of assise were £36 in the Lord Keeper's lifetime, and it seems to have paid for itself, in his day, with the help of substantial fines and a copyhold which was turned into a little demesne. But his son soon got rid of it.

To these examples we might add a property like the Hundred of Blackburn, where only the oat rents were flexible, and the value in 1700—about £30—might be only £10 higher than it was in 1600; or the majestic Liberty and Franchise of Bury St Edmund's, in respect of which a voracious monarchy was able to recover £3100 in 1628 for supposed flaws in the Lord Keeper's title. But allowing for all possible variations in the history, we have no reason to suppose that the estate as a whole did not bear up well—and very much better than some of the generalisations about the difficulties of landlords in a period of inflation have led us to expect.

CONCLUSION

On 9 December 1613 Sir Robert Drury, of Hawstead, Suffolk, replied to an enquiry from his wife about a man who wanted to rent one of their farms: 'he may chouse which ferme he will have, and Adams shall have the other, and I will make a lease for 12 years, But not a penny onder 10 shillings the acre, for as the pryse of thinges ryseth, I will warrant you, you shall see the pryse of Lands ryse much or sixe months be passed'.[1] If the usual opinion of economic historians is correct, agricultural prices had been leading the inflation, so the farmers who

---

[1] Correspondence, Bacon MSS. (Chicago).

were selling corn, meat and wool on this rising market cannot have had much to complain of. As for the price of land, Sir Robert Drury's figure suggests a tenfold increase since the opening decades of the sixteenth century, when the monastery of Bury St Edmund's was rating land at 8*d*., 10*d*., and 1*s*. an acre, and the standard fine of 2*s*. an acre probably represented twice the annual rent. How much further it went we are uncertain.[1] We have seen pasture fetching 13*s*. an acre in 1637, and we know that the Park at Redgrave, valued at 6*d*. to 1*s*. an acre in 1545, was rated at 11*s*. 8*d*. an acre in 1702, after a long period of stability. Obviously the increase must have exceeded any rise in the cost of living, and the only question, therefore, is whether the tenurial arrangements, and the habits of landlords, enabled them to get their share of the rising income.

The evidence we have collected in this chapter, being no more than a handful of cases, provides no excuse for dogmatism, but it is certainly suggestive. We began by pointing out that sheep-farming, which played an important part in the income of the gentry of this region, was exempt from any of the rigidities which are supposed to have handicapped the rentier, and we gave reasons for thinking that the money income of the flockmaster may have increased from 450 to 700 per cent between 1520 and 1640.[2] As for the rentier, we have shown how the values of leases could be improved, over the whole period, up to 1000 per cent and more; how the lease of twelve, fourteen, or at most twenty-one years, enabled adjustments to be made with some regularity; how corn rents ensured an automatic adjustment, as far as they went; and how the inflexibility of copyholds could be easily tolerated when there were these opportunities in farms. We have found no reason for thinking that any novelties, in the way of psychology or estate-management, were needed to accomplish these results, or that they involved any special handicaps for tenants after the era of Kett's

---

[1] We have not yet consulted J. Spratt, 'Agrarian Conditions in Norfolk and Suffolk 1600–1650' (M.A. thesis, London University, 1935). It has been stated, on the basis of this work, that 'the rent of arable rose sixfold between 1590–1600 and 1640–50 and of pasture and meadow between two- and threefold' (E. Kerridge, *op. cit.* p. 17). In the absence of the precise rates, it is not clear how this compares with our findings.

[2] See pp. 194–6 of this chapter.

rebellion. We are inclined to think that the image of the 'bourgeois landlord' is a myth, which was propagated by historians who erroneously supposed that a conflict between middle classes and working classes in the nineteenth century demanded an earlier conflict between 'feudal' landlords and 'capitalistic' landlords in the sixteenth; whereas all that we find in the sixteenth is the traditional shrewdness which had been applied by all classes to market activities for long enough. As for 'impoverished landlords' or 'declining gentry', we do not doubt that they existed, but we cannot see why the agrarian history, *per se*, should have produced them in any great numbers.

It may be objected that the proofs submitted, outside the scope of sheep-farming, depend entirely on the availability to the landlord of farms with adjustable leases. A manor composed wholly of copyholds of inheritance, or a manor where the demesne had been leased for a very long period of years, must have resisted improvement. This is true; but it has yet to be shown that the gentry were heavily handicapped by such conditions.

So far as the long lease is concerned, we must first recall that the only landlords in this region who seem to have granted them on a large scale were the crown and church, and that in these cases the gentry were the direct beneficiaries. Most of the estate records of the bishopric of Norwich were burned in the fire at Ludham in 1611, but the manuscript notebooks of Anthony Harrison, who had come to Norwich in 1602 as bishop Jegon's secretary, are a revelation of how the long lease, and the lax book-keeping of the diocese, played into the hands of the county families.[1] Harrison tried to be the faithful steward, after three generations of spoliation, but his hands were often hopelessly tied. Bishop Rugge—'that grand spoiler'—had begun the history at the Reformation by disastrous exchanges and a whole spate of long leases. In 1588, while Rugge's leases were only half-spent, Bishop Scamler was obliged to give an eighty-year lease to the crown (it was assigned to Sir Thomas Heneage) of a large number of manors, with the bishopric

[1] 'Collections concerning the Diocese of Norwich', Reynolds Chapel, Norwich Cathedral. I am indebted for my introduction to these manuscripts to the courtesy of Rev. J. F. Williams and T. F. Barton, Esq.

retaining nothing but the ancient rents. Thus the demesnes of Horning, which Rugge had leased in 1545 for seventy-five years, would produce only £2. 10s. a year; Horning Hospital, leased in 1546 for ninety-six years, £5. 6s. 8d. Nor was it only that the episcopal rents stood still while others absorbed the ballooning increments. It was Harrison's fear that land would be lost forever under a system where no sworn officer was charged with a clear responsibility for preserving a record of the leases, and where the Keeper of the Palace had often been willing to 'gratify the gentlemen of the county' by allowing them to remove the counterparts of their leases, and other evidences, from the episcopal archives. He wanted to protect the future interest of the see by compiling as good a record as he could, against the day when leases would lapse; but it must have seemed like the Greek kalends for many of the lands. On 10 November 1662, Charles II asked the bishop to renew, for the benefit of Lord Townshend, Sir William Doyly and Sir Robert Kemp, lands which their families had held 'for divers ages' at the old rents. The rents were to stay the same, notwithstanding a recent order that they should be at least doubled, and only a 'reasonable' fine should be asked.[1] Harrison's successors might well have groaned, How long, O Lord, how long?

Who were the beneficiaries? Harrison named, besides those mentioned, Sir William Paston, Sir Thomas Barney, Sir Miles Corbett, Sir John Pettus, Sir Edward Blenerhassett, Sir William Woodhouse and many more; in other words, the gentry, usually premier families, but also others. And to all who fattened on the continued existence of the see of Norwich, we must add those who were 'gratified' in the last days of the monasteries. It was Sir William Buttes, the rising physician, who received a ninety-nine year lease of the manor of Thornham from the dean and chapter of Norwich in 1638; it was the Crofts, a well-known West Suffolk family, who got a ninety-nine-year lease of the manor of Playfords in Barnham from Thetford Priory in 1535; and William Marston, yeoman, who got a ninety-year lease of the manor of Apsebury, in Hertfordshire, from the abbot of St Alban's. To these three cases, which have been found on the manors examined

[1] Townshend MSS., Garsett House, Safe 2, Norwich.

in this study, a few more could be added. They are unlikely to have formed more than a small fraction of all the lands in the area, but those who received them were obviously enjoying a good thing.

Were there any circumstances in which the gentry would be victimised by the long lease? We have already referred to the fact that it was not the practice of the ordinary landlord of this area to grant beneficial leases; the normal term of years ran between twelve and twenty-one. The only exception, on the manors examined, was a sixty-year lease of Foxearth which was granted to a daughter of the family on her marriage in 1524; but though this affected the distribution of the income within the family, it was no obstacle to the raising of rent. Some cases can be imagined which would involve hardship—the grant of an unusually long term to a farmer before the inflation began, the desperate sale of a long lease for ready cash, or the purchase, at an early date, of a monastic manor which was burdened with such a lease. The embarrassments of these leases must have been obvious to everyone by some such date as 1550, and one would expect the price at which they changed hands to have reflected the rigidity, unless the buyer had some other motive for paying the usual rates. The one case in which Nicholas Bacon bought a manor so burdened, after the early years, seems to have involved no special hardship. He paid a twenty-year purchase for Playfords in Barnham in 1560, that is, about £150 for a fixed rent of £7. 13s. 4d. from John Crofts. During the thirty-five years which his family held it, the rent decreased to £7. 6s. 8d., as they sold off one scrap for £20 and another for an unknown sum which may have been about the same; then in 1695 they sold it to the Crofts, whose lease still had forty years to run, for £160.

As for the other source of rigidity, copyholds of inheritance, it is true that some manors existed which were made up of little else. We have met a few of them on the Bacon and Cornwallis estates. Only a well-to-do landlord, who wanted them for their position, could afford to keep them, for even where the fines were uncertain, there are indications that the best that could be done was to raise the profits of court to about the same annual value as the rents of assise. It was on this basis that the fines on the Redgrave Estate, which were all 'arbitrable', were valued when it was sold in 1702.[1] But how many manors were made up wholly, or largely, of rents of assise? We have found only a tiny handful, and we have seen that manors where rents of assise accounted for as much as a third or a half of the income in 1530, were not so burdened that they could not soar with the help of their farms. Here again, we may perhaps say that if there were many victims, they have still to be shown.

The presumption we are pressing in favour of landlord prosperity would, of course, be altogether stronger if we were able to compare their expenditure with their income, and show that the latter kept pace with the former. But no one, so far, has been able to compare expenses with income. We were only able to do so in one case, for a limited period—the lifetime of Sir Thomas Cornwallis, in which it seemed that the curve of rising expenses were flatter than that of income. If many studies could be made, we would doubtless discover individual instances of poverty—bankrupt Banyards, spendthrift Wodehouses, victims of the law courts like Thomas Hales, or of too many grown-up boys, like John Winthrop. An inflation of agricultural incomes was no insurance against folly or misfortune or unusual family circumstances; and of course there were fluctuations in the upward cycle, and a flat plain at the end instead of a further rise, all of which may have involved problems for particular families. But our guess would be that the majority fared well enough. We are obviously unable to agree with one historian, that a threefold rise in the cost of living was only met on the best-managed estates,[2] for the estates we have examined show a far

---

[1] The formula for each manor ran 'the fines being arbitrary are on the average accounted to be of equal value with the quit rents'; a Particular of Sir Robert Bacon's Estate in Suffolk, Holt-Wilson MSS. S 1/11; Box 72 (6), E.S.R.O. It was common earlier in the century to consider them worth half as much as the rents of assise, and to offer a thirty-year purchase for the latter (which would include the average income from profits of court) while the demesnes were rated at twenty years. Thus a prospective purchaser of Foxearth wrote in 1654, 'as for the profitts of court (they being not certayne) I know not how to bring them under a certayne valuation; and therefore thinck it the more equall way (as it is also the most usual) to value the rents of assise att 30 yeares purchase which considering the charge and trouble of collecting, and keeping courtes is a full value of them'. This purchaser was offering an eighteen-year rate for the demesnes. However, other cases are known in which a forty-year purchase was offered for the rents of assise, which comes to the same thing as Sir Robert Bacon's formula.

[2] H. R. Trevor-Roper, 'The Gentry 1540–1640', *op. cit.* p. 13: 'Economists seem generally agreed that the value of money, by 1640, had declined to one-third of the value which it had had

greater increase than that, and, whatever may have happened to the cost of living, it is difficult to believe that the rising income was not equal to it.

There is one other test which may support these guesses. Such efforts as we have made to compare the ruling families of Suffolk in 1640 with those in 1540 have not impressed us with the instability of their class. There are obvious difficulties about pursuing English local history from a residence in Chicago, and the guerilla warfare which has been waged by some of the controversialists in the recesses of family history is a reminder of its problems. Nevertheless, we are tempted to guess that continuity, rather than change, is the keynote of this county, and perhaps of Norfolk, too. If we had to add another category to a debate which already invites an Occam's razor, we would propose, for this region, 'the perdurable gentry'. Apart from a few Bacons that rose, a few Heydons that crashed, and rather more who disappeared through lack of male heirs, it is an interesting possibility, after all the talk of rise and fall, that the rest may just have endured. If so, it would be something of an anti-climax; but to one student, at least, the agrarian history of this century has turned out to be far more prosaic than he ever expected.

in 1540; on the other hand, only the best managed estates were so improved in the same period that they yielded to the landlord at the end of it three times the rent which they had yielded at the beginning.' Dr Kerridge reached similar conclusions to this author about the movement of rents in Wiltshire, but the difficulties of dealing with long leases and large fines, which were the norm in that region, must have introduced great complexities into his calculations. It is also not clear to this author that the rise in rents can have led the rise in prices; Sir Robert Drury's letter, already quoted, suggests the more usual view.

INDEX OF PLACES

217

Index of Places

Index of Places

INDEX OF PERSONS

220

Index of Persons

Barnard, Sam, 136
Barney, Sir Thomas, 213
Barnham, Alice, *see* Alice Bacon
Barnham, Benedict, 104 n
Barrow, Mary, 91, 92, 199
Barrow, Thomas, 92, 199
Barwick, Richard, 150, 159
Bedingfield, Eva, *see* Eva Yaxley
Beza, Theodore, 98
Blackman, Anne, 29
Blackman, Robert, 29, 86
Blenerhassett, Sir Edward, 213
Boldero, Francis, 86 n, 87
Bosom, Robert, 71, 78, 83
Bourchier, Susan, 169
Bretton, William, 75, 76
Bridges, Thomas, 206
Broke, John, 86 n
Browne, Sir Valentine, 9, 87 n
Bryene, Alice de, 91
Bures, Anne, *see* Anne Buttes
Bures, Bridget, *see* Bridget Buttes
Bures, Henry, 91, 196, 197, 198, 199
Bures, Jane, *see* Jane Buttes
Bures, Mary, *see* Mary Barrow
Bures, Sir Robert de, 91
Buttes, Anne, *see* Anne Bacon
Buttes, Anne, née Bures, 91, 92
Buttes, Bridget, 91, 92, 198
Buttes, Edmund, 92, 198
Buttes, Jane, 91, 92, 198
Buttes, Thomas, 4, 11, 92, 93, 198, 199, 200
Buttes, Sir William I, 20, 40, 91, 196, 197, 213
Buttes, Sir William II, 92, 93, 198, 199
Butts, Robert, 122, 125

Cage, Isabel, *see* Isabel Bacon
Candler, Rev. Matthias, 100 n
Carman, Richard, 159
Cary, Robert, 32 n
Catlin, Sir Robert, 9, 92
Cecil, Sir Robert, 104 n, 106
Cecil, Sir William, Lord Burleigh, 4, 24, 26, 33, 40, 41, 42, 43, 58, 59 n, 91, 102, 103, 104, 174, 175
Cheke, Sir John, 39, 41 n, 42
Cocker, Christopher, 87 n
Coggeshall, Elizabeth, 75

Coggeshall, John, 46, 75, 86 n
Cooke, Anne, *see* Anne Bacon
Cooke, Sir Anthony, 26, 40, 42, 43 n, 72
Cooke, William, 24
Corbett, Sir Miles, 213
Cornwallis, Alice, *see* Alice Southwell
Cornwallis, Anne, w. of Sir Thomas, 146, 149, 150, 158–9, 173
Cornwallis, Anne, w. of Charles Cornwallis, 170, 171
Cornwallis, Sir Charles, 142, 170, 171
Cornwallis, Elizabeth, dau. of Sir Thomas, *see* Elizabeth Kytson
Cornwallis, Elizabeth, relative of Sir Thomas, 165, 171
Cornwallis, Francis, *see* Francis Withipole
Cornwallis, Sir Frederick, 142
Cornwallis, Henry, 170
Cornwallis, Sir John, 142, 143, 144, 147
Cornwallis, John, grands. of Sir Thomas, 160
Cornwallis, Lucy, 171, 177
Cornwallis, Margaret, 170
Cornwallis, Mary, 160, 170, 173, 174, 176
Cornwallis, Richard, 143, 170
Cornwallis, Sir Thomas, 11, 19, 20, 60, 142: income (1540–95), 143–58, expenditures (1557–97), 158–78; 215
Cornwallis, William, father of Sir John, 142
Cornwallis, William, s. of Sir John, 144, 170
Cornwallis, William, s. of Sir Thomas, 155, 156, 160 n, 163, 166, 171, 172, 173, 177
Cranfield, Lionel, 107 n
Cranmer, Thomas, 33, 34, 42
Cresswell, Richard, 86 n
Crisp, Ellis, 120
Crisp, Mary, *see* Mary Cullum
Crisp, Nicholas, 120, 137
Crisp, Sir Nicholas, 120, 133, 138, 140, 141 n
Crofts, John, 187, 214
Cromwell, Oliver, 196
Cromwell, Thomas, 33, 34
Crowe, William, 158
Cullum, Daniel, 118
Cullum, Dudley, 137, 138

221

Index of Persons

Index of Persons

Index of Persons

INDEX OF SUBJECTS

Index of Subjects